SWINDON APPRENTICE

2-8-0T 5236 with new cylinders having enlarged steam chests and outside steam pipes heads a tanker train to Ebbw Vale steelworks.

SWINDON APPRENTICE

A. E. DURRANT

*All photographs are by the author,
unless otherwise credited*

RUNPAST PUBLISHING
CHELTENHAM

British Library Cataloguing in Publication Data
Durrant, A. E. (Anthony Edward, 1929–)
    Swindon apprentice.
    1. England. Railway services: Great Western
Railway, history – Biographies
    I. Title
    385'.092'4

    ISBN 1–870754–10–7

Photoset, printed and bound by
Redwood Burn Limited, Trowbridge, Wiltshire

Contents

A STEAM ENTHUSIAST

What starts a person on the road to becoming a steam locomotive enthusiast? In some cases, it is familiarity – steam trains are used as transport to and from school or holidays, perhaps the ancestral semi-detached backs onto the Great Something main line, or a relative works on the railway. All these are easily understandable, but account for quite a small proportion of known enthusiasts. In the case of the author, his early boyhood might almost have been contrived to keep him away from the steam locomotives which moved most of the traffic on British railways, parents having settled on the electrified suburban area of the Southern Railway. Outings and holidays were taken in father's motor car, and opportunities to see steam in any form were limited to looking at the 0-6-0 shuffling wagons at Sunbury goods yard, when father went to pay his coal merchant's account, glimpses of the narrow gauge 0-4-2T at Hampton water-works, and the annual treat to a London West End pantomine, where the best remaining memories are of massive steam engines steaming and barking under the canopy of Waterloo station.

Family relatives provided no background for one who eventually opted for a railway mechanical engineering career, there being none engaged in either railways or engineering! Father, and several close male relatives were munici-pal accountants, with Grandpa borough treasurer of Woolwich. Of several uncles vaguely remembered, one was an army NCO who seemed to spend weekends polishing brass buttons, and whose conversation was mainly about trenches and machine guns. There was another, dimly recalled, a missionary in Uganda, and probably partly instrumental, inadvertently, in producing the monster known as Idi Amin! A third avuncular memory is of a lugubrious character who operated one of those brown pubs with tiled walls which infest south east London, dispensing lukewarm beer to the local Gorblimeys. The distaff side is less well remembered, and seemed to consist mainly of vast females having enormous udders, clothed in dark materials with flowery patterns, well saturated with lavender water. One exception was father's sister, quite beautiful, who had danced on the Paris stage with the Tiller Girls, and who probably balanced out the Uganda missionary in overall effect upon a youth who for no apparent reason was fascinated by railways in general and steam locomotives in particular!

Reviewing the above, there is no logical reason why the author should have become so fascinated by steam, other than the perverse logic of its being rarely seen and bordering on the unattainable. The 1939–45 war years totally reversed this situation, plunging him into a veritable orgy of visual and aural steam experiences, all of which simply fanned the flames of 'steamania''.

1

SCHOOLDAYS

In 1939, when war broke out, the family was living in suburban Sunbury-on-Thames, but with thoughts of possible air raids upon London, was evacuated to share a house with some elderly maiden aunts at Burwash Common, a remote hamlet in the Sussex weald. Not in itself graced by a railway, there were two lines vaguely serving the area, one of which was the main line to Hastings, with Ticehurst Road station some 2½ miles distant. To the West was Heathfield, our nearest main shopping centre, on the Tunbridge Wells to Eastbourne line. Both lines were all steam, to my great satisfaction, and although little contact was made, I was delighted to recognise locomotives previously encountered only in the Hornby tinplate train catalogues. The Hastings line produced L1 and 'Schools' 4-4-0 tender engines, while Heathfield provided inside cylinder 4-4-2T (probably I1X) which to my untutored eye were the Hornby prototypes. At this stage it should be mentioned that my parents were probably unaware of how deep the steam fascination had been rooted, and my only 'railway' reading was of toy catalogues and the 'Meccano Magazine' which always had some rail news. There was, in fact, little else available, about none of which I knew.

The Battle of Britain proved the turning point. Suddenly, the 'safe' skies over Sussex were full of wheeling, diving, fighting aircraft, vapour trails clear in superb blue backdrop, while every now and again, a small cruciform speck belched black smoke and plunged to earth. To a schoolboy it was a marvellous show staged for our benefit, and we stood on local hilltops better to enjoy the action. Mother (as mothers are wont to do!) was driven to distraction by the thought that a Junkers, Heinkel or Messerschmitt was going to flatten her brood as it crashed in some local field, and arrangements were made for evacuation number two! Father came and collected us in his car, for which he had managed to obtain some petrol, and we drove for an interminable time, probably some three hours, to Zouch Farm, Culham, Oxfordshire. Zouch Farm was a large, manor style farmhouse, and we were made welcome by farmer Saunders and his family and allocated a suite on the ground floor, facing south, towards the river Thames of former Middlesex familiarity. As an animal lover,

During the author's early wartime evacuation, to Sussex, these former LBSCR 4-4-2T class I1X were often seen at Heathfield. 32005 at Brighton works 1951.
(A. C. Sterndale)

life on a farm was fascinating, with every form of domestic animal in profusion. There were the enormous wooden barns redolent of hay and assorted sacked grains, and the stark steel wheeled tractors, open to the elements, of whom farmer Saunders favoured Fordson and Allis Chalmers.

Overriding the fascinating mysteries of farmyard life was the fact that Zouch Farm was bisected by the Great Western Railway's main line from Didcot to Oxford. Our living rooms overlooked the watermeadows sloping down to the Thames bridge, beyond which Appleford Halt could be dimly perceived. On cold winter mornings, numerous plumes of steam indicated intense activity at what were later discovered to be Didcot and the immense ordnance depot just west thereof. The Didcot-Oxford line was probably busier during wartime than at any period in its existence, as a vital North-South-West link, such that here, to a steam-starved enthusiast, was steam in profusion! The limited range of the Hornby catalogue was immediately rendered redundant by the assortment of locomotives passing by, but fortunately father, on an early visit by rail, had picked up a couple of those splendid GWR locomotive publications at Paddington station, thereby providing me with a means of identifying many locomotive types, and by comparing published dimensions, an initial insight into the technicalities of what eventually would be my chosen career.

2-4-0 1336, ex-MSWJR, on its home metals climbing from Rushey Platt to Swindon Town in 1952. Sister 1334 was a familiar sight at Culham during wartime evacuation.

Almost any GWR type could be seen at Culham, with the exception of 'Kings' and the 47XX large 2-8-0. Tank engines were rare, apart from a regular Oxford 61XX working, with the result that the occasional appearance of a heavy 2-8-0T or 2-8-2T was a matter of congratulation. All tender engines were commonplace – Castles, Stars, Saints, etc, 28XX and ROD 2-8-0s, Churchward and 'Aberdare' Moguls and all the remaining 4-4-0 types including 3265 'Comet', and 2-4-0 1334 which often headed the pickup goods. Perhaps the most unusual type seen at Culham was the GWR's most profuse breed, the 0-6-0PT, seen running light from time to time en route to or from Swindon works.

Furthermore, there were 'foreign' engines. The Southern was represented by 4-6-0s with smoke deflectors which turned up from time to time on freights, and by a 2-6-0 which passed by daily except Sundays on a passenger train which alternated between Southern and LNER coaches, the latter including several in green and yellow livery. I write these notes within the then limits of my knowledge, as the only classes I could identify were the native Great Western's, due to possession of the railway's own publications. The LNER was repre-

sented initially by Robinson 2-8-0s, presumably working down from Wood-
ford, and these I found fascinating with their deep throated exhausts and
clanking rods, keeping time with their waddling gait and wagon-type three link
couplings which swung from side to side for all the world like the dewlap on
one of farmer Saunders' milch cows! On Sundays, to make up for the absence of
a Southern Mogul, there was an LNER passenger train, hauled usually by an
'Atlantic', with occasionally a 4-4-0, 2-6-0 or 4-6-0 as substitute. The LMS was
represented by small 0-6-0 often used on the pickup goods, and one such was
the first locomotive whose number I noted down. Front cover of the 'Meccano
Magazine' had featured such a small 0-6-0, and I was certain it was one which
appeared at Culham. How wrong I was – clutching the scrap of paper upon
which the actual engine had been noted, the numbers were far apart! In fact,
the magazine featured an old LNWR 'Cauliflower' while those on loan to the
GWR were Midland class 2F!

   From time to time we actually used the railway as transport to Abingdon, the
nearest shopping centre. The only bus service was an Abingdon-Dorchester
schoolbus, run by a small private company using little long-bonnet type buses,
and on market days only, an Oxford Bus Co service in the opposite direction.
When it came to such shopping chores as buying clothing, Saturday was the
only time, and this meant the morning train to Radley, almost invariably
hauled by 5973 'Rolleston Hall', and changing onto the push-pull branch train
to Abingdon handled by a 48XX 0-4-2T. Thus the short shopping expedition
round two sides of a triangle resulted in four train rides, to mother's exasper-
ation and my delight.

   It was while at Culham I made my first 'steam safari'. After a good Sunday
lunch on a winter's afternoon those plumes of steam down the line beckoned,
and taking my young brother Alan in tow we set off to investigate. Across the
fields to the river was familiar ground, but then we had to walk over the railway
bridge. Waiting for a train to pass first, thereby leaving a 'clear section' we
followed through and then took to the fields to avoid being accosted at the next
station, quite close by (unknown to us, it was Appleford Halt, unmanned). The
fields were newly ploughed and soggy with rain, greatly impeding progress,
and it was some time before reasonable going was regained. Steam plumes
were still a long way off, but on we plodded mainly trackside, until Didcot
North Junction. Again avoiding authority, a long detour was made during
which time an early winter dusk fell, and we eventually arrived at the south
side of Didcot station, exhausted, and in no state to walk all the way back as
initially planned. I had a few coppers pocket money, and approached the
booking office. 'Please Mister, how much is a train to Culham?' The clerk,
clearly something of a joker replied 'About £10,000'. 'No, I mean the ticket'.
Disaster, the last train was just leaving, and we had missed it! Luckily we knew
the farm 'phone number, and even more luckily father was 'home' for the
weekend. So after the clerk kindly telephoned for us we waited while father,

with the farmer's daughter as navigator over the devious route of country lanes, finally collected us, tired, cold, and hungry! An inauspicious start to years of train chasing worldwide!

BACK TO LONDON

Sometime after this episode, the Battle of Britain was over, and we were returned to the London area, but as our house in Sunbury was occupied, we rented another at Hampton, on the same line. Fairly soon, Ian Allan produced his first publication, the ABC of Southern Locomotives, and I invested my pocket money in a copy. Here at last was information on the local locomotives, and I proceeded to identify those seen at Hampton, thereby becoming one of the first 'loco spotters'. Hampton had a fair sized suburban goods yard, mainly for coal traffic, and this became a Mecca on Saturday mornings. Nothing like it exists today, and the sights, sounds, and smells are worth recording. Coal was brought in mainly by private owners' open trucks, small, four wheeled, wooden affairs, like matchboxes on wheels. It was shovelled into sacks by sweaty, swearing men, then stacked onto road vehicles for local delivery. There were a few lorries, but most local delivery was by horse drawn cart. Thus, the unforgettable odour of coal dust, horses (and their dung), sweaty men, plus the

Maunsell *King Arthur* sweeps through Clapham Junction, Waterloo bound, typifying the author's first successful wartime trainwatching expedition.

steam odours of the shunting engine. All contributed sounds: shouting men, stamping, whinnying, and blowing horses, and clink-clank-clonk of wagon buffers, distinctive scrinching noises of three-link couplings tightening, sad moanings of flanges binding on rails, and the rattle-rattle-rattle of a loose handbrake lever. Above all were the engine noises. The shunter was usually a K10 or L11 Drummond 4-4-0, nicknamed small or large 'hoppers', possibly due to their propensity for slipping. At virtually every start, there would be a slip, and as the wheels gyrated there would be a loud 'bloinggg' from the coupling rods, a most distinctive sound peculiar to four-coupled locomotives. The rather unsuitable 4-4-0 shunter picked out all the empty wagons and lined them up for a 700 class 0-6-0 which later in the day collected them from stations along the line for transfer to Feltham yard.

Having by now the steam bit between the teeth, as it were, I was eager to explore further, and the former pedestrian fiasco at Culham was no deterrent. Clapham Junction was not far up the line, again a Sunday afternoon was chosen, and again it was a gloomy winter's day. I had no idea what to expect, and was amazed at the size and complexity of the place. Even on a quiet Sunday afternoon there was plenty going on, and armed with my 'ABC' locomotives could be identified when noted. Several main line trains were headed by 'King Arthur' 4-6-0, and probably the odd 'Lord Nelson', and far over on the Brighton side a few I3 4-4-2T came and went. In the middle of it all were the carriage sidings shunted by a couple of O2 small 0-4-4T and the delightful little 0-8-0T 949 'Hecate' which to my amazement loose-shunted bogie carriages around like empty coal trucks in a local goods yard. Larger M7 0-4-4T worked empty trains to and from Waterloo. It was all new and fascinating, as was the last train seen before going home. There were electric trains everywhere of course, with twelve electrified through running lines, and they scuttled to and fro, spitting sparks of frustration at every gap in the conductor rail, but in the background there slowly emerged the sound of a steam engine working hard at low speed. At the London end, North side, steam and smoke appeared, under which was the strangest locomotive I had ever seen, an 0-6-2T, LNER, with enormous pipes each side of the smokebox, rising into a loop, and plunging into the side tanks. From the chimney came a muffled, asthmatic exhaust beat, totally unlike the sharp Great Western bark, and the painful progress out of the gathering dusk conjured up thoughts of a dinosaur crawling out of some primeval swamp! It was only an Ivatt class N1, later to become familiar, but a pointer towards further explorations around London.

Unknown to me at the time, indeed for many years later, London was the biggest steam centre in the whole world. Served by four mainline railway companies, there were fourteen mainline passenger termini of which five were totally steam operated and another two predominately steam. The six Southern termini had a lot of steam, even though this was swamped by a vast electric service, and indeed the Southern had more steam locomotives in the London area than any other railway. In round figures, within about a dozen miles from the various termini there were nearly twenty locomotive sheds having between them an allocation of about two thousand locomotives of nearly two hundred different classes. In addition, every day saw many other locomotives and classes working in from the provinces. A steam paradise!

Having successfully completed the Clapham Junction trip (and to my parents, returned safely home), further trips were rapidly instituted, mainly on an all-day Saturday basis, as there were more trains to be seen. At first only the termini were explored, taking the Southern electric to Waterloo thence underground to various locations. Except for a few places like King's Cross and London Bridge, this meant that little freight was seen, and as knowledge of where marshalling yards and freight loco depots was slowly acquired, further expeditions were made to these also, often involving runs in steam hauled suburban trains. Also, I was given my first bicycle, and this was utilised effectively to reach vantage points on nearby main lines, to Esher on the Southern, Hayes on the GWR, Northolt Junction to see the GC locos, and furthest to Kenton where GCR and LNWR lines crossed. Another favourite Southern place best reached by bicycle was Feltham, where always would be a couple of massive Urie 4-8-0T slowly pushing wagons over the hump – whoof, whoof-clank, whoof, whoof-clonk, an apparently irresistible force contrasted by the little Adams 0395 class 0-6-0 scurrying about on lighter, level, shunts.

Even in wartime, the Southern was relatively clean and bright, and each terminus quite different in its traffic and the locomotives seen. Waterloo had the main lines to Bournemouth and the West of England, mainly handled by 'King Arthurs' and 'Lord Nelsons', while the strange Bulleid Pacifics were just starting to appear. Basingstoke locals rated odd 4-6-0s such as Drummond T14s, N15X 'Remembrance' class, and the lesser H15s. 4-4-0s were rare, unlike Charing Cross which saw mainly 'Schools', L, L1, and various Wainwright locos and their rebuilds, D, D1, E, and E1. H class were used on empty stock. Victoria was different again, with 'Arthurs' and 'Schools', plus main line tank engines for the Oxted line, I3s and occasionally the handsome J1 and J2 4-6-2T. Empty stock was largely worked by the neat E2 class 0-6-0T.

The least impressive railway was the LMS, somehow always grimier and more unkempt than the other lines. Euston was difficult from which to see what was going on, and I tended to go out to Willesden Junction, where there would be shunting and activity on the high level line added to the main line. Stanier's superb streamlined 6220 class looked particularly scruffy in overall grime, with bits of blue or red showing through – somehow a smooth surface shows up dirt more than one broken up by protrusions. Mainstay of the services were the 'Scots', then unrebuilt and fat bellied, aided and abetted by 'Patriots' and 'Jubilees', all of which produced an undulating roar when worked hard, as was invariably the case on the climb out of London. Watford locals usually rated Fowler 2-6-4T, and Bletchley trains were mainly hauled by their stud of 'Prince of Wales' 4-6-0, including 25845 with outside Walschaerts gear actuating inside valves. Out on the main line, the endless procession of coal and goods traffic heading into London was still mainly in the hands of LNWR 0-8-0s, their archaic appearance and snuffling, wheezing, clanking noises belying an apparent ability to move substantial loads at steady, relentless, speeds.

Willesden Junction had some early diesel shunters, of the 0-6-0 type with jackshaft drive, and even then I found these uninteresting. What was interesting were the engines used on carriage shunting and empty stock workings to and from Euston. These comprised 'Cauliflower' 0-6-0, the 0-6-2T version thereof, and the smaller wheeled 'Coal tanks'. Even on the rather low platforms of Willesden Junction, I found I could look over their boilers, and when they moved some strange motion could be seen moving *up and down* between the frames, instead of the usual fore and aft. I had probably not even heard of Joy valve gear then, and certainly did not recognise it – the whole aspect of these little, low pitched, engines seemed exceedingly quaint and antediluvian!

St Pancras, unlike Euston, was totally open. One could see everything that went on, not that it amounted to much. Principal trains had Jubilees and class 5 4-6-0, while Compound and class 2P 4-4-0 were common. Gentle Johnson 0-4-4T handled carriage shunting and empty stock, and often banked main line trains up the gradient past the gasworks. Shunting in adjacent Somers Town goods depot was by Midland class 1F 0-6-0T, several with open back cabs, while right in the middle of the station was a horse, which by means of ropes and capstans, shunted onto a lift trucks loaded with best Burton bitter beer, destined for distribution from the cavernous cellars underneath the platforms. To see the heavy coal traffic, one needed to travel out to Mill Hill, a fascinating experience. Motive power would be a Fowler class 3P 2-6-2T or sometimes the Stanier version, one vying with the other for the most feeble suburban engines in London. Up through the cuttings and tunnels, dank, dripping, and smoky, they would plod, shuffle clank, shuffle clonk, wearily dragging half a dozen drab maroon coaches at speeds which regular users must have found exasperating. Barely a glimpse could be seen of Kentish Town shed, but once past Cricklewood the goods loco shed and extensive yards were easily visible at a slightly lower level. Lots of Midland 0-6-0, tank and tender, for the lighter duties and shunting, Stanier 8F in profusion, and the main big game in London, *Garratts*! A day at Mill Hill would produce between six and ten Garratts on coal trains and empties, for this was the very line for which they were designed, although the smaller 8Fs seemed able to handle much the same trains.

The other LMS station of interest was Fenchurch Street, where yet again localised locomotive varieties were evident. The principal trains were handled by Stanier 3-cylinder 2-6-4T, lovely engines running with clockwork-like precision, on massive suburban trains of eleven coaches. The station was actually owned by the LNER, who ran a few trains at rush hours, but most of the service was LMS. The second type in use were the LTSR 4-4-2T, looking vaguely like tank versions of Midland compounds, and with similarly deep, roaring exhausts and clanky rods. These shared the same power class, 3P, as the miserable Fowler 2-6-2T at St Pancras, but in actual performance they were like chalk and cheese, the Tilbury tanks being able to roar along at good speeds with heavy loads.

THE LNER

Three main constituents comprised the LNER presence in London, each being totally different! To the West lay Marylebone station, close to GWR's Paddington, and in the early 1940s this was still very much Great Central territory. Suburban work was mainly in the hands of Robinson's 4-6-2T class A5 seen on a brief visit to Marylebone itself, but most often at Northolt Junction, more rewarding with freight traffic also plus some Great Western. It was some time before I realised that some of these big tank engines had the opposite wheel arrangement of 2-6-4T, these being L1 class freight tanks often used on peak hour suburbans. Other Robinson types seen were B1 and B3 4-6-0, C4 Atlantics and D11 4-4-0 on passenger work, with B7, B8 4-6-0, plus O4 2-8-0 on freights. N5 0-6-2T handled shunting. Actual LNER types were less common, some B17 4-6-0, K3 2-6-0 and little else.

King's Cross was the London centre for Wagnerian performances, despite Germany being then the enemy! With fourteen platforms squeezing rapidly through a maze of pointwork into six lines, uphill through three double track tunnels, it was perhaps the most difficult start out of London. Combine this with the heaviest passenger trains in use, often over twenty coaches, and Gresley locomotives which despite the theoretical torque advantages of three cylinders were extremely slippery, and one had the makings of an exciting spectacle. The overture started with an N2 emerging from one of the tunnels at frightening speed, clatter clatter clatter clatter BLONG BLONG BLONG as loose axleboxes and motion bounced between the frames and the three coupled axles crashed across the nearest pointwork. Behind trailed a score of brown coaches disappearing into the station's maw at unabated pace until a squeal of tortured brake blocks averted disaster just before the bufferstops!

The slow movement comprised a large, eight wheeled, non-bogie tender emerging from another tunnel, followed by the cab, wide firebox, and large boiler of a Gresley Pacific. Automatic couplers gently kissed and consummated, and with a sigh of satisfaction vacuum lines were united. Electro-mechanical pointwork whirred into action, colour light signals flicked to green, and an indicator changed to 'ML'. Whistles shrill as tardy passengers are hurried aboard and the guard gives 'rightaway'. From the engine a *castrato* squeal from the Great Northern whistle shows the driver has understood, and a sniff from snifting valves show the regulator has been opened. Play in axleboxes and motion is taken up with a Klong!, and a wheeze of steam leaks from a gland between the frames. Suddenly, mayhem breaks loose! A thunderous roar from the chimney is accompanied by whirling wheels and flailing rods and although the driver acts quickly to close the regulator, steam in the main steam pipes and superheater continues to power the slip for a couple of revolutions. Afterwards the roaring stops, and spinning wheels decelerate until tyres again grip rails with a final confirming clank from the motion. Normal departure from King's Cross demanded several encores until the prima donna pacific was finally heard executing muffled tantrums from within the smoke-belching tunnel mouth. Meanwhile the N2 sat smugly at the buffer stops making no attempt to help the struggling Pacific. Such was King's Cross, where always there was plenty to see and hear.

The final LNER station to consider is Liverpool Street, certainly the busiest all-steam passenger station in the World at that time, and possibly at any time. By 1912 six approach tracks carried about 1200 trains daily, and whilst this declined later, increased rail usage during the war probably meant that about a thousand trains daily used the station. Mother always knew when I had been to Liverpool Street, by the combined effect of blissful expression and blackened appearance! Due to weight limitations on the Great Eastern system, LNER's largest locomotives were absent, and the biggest main line locomotives normally seen were the 'Sandringham' class 4-6-0 with, occasionally, a larger K3 Mogul. GER's excellent little B12 class 4-6-0 predominated, while lighter country trains used the old 'Claud Hamilton' class 4-4-0s with seven foot wheels, whose coupling rods reverberated under the overall roof like a carillon of bells in an immense cathederal.

Most trains were suburbans, consisting of two, five-coach articulated sets, making ten coaches in all. For outer services one saw a few Gresley 3-cylinder 2-6-2T, rolling in with rods all a-plincklety-plonk, but most trains used the small GER 0-6-2T of class N7, excellent little machines with high accelerative capacity. There were not enough of these to run the service, about a quarter of which still used the gallant little 2-4-2T of classes F4, F5, and F6, seen battling up Bethnal Green bank with ten coaches designated for such destinations as Loughton, Epping, or Ongar, all today handed over to London Transport tube services over the same lines. Very smart operating was the order of the day. A train rolled into the terminal platform, and engine immediately uncoupled. Meanwhile, at the outer end, points were changed and the new engine backed onto the train, coupled, and airbrakes connected. During this time about a thousand passengers crammed into the cramped compartments and it was time for off. As the train accelerated out, the incoming engine followed up close behind until points and signals directed it into the engine siding from which it would soon emerge to take over the next train. Much is made of the operational efficiency of multiple unit electric trains, but it could be credibly claimed that at Liverpool Street, engines were changed and ready to go in faster time than an

A clear winter's morning sees 5076 *Gladiator* accelerating from a signal check at Old Oak Common with a Paddington express.

electric motorman could walk ten coach lengths along a crowded platform! Such was the reality of the world's most intensive steam suburban service, carried out by incredibly small locomotives. The theme tune was the pant of Westinghouse airbrake pumps. There may have been moments at Liverpool Street when no locomotive was actually moving, but there was always an active brake pump, either gently reciprocating to combat leakage in the system, or bashing away like a demented jazz band, recouping air pressure after a screeching, time saving, brilliant stop. Pah Tah, Pah Tah, Pah Tah – the Cockney rhythm of Liverpool Street station in steam days.

PADDINGTON

The urbane Great Western operated from Paddington station on a route which ran along, rather than climbed out, of the Thames basin. Thus, gradients were less severe, a condition of which I was then unaware. From Paddington, the 'Kings', 'Castles', and lesser 4-6-0s accelerated their trains with practised ease and rarely a trace of slip, and from a platform end viewpoint it was evident that the smaller engines of the Great Western were making a better job of things than, say, the massive Pacifics of the LNER. This was perfectly true, as was even demonstrated on the LNER in bygone days, and I was suitably impressed. Similarly, GWR suburban trains operated with a briskness unknown on other steam services, and were comparable in overall speed with Southern's electrics. My original steam residency had been on the Great Western at Culham, creating familiarity, and later sojourn in London had shown that however interesting, and even amusing, were the other company's engines, GWR was the way to go.

Fate combined to finalise things when Hitler started to rain his V bombs on London. After a harrowing night when houses either side of us had been demolished while we cowered in the cupboard under the stairs, first move was a rapid return to Zouch Farm. That in itself was fine, but educationally I had reached the then minimum school leaving age of fourteen. Having passed the entrance examination for Twickenham technical school an attempt was made to enrol me in the equivalent at Oxford, but this was over full. For a while there was thus a hiatus in my formal education, and during this period I worked on a correspondence course for basic mechanical engineering, living on the farm. This was delightful, no hour-by-hour schedules, just get the job done on time and submit it. Somehow, I had heard about premium apprenticeships at Swindon, and one day went there to find out what it was all about. In all youthful innocence the staff department was invaded, and probably much amusement incurred by my asking about a job 'designing locomotives.'

It was explained that entry to the drawing office was governed firstly by satisfactory completion of a five year apprenticeship in the workshops, and secondly by studies culminating in the National and Higher National Certificates in Mechanical Engineering. Forms were provided for completion, and to my delight I was given a brief trip round the works.

Meanwhile, at Culham, the railway scene had somewhat changed. The GWR constituent was unaltered, except that I was better informed since Ian Allan had produced an ABC of GWR locomotives, and I had also obtained *British Locomotive Types*, a book containing over a hundred diagrams of British locomotives, with their principal dimensions, fulfilling my need to know more about locomotives than their simple existence. The Southern train, now known to be a Newcastle-Ashford through service, avoiding London, was identified as being hauled by the U1 class 2-6-0, and the locomotive on the Sunday LNER train, then known to be a Sheffield-Swansea service, was normally an Ivatt Atlantic, interspersed by occasional Great Central types. Wider horizons were encountered almost simultaneously by the appearance of War Department 'Austerity' locomotives, and real 'Foreigners' in the shape of USA Army 2-8-0s which rattled and banged along, tenders bouncing on freight car bogies with jingling brake rigging. Perhaps this early exposure to real *foreign* locomotives, at an impressionable age, prevented contamination with the parochial paranoia which infests so many enthusiasts today.

Wartime Wonder 1. Living in rural Oxfordshire, the author was amazed to see, originally unannounced, numerous 2-8-0 lettered U.S.A. Transportation Corps. This example, JDZ 37.031, was photographed later in Jugoslavia.

With the war in Europe, and invasion of France, under way, there was much military traffic, and a visit to Abingdon involved my first derailment, when 0-4-2T 4848, the regular engine, backed the auto coach onto some empty RECTANK bogie wagons for conveying army tanks. The siding had catch points, which someone forgot to switch, and we pulled a wagon off the track. This was abandoned, and we continued as a pure passenger train. On another occasion, 4848 was 'off' for some reason, and we had '517' class 1159 on the train, the only occasion I was hauled/pushed by that class, no different basically to the 48XX class. One afternoon, looking out of the room at Zouch Farm, there appeared at Appleford bridge a doubleheader. This in itself was rare enough, I cannot recall another, but behind the clearly GWR profile of the leading loco-motive was a large parallel boiler, gleamingly clean. Leaping out of the window and galloping across farmer Saunders' field, lineside was reached in time to see a military ambulance train doubleheaded by a 'Bulldog' and an ex Great Eastern B12/3! After that, the B12/3s were often seen, but always solo, and I sometimes wonder whether this was the only occasion when Great Western and Great Eastern locomotives were doubleheaded.

Heavy tank engines were seen from time to time, and for some curious reason they were noted to be from Llanelly shed rather than from the more obvious nearer depots that had such engines, possibly as a result of some peculiar cyclic working. 5220 and 7220 appeared several times, to my dis-appointment, as I still collected numbers and these 'rare' classes turned up the same engines. One day 5220 appeared on the local pickup, and the loco crew, unused to such power, had wagons hurtling down the sidings to the great anxiety of the shunter who had to pursue them and apply handbrakes!

Writing of 2-8-0T, having acquired a drawing board and tee square for my correspondence course, a first attempt at locomotive 'design' was attempted. What this amounted to was a GWR 2-8-0T modified to include Walschaerts valve gear plus improved cab and bunker similar to those on Stanier's 2-6-4T. This showed a basic urge to improve upon locomotive design as found in many progressive engineers. However, in recent years one reads about schemes to restore locomotives 'to original condition', a strange idea which basically means scrapping improvements found necessary to improve an originally unsatisfactory design!

Yet another re-evacuation, the last, was effected late 1944 when we returned briefly to London and were incorporated into an official evacuation scheme rather than a private effort. Well I remember the incident. Because there was a war on, everything was 'secret'. We assembled secretly at a local school, and were loaded into a convoy of large red London Transport double deck buses, which proceeded secretly in broad daylight to St Pancras station. Here we were secretly loaded onto a train of LMS bogie coaches, for which a 'Jubilee' had been secretly rostered. Our destination was Top Secret, but by elementary logic seemed to be North of the Thames.

TO YORKSHIRE

The train run north was the longest journey experienced at that time, even though less than two hundred miles. Nevertheless, it was full of interest, with the Jubilee on the front making its typical undulating roar, traversing totally unfamiliar country seemingly netted with many lines crossing over or under, joining or diverging, to unknown destinations. Swollen with wartime traffic, nearly every line seemed to have a freight train but there were few surprises in the motive power seen, mainly familiar LMS types of 4-4-0, 0-6-0, 2-6-0, 4-6-0, 2-8-0, and Garratts. At Kettering an old outside framed 2-4-0 was spotted and somewhere along the line was seen an 'Austerity' 2-10-0, with its seemingly endless row of coupled wheels. In fact, there was one more pair than I was accustomed to, but the mind can become so circumscribed by the familiar that anything slightly outside becomes bizarre! For this 2-10-0, I had to *count* the wheels before realizing what it was. Many years later, in Austria, the opposite occurred when I was puzzled by an unfamiliar looking 2-10-0 only to suddenly realise I was looking at an ex-Württemberg State Railways 2-12-0! These were so beautifully proportioned that there were more wheels than at first seemed the case.

At Leicester we were informed of our destination, Sheffield, and eventually, with its characteristic tinklety tonklety, tinklety tonklety sound, the Jubilee rolled under the roof of Sheffield Midland station. After much confusion, we

Wartime Wonder 2. The author's first sight of a ten-coupled WD was an eye-opener, the fifth axle being one more than any loco seen before.

were billeted with a retired greengrocer and his wife in the Graves Park area, a funny old couple. The old girl spent most of her time shuffling around muttering 'Oh dear' to herself while 'T'owd chap' lazed in front of a fire upon which he frequently expectorated, with much resultant sizzling.

There was some time before school term commenced, and this was spent exploring the local railway scene and absorbing the plethora of new sights and sounds. From the billet, it was possible to walk through Ruskin Park down to the Midland main line near Heeley, a four track section used by familiar Midland and LMS types, although there were some 4-4-0 variations in the shape of the earlier class 2P with straight running plates, and the larger 3P, 700 series, not seen in the London area and used on freight duties. A morning local to Nottingham was powered by a small boilered LTSR 4-4-2T, like us, evacuated from London, and this turn once produced a Stanier 3-cylinder 2-6-4T, similarly exiled. An evening turn looked out for was the empty stock of a train from York via Pontefract which proceeded to Heeley sidings with the LNER engine bringing the train in. Usually this was a D49 'Hunt' class, with occasional variation such as a B16, but the highlight was an engine which at first seemed to be a 'Hunt' but was too long. As it hove closer into view, it was seen to be No 732, a Raven C7 rebuilt with D49 type poppet valve cylinders, etc.

Most through freight avoided Sheffield, but there was plenty to and from the local steelworks and other industries, hauled by the usual locos, including occasionally a Garratt. There was an evening train to some waste disposal dump, almost invariably hauled by class 2F 3666, with chalked name 'Enoch', and of course known as the 'Shit Train'. 0-8-0s came and went from unkown destinations, occasionally the Fowler type, but more often the LNWR species with their distinctive sound effects – 'CHA CHA wheeze klong, CHA CHA wheeze klong'. A very rare visitor one evening was 25292 'Medusa' which arrived from the south on a freight. What it was doing at Sheffield Midland cannot be imagined, but it was the only LNWR 4-4-0 I ever saw working a train.

Far more interesting than the LMS was the LNER at Sheffield Victoria station. Access was by tram along the Brightside Road to the Wicker arches, where rail crossed road on a high viaduct. A long series of stairs climbed up to a vantage point by the platform end, high over the city, looking across the tracks to the Wicker LMS goods station (terminus of the original Sheffield to Rotherham Railway), in which several 0-6-0T constantly shunted. There was a wonderful atmosphere of locomotive smoke, industrial haze, and a malty bouquet from the local brewery, which vintage blend should have been bottled and laid down in a suitable cellar for the benefit of posterity.

Locomotive types seen at Victoria were of such wondrous variety that it was almost impossible to leave the place – on my first afternoon about ten totally new classes were encountered. Nearly all the Great Central passenger classes were to be seen, swarms of Directors and Atlantics each of two series, all sorts of 4-6-0s with inside, outside, or four cylinders, each cylinder arrangement coming in at least two wheel sizes to boot. There were 4-4-2T clattering in from Barnsley, Ivatt Atlantics, Gresley Pacifics, V2s, and B17s, and what was then a rarity, Thompson B1 8307 *'Blackbuck'*. Shunting was done by N4 class 0-6-2T, of which I think virtually all the class were Sheffield based, as were several other numerically small classes such as B5 and D10.

All the above pale before the freight workings, which mostly used the back roads behind the station screened from sight by a wall reaching down to about platform level, below which one could see the wheels and motion of whatever waited at signals for a clear road. Freight locos came in an even greater variety comprising numerous origins, wheel arrangements and cylinder styles. Possibly 80 to 90 percent of freight was handled by four main classes, each different to the others, in an orgy of non-standardisation alien today. First and foremost were Robinson's O4 class, 2-8-0 with outside cylinders, strong and sturdy with softish yet powerful exhaust beats, timed by big ends having loose brasses which collection of several components came together twice per revolution with a kind of 'clock' noise. With three cylinders were the Gresley K3s, similarly

Darnall shed in wartime was the Mecca for local enthusiasts, some rare loco type often being present. Twenty years later finds various Great Central 2-8-0s, some rebuilt with Thompson boilers.

imperturbable, but with a whistling type exhaust rather reminiscent of a GWR 'Hall' except for the syncopated rhythm from which one beat was often absent. Machinery noises from this class were much more violent.

Two inside cylinders were represented by Gresley J39 0-6-0, with a good crisp exhaust beat almost drowned by an incredible percussive cacophany of machinery with a 'clack clock blong clock' scoring. Four-cylinder propulsion provided the class B7 'Black Pig' 4-6-0 with typical Robinson deep throated exhaust and yet different, though less violent, machinery noises. Between these four main classes all manner of other types appeared on freight. Gresley O2 2-8-0 making the most fearful clashing and banging noises loped through from the Doncaster direction, J11 'Pom pom' 0-6-0 on local freights, various 0-8-0 including native Q4, rather like an O4 minus pony truck, giving a freedom of lateral movement making them wiggle lasciviously like Eastern dancing girls! Workings from the Northeast often brought B16s, Q6 or Q7 classes, and whatever else was allocated within the GC, GN, or NE sections 100 miles from Sheffield was likely to appear on a wartime freight. Due to the climb over the Pennines, many freights were banked out of Sheffield, usually by a local N4, or perhaps a J50 tank engine, often with a J11, and occasionally with something unusual or even bizarre, of which the extreme example was an Ivatt small boilered Atlantic which once only appeared pushing not much more than the guard's van of a train hauled by an O4. The great element at Sheffield Victoria was uncertainty, particularly on freights, one never knew what locomotive would next appear.

Wartime Wonder 3. At Sheffield Victoria appeared a loco with a totally new outline but carrying an O4 class number. Several were seen before details were published. In later days this Thompson O1 rebuild is seen near Nottingham.

From time to time one saw totally mystifying locomotives, this being the period when Edward Thompson was composing his enigmatic variations upon several themes. One such occasion was a 2-8-0 seen rolling in from the Manchester direction, bearing an O4 number, but with outside valve gear and totally alien appearance. Then there was a lean and rangy looking 4-6-2, 3697, which worked Manchester trains for a while, seemingly tacked on to a batch of V2s, which was in fact the case. Yet a third surprise was an 0-8-0 with correct Q4 number, but with side tanks and no tender. In the fullness of time all these mysteries were duly explained, but they added to the aura of unpredictability which permeated Victoria but only rarely surfaced at Midland.

Once school was started, train spotting was largely reduced to weekends, and within the limits of pocket money, excursions were made to various locations which looked interesting on such maps as were available. South of Sheffield, on the Midland, Dore & Totley station was a cheap excursion where a triangular junction joined lines from Sheffield, Chesterfield, and the Hope Valley. Within the triangle was a small disused quarry with narrow gauge track and a wagon which we pushed up and rode down upon between rushing to one of three sides to see what passed. Hasland and Westhouses sheds, near Chesterfield, each had about three Garratts, and it was common to see such a loco heading along the Hope Valley from this southern direction.

Chesterfield itself was interesting. Four tracks from the Erewash valley, virtually all freight, converged with two tracks from Sheffield, just north of the station, into a bottleneck of four tracks only through the station. To the south, three double track routes diverged through Nottingham, Toton, and Derby, making six running lines again. Early Saturday mornings were fascinating to behold. The two platform lines remained clear for passenger and faster freight trains, but the two 'back' lines were a virtual conveyor belt of slow moving freight traffic, permissive block and nose to tail at walking pace. No matter whether the train engine was a Johnson 2F, a Jubilee, or a Garratt, the plodding parade crawled past. Presumably this condition existed throughout the week, but by Saturday afternoon things had thinned out sufficiently for trains to pass at twenty mph, the little four wheeled matchboxes-on-wheels bobbing over rail joints like a procession of Chinamen bowing obeisance to their Mandarin. Sunday was presumably very quiet, for even Britain, fighting for her existence in total war, tried hard to obey the eleventh commandment, 'Thou shall not run freight trains on the Sabbath!'

Doncaster, eighteen miles away, was a favourite Saturday outing, return half fare being about one and sixpence. The morning train usually caught was worked by a Robinson B5 4-6-0, giving a delightful ride with sounds of deep exhaust and clacking big ends rolling back along the train, or reverberating from the miles and miles of sidings past Sheffield's massive steel works, full of trucks, with Parker N4 0-6-2T and industrial saddle tanks busily sorting out loads and empties with industrious energy. After clearing the Rotherham

A bleak winter's day at Doncaster, similar to those experienced at Sheffield in 1944–5, though probably with more action evident.

complex industry thinned out slightly until Mexborough hove into sight with locomotive shed at lower level, crammed with normal freight engines, and occasionally a glimpse of a three-cylinder 0-8-4T making ready for a stint at Wath marshalling yard, or even U1 Garratt 2395 perhaps on shed for washout. Incidentally, local railfans knew that the Garratt worked Worsboro' bank, but we could not find the place on such limited maps as were available in wartime, and there was no passenger station there. Thus we never got to see Britain's biggest locomotive working on its designed duties, even though they were but a dozen miles from Sheffield. After Mexbro', the line went quite rural, past Conisbro' and its castle, until a clatter round a sharp left hand curve brought the train into Doncaster station, teeming with asthmatic Ivatt engines, off-beat roaring and clanking Gresley monsters, and gentlemanly Robinson types.

By far the most enjoyable trip from Sheffield was to Manchester, rather further, and into the five bob fare range. I once made the trip via the Hope Valley route, hauled by a soggy Midland 4-4-0 which struggled to drag three or four coaches over the Pennines to Manchester Central station. Here was seen a

Pollitt D6 4-4-0 on a passenger from somewhere, perhaps the trip's highlight, and continuation was on the CLC route behind a J10 0-6-0 which again gave an uninspiring performance. At Chester were GWR engines, Bulldogs and mainly odd types, and I was pleased to get a sniff of these, to hear the pish-tish of vacuum brake pumps, and the rude, farting, noises made by several classes.

The *real* way to visit Manchester was by LNER, from Victoria station. At the head of a substantial train would be a Gresley V2, sitting on the Wicker arches surveying a scene which Lowry should have painted. From the right away it was uphill going, past grimy factories, the remains of Neepsend loco shed, some derelict industria, then quite suddenly into bleak moorlands. As the V2 accelerated through echoing cuttings and retaining walls, the fantastic Gresley two-and-a-half cylinder beat flowed back past young Durrant, head out of the first compartment. Da-da-dum, da-clank, da-da-dum, da-clank, da-da-dum, da-clank. Gathering speed through a grey, misty, countryside, the chimney top roar changed to an undulating thunder, shouting defiance at leaden skies of rain-filled clouds grimly holding their impregnable Pennine hilltop positions. Below the running plate, a regular clank-clonk, clank-clonk, bounced back from sheep-retaining drystone walls, and lonely, bleak, places like Thurlstone glided by.

At Penistone, the coal hauling artery from Barnsley and Mexborough joined, with a clatter of pointwork, and there would be an ex L&Y 2-4-2T on the LMS connection to Huddersfield. From then onwards, every passing loop held a freight, sometimes two, huddled together like sheep sheltering from the cold wet mists of the Yorkshire/Lancashire borderlands. Many freights were banked, and to cope with the pressure of wartime traffic all sorts of strange machines were to be seen, some remembered being Robinson inside cylinder 2-6-4T, Gresley non-condensing N2 0-6-2T, and perhaps most unlikely, an ex-Metropolitan 0-6-4T, clearly more at home amongst the Chilterns than battling against the harshness of the Pennines.

After skirting Wortley reservoir, pressure from the all conquering Pennines increased, and no matter how the train squirmed and wriggled in evasion, the V2 eventually had to give a squeal of despair and plunge into one of the Woodhead rabbit holes. Within the subterranean darkness, exhaust roar and wheel rumble blended into a frightening intensity, as through gaps in the swirling smoke wet walls of the tunnel were momentarily lighted from the dim carriage illumination. Amongst the cacophany of noise, only two sounds were identifiable, the dum-dum, dum-dum, from the coach's leading bogie, and the Gresley clank-de-clonk, clank-de-clonk from the V2 ahead, each soporific in its regularity. In case the driver himself should be induced into actual slumber by all this, the railway had installed a monstrous alarm clock in the form of a treadle operated bell at the summit actuated by the wheel flanges, whose shattering DING DING DING eclipsed all other train sounds, and would have awoken the Devil himself.

Emerging with a rush, and speeding past scarcely noticed Woodhead station, with its low platforms, brakes squealed to halt the train at Dinting with nameboard so strangely laid out that 'DINTING change for GLOSSOP Central' seemed to read 'DINTING GLOSSOP, change for Central' There would be a C13 4-4-2T on the branch train, and as we neared Manchester more of these stout-hearted engines would be passed, thrashing out through the suburbs on local trains. Gorton shed and yards would be eagerly scanned for strange engines, perhaps D6 or D9 4-4-0s, inevitably some small wheeled B9 4-6-0, and the ex-LD&EC Kitson 0-6-0T works shunter. Across the way, nothing could be seen of whatever Beyer Peacock were building, although sometimes their little works shunter could be seen. Rolling into London Road station, we might race a lean Fowler 2-6-4T, or a pompous 'Royal Scot', tinkling in along the parallel LMS tracks, before passing the F1 2-4-2T on the GC station pilot duty.

Once in Manchester, the local Mecca was Victoria & Exchange stations, back-to-back termini with through tracks and a single platform from one end of Victoria to the other end of Exchange. These combined stations were possibly

Former L & Y locos exerted a strange fascination on the author. Barton Wright 0-6-0ST 11305 is seen at Horwich Works, still with LMS number.

the busiest in the country, second only to London's Liverpool Street, and since it was impossible to watch both ends together, Victoria was the highpoint. There was an electric service to Bury, with strange heavy looking stock, but everything else was steam. The great attraction was the plethora of ex L&Y locomotives to be seen, numerous 2-4-2T of all types, apparently working turn-in, turn-out with standard 2-6-4T, 0-6-0 on local freights, and also on banking duties which started right in the middle of the station on the through West-East freight lines! There were Fowler 0-8-0s with sharp, very un-Midland exhaust, and their huge L&Y conterparts, with massive boilers perched on eight closely spaced wheels, looking rather like circus elephants balanced on tubs. Perhaps twice daily, there would be a Hughes 4-6-0 on a train from Blackpool, all this mingling in with standard LMS types, some LNW 0-8-0, and even the odd Midland class, hardly capable of coping with the daily duties performed by their sturdier contemporaries.

In the time I was in Sheffield, one lengthy (for a wartime schoolboy) trip was

Quite amazingly, the Fowler regime on the LMS built hundreds of these archaic 0-6-0s as its standard goods class, while on the GWR, Aberdare 2-6-0s of roughly the same size, capacity and technical content were being scrapped.

south to Birmingham. Apart from a desire to see some more Great Western steam, I had been involved in the usual schoolboy type arguments about 'who had the best locos'. Of course, the Sheffield contingent were divided amongst two 'teams', LMS versus LNER, and I was a disruptive factor in bringing in GWR as a contender. One day, in class, I sketched a GWR 2-8-0T, these chunky and powerful machines being then my favourite, the resulting drawing being greeted with derision. '2-8-0 always have tenders – there is no such thing as a 2-8-0 tank engine'. Certainly true by their local experience. Since Birmingham was easily reached by the Bradford-Bristol expresses, it was simply a case of issuing a challenge to at least *see* some GWR locos, although a 2-8-0T could not be promised. The fare was well over five bob, a fairly daunting amount those days, but I saved up carefully as did only one other brave compatriot. The others regarded entering GWR territory as akin to mounting a mission amongst cannibals, even the more affluent eventually taking the chicken run. Pity I cannot remember the name of my sole companion, although his face, forty years later, lingers in my mind. We saw strange LMS locos around Burton, several odd 0-4-0T and 0-4-0ST new to both of us, together with those low numbered 2P 4-4-0. There were main line locos, Scots and Pacifics glimpsed at Tamworth, and Kirtley 0-6-0 with double frames around Saltley. Even from the LMS viewpoint, it was a voyage of successful exploration.

Somehow we found our way to Snow Hill station, and within its stygian shadows the Great Western came to light to an outsider. Two things first claimed attention, the sharp crack of the Swindon exhaust beat, and the proliferation of 'namers', ie locos with names, plentiful on the GWR but less so in Sheffield. While all this was sinking in I was proudly acting like a host showing off his own estates. Perhaps the highlight came when a slow, sharp, steady exhaust blasted out from the northern portal, and to my delight, it was produced by a 52XX 2-8-0T! I could hardly have been more delighted had the thing been personally designed and built, but there, vindicated, was the strange notion that such a machine existed. My Sheffield friend was suitably impressed. Later we took a suburban to Tyseley, and he was further impressed by the way what appeared to be a small 2-6-2T accelerated and ran. Behind the shed, not in steam, was a 72XX 2-8-2T which rather overwhelmed him, and later, in the presence of peers, he had to admit the GWR had something after all! The final highlight was returning to Snow Hill station and meeting a local at the platform end. After being mystified by our outer space accents, one pure River Sheaf, and the other a mongrel mixture of London, Sussex, Oxford, and Yorkshire, he approached and in the purest English, as doubtless enunciated by Shakespeare himself, asked 'Wheer duz yow coom fram?'

Eventually the war in Europe came to an end in 1945, and we were re-patriated south again, on VE Day itself, by a very slow train which ran via Derby, Nottingham, and Melton Mowbray, replacing several services can-celled due to the celebrations. In contrast to the busy tracks seen on the

Churchward's 2-8-0T, designed for heavy work in the wet and misty Welsh valleys, were probably the most sure-footed design in Britain – it was almost impossible to make them slip.

northbound run, there was hardly a train to be seen, but all the loco sheds were crammed full of somnolent motive power.

During the war, successive evacuations had upset the normal programme of formal education, and I had striven to gain knowledge in half a dozen establishments ranging from a village church learnery to grammar and technical schools. Whatever may have been lacking on the formal side, my informal education had gained considerably. Under normal peacetime conditions all would have been carried out in a steady suburban environment devoid of variety. Instead, this had been enriched by residence in places varying from a remote farmhouse to a busy industrial city, together with exposure to an equally rich spectrum of British people and their assorted and almost mutually incomprehensible accents. On the steam locomotive front, my chosen *raison d'être*, development was from a state of underexposure, in 1939, to a situation in 1945 where I had lived on all of the 'Big Four' mainline railways, had seen a remarkable variety of their locomotives, and in the shape of the US Army S160

2-8-0s had even been exposed to foreign practice, albeit at home. Since the prospect of starting yet another school was unattractive, the papers obtained on the earlier visit to Swindon were exhumed, and to my intense satisfaction submitted to the GWR staff office at Paddington.

2

PROBATIONER

With father still tied up with wartime matters, grandfather took over the task of setting me up at Swindon, and the initial meetings at Paddington. These were disappointing to me, since my scanty locomotive technical knowledge was not called upon at all, and only general educational matters discussed. To fill in the time before my premium apprenticeship commenced, I took a job at a small engineering works at Burwash, operating a hand press, a lowly enough job but good at getting the 'feel' of engineering. With the small wages thus earned, a bicycle was purchased – a large, second hand machine, eminently suitable for a farm labourer. With this independent transport I cycled out evenings and weekends to the local railway lines. Evening trips were to Mayfield, where assorted 'Brighton' tanks came and went on locals, or to Robertsbridge, where the evening's 'bag' usually included several 'Schools' and an L or L1 4-4-0, plus an N1 2-6-0 on a through freight. Weekend rides went further afield to Tonbridge, Tunbridge Wells West, Brighton, and on one exhausting ride, to Ashford. On one of the Brighton trips, sitting on the hill overlooking the shed, I was amazed to see a new Bulleid Pacific with a number about 21C103 or 104. To me, it was indistinguishable from a 'Merchant Navy', and I marvelled at over a hundred of them being built whilst I was in Sheffield! This was not so naive as may be thought today, as during the Sheffield sojourn, the LMS finished off the 54XX series of Class 5s, and suddenly all manner of new locos appeared from Crewe and Derby, numbered in the 49XX, and later, 48XX series, such that this sort of thing was not unusual. What I did not know was that I had seen one of the first of a new locomotive class!

Getting back to things Great Western, Ian Allan had by then published one or two editions of his GWR ABC books, and what I found most mystifying were the numerous locomotives with three-figure numbers, usually listed laconically as, say, '0-6-2T TV'. At that time, all but a handful of true GWR locomotives had four-figure numbers, and anything less than that, such as aged panniers 907 and 992, seen at Didcot and Swindon respectively, seemed to have a vaguely prehistoric atmosphere. The discovery of so many low numbered engines, about which virtually no information was given, was something to be investigated. Names of former railways, such as Barry, Rhymney, Port Talbot etc showed that most of these mysterious locomotives ought to be in South Wales, the relevant 'research' being the station index in the GWR timetable. Were all the 0-6-2T RR the same, or did they form several classes? What did they look like? Were they big or small, old or new? Suddenly there was a large chunk of my favourite railway about which I had less information than the locomotives of the other three groups.

Since I had never before left home, apart from the odd Boy Scout camp, grandfather in his wisdom thought it would be a good idea for me to go on a one week trip to South Wales, satisfying me in meeting all these locomotives, and satisfying *him*, in view of my imminent departure to Swindon, that I was capable of existing outside the comfortable confines of home and family. Accordingly I was despatched on this adventure, in July 1945, with a booking at the YMCA Hostel, Cardiff. It was, in effect, my first visit to a 'foreign' country for although no passport nor alternative currency was needed, Wales is a country with its own language and proud traditions, and whilst part of Great Britain, was in no way part of *England*! The great adventure started with a train to London (probably 'Schools' hauled), across the inner circle to Paddington, then a 'Castle' on the Cardiff train. As far as Swindon, it was familiar territory, then heading West, approaching the Severn Tunnel, we rumbled down through cuttings and dank tunnels, at the standard GWR 55 mph, crossing freights assisted by extremely grimy 3150 class 2-6-2T. Into the bore, under the river, then out the Welsh side to Severn Tunnel Junction with its marshalling yards. Scanning anxiously, there were my two first Welsh locomotives, ex B&MR 0-6-2T 11 and 332 working the two hump yards, and looking disappointingly standard with their Swindon boilers.

Newport produced lots of my then favourite class, the 2-8-0T, but none of the Welsh types. The only surprise there was an ex-LNWR 0-6-2T on a passenger – I had no idea then that the LMS penetrated so far into GWR territory. After Newport, a few miles of bleak country, then with clattering wheels echoing from rows and rows of goods trucks, we rolled towards Cardiff through seemingly endless yards in which, joy of joys, were 'strange' locomotives. 57 and 72 are numbers etched into my mind, massive looking 0-6-2T with fat, domed, boilers, of somewhat Great Central appearance, and quite un-GWR. Alighting at Cardiff General station, doubtless slightly bewildered, an '0-6-2T TV' was blasting out briskly with a suburban train. The loco had a Swindon boiler but otherwise was quite different. It was, of course, a Taff 'A', a superb locomotive with which I was soon to become familiar. Somehow the YMCA was found, and at supper I met Guy Kerry, resident, and working as a draughtsman at Caerphilly works. Learning that I was about to start at Swindon (where Guy had served his time) a visit to Caerphilly was fitted into my schedule.

South Wales was an eye opener. Quite a lot of these low-numbered engines

The author was fascinated at an early date by engines like unrebuilt Rhymney Railway class AR no. 35, rolling down the TVR main towards Radyr in 1950.

were seen, and to even my inexperienced eyes, they were of several basic types for each constituent, while many had been fitted with Swindon type boilers. As to dimensions, I had no clue, but certainly they were no mean machines. The Taff 'A's' worked many of Cardiff's suburban 'Valley' trains, turn about with the later and larger 56XX 0-6-2T, and on passenger trains there seemed little to choose between the two classes. Much later, I discovered that the rebuilt 'A' class, with Swindon boiler, had the same nominal dimensions (cylinders, wheels, boiler pressure, and tractive effort) as the Fowler 2-6-2T encountered at St. Pancras. When it came to performance the similarity ended. Where the Fowlers struggled out of London with half a dozen coaches, the Taff literally galloped up the valleys out of Cardiff, hauling eight coaches, on schedules little inferior to those of the 'Southern Electric'. To see, and hear, a Taff 'A' starting eight coaches out of Dingle Road halt, on I think 1 in 36 gradient, was a moving experience. They had balanced slide valves over the cylinders, and rather later in my Swindon career, discussing these engines, some wit claimed that upon opening the valve to exhaust, there was just "one bloody great hole from the cylinder to the top of the chimney!" Certainly, the sound of these engines agreed with this description. After the foul Fowlers, the same nominal dimensions were perpetuated by Stanier, and even by BR on their class 3 2-6-2T of

Swindonised Taff Vale A class 387 has GWR pattern tanks but retains TVR cab, as it brings empty stock into Barry.

Rebuilt Rhymney Railway AP class no. 80 accelerates up the valley from Llanbradach with a train for Rhymney.

series 82000, some of which were allocated to South Wales. For those in the know, even the BR standard locos were given lower loadings than the Taffs, although they were otherwise quite good little locomotives, but ultimately, the Taffs were the oldest and the lightest of various 'similar' classes, and could outperform any of the more 'modern' replacements. Is there a lesson here?

Performance of the Rhymney 0-6-2T seemed less sprightly, but still adequate for these heavy services. At the time, two passenger engines still retained their Rhymney boilers, but the others were Swindonised. The RR freight haulers were more at home, one felt, on such duties, ambling along imperturbably with long strings of coal trucks. Many of these retained RR boilers, some until scrapping.

The trip to Caerphilly works was of great interest, not that I understood much of what was going on, but further interesting locos were undergoing overhaul including an Alexandra Docks 0-6-2ST with outside cylinders, a very strange beast, and an 1101 class dock tank from Swansea, one of only a dozen GWR locomotives with outside Walschaerts valve gear. Those few days based on Cardiff were quite outstanding. From the YMCA one could hear the mellow,

GWR smaller 2-6-2T were designed for west country branches, but use expanded to include suburban duties, notably around Bristol, and later in South Wales on push-pull workings.

warbling whistles of incoming trains, and the sharp bark as 56's and Taff 'A's' accelerated out to the valleys. It was much more exciting than London or Birmingham, and unknown to me at the time was the fact that about a quarter of GWR's locomotive stock was allocated to depots within some 25 miles from Cardiff, and this comprised a variety of classes found nowhere else on the system. None of this deterred my enthusiasm for things Great Western.

Came the appointed day, and Grandfather travelled to Swindon, with me in tow, to start work. We stayed at the Goddard Arms hotel, in old Swindon where the former country market town atmosphere still prevailed. Wartime restrictions remained in force, and accommodation in industrial towns was controlled through the labour exchange, who provided a few possible addresses. Hence, I exchanged my comfortable room at the 'Goddards' for the attic bedroom in Mrs. Morris' boarding house at the bottom of Rolleston Street. Grandpa returned to Sussex, and I was on my own! Sunday was spent doing some train watching at Swindon Junction station, and making a trial run to the works entrance to determine the requisite walking time.

Monday morning arrived with a dismal blast upon the works hooter at 07.00, echoing throughout the town and surrounding countryside awakening any still in the land of Nod. Eager to start, I was already in Mrs. Morris' kitchen, consuming a hasty breakfast before setting off well ahead of the necessary hour. Three further hooters were sounded, warnings at 7.45 and 7.50, followed by the 'start work' hooter at 7.55, and in these final minutes, the streets around the works entrances swarmed with thousands of workmen, clad almost to a man in drab fawn raincoats and cloth caps. They arrived by every form of transport., Many walked, shuffling heavy boots relentlessly along the pavements, while others rolled in on bicycles. Hordes from the more outlying suburbs converged in Swindon's blue and cream buses, crammed to the roof despite the limited number of standing passengers in theory permitted. On the older 'buses, with outside stairs to the upper deck, they could be seen, sunshine or rain, in full occupation of this rearguard position. For those resident in more remote areas, Highworth, Wootton Bassett, Purton or Chiseldon, the GWR laid on trains, usually a 45XX and two coaches, which sped into the junction station with a tankle tankle tankle of lightweight rodding keeping pace with furiously revolving 4'7½" wheels. In those days, a motor car was out of the question for most, and even the lordly, bowler-hatted, chief foremen rode by 'bus from the select suburb of Coate Water.

Caught among this throng, I was dragged into the maelstrom of seething humanity, and sucked through the main works entrance into the subterranean tunnel beneath carriage works and Bristol main line, to emerge at the ramp between the main offices and 'B' shed. Here was the central time office where the ritual of 'checking in' was learned. Each employee on the wages staff had a number, and this was stamped on a pear shaped piece of brass, about 1½ inches across, the small end of which was pierced to hang on a hook. For the first month I was on probation and checked in at the main time office, but once pronounced satisfactory was renumbered and reported to the shop check board. This was a large box, studded with numbered hooks, from which one removed one's check upon arrival. At 7.55, when the last hooter blew, the shop timekeeper (known as the 'checkie') slammed down the glass covered lid, noting as absent owners of any checks remaining on the hooks. Slightly late arrivals were allowed another go, with loss of 15 minutes pay, known as 'losing a quarter', but anyone later than this would have to see the foreman (the 'gaffer') for reprimand and further pay loss. On paydays, the normal check was exchanged for an oval copper 'pay check', which in turn was handed in exchange for a pay tin, like a small metal snuff box into which was stuffed pay and wage sheet. At the end of a normal day, when the final 'cease work' hooter blew at 5.30 pm, pandemonium reigned as every man threw his check more or less in the direction of the check board and sprinted out to 'bus, cycle shed, or whatever, leaving the 'checkie' to gather up the checks and hang 'em on the hooks!

Like all apprentices, my probation period was spent in the 'B' shed wherein were repaired tenders, small tank engines, and a few of the smaller tender engines such as 0-6-0 and 4-4-0 types. I cut my engineering teeth on the tender gang, and soon discovered that real engineering was totally unlike the almost clinical conditions previously experienced in school workshops. Put to work stripping the water pickup gear beneath a tender it was rapidly apparent that after several years and many miles in service there was not a single nut which would budge for a mere spanner! Each had to be split by means of a hammer and cold chisel, a laborious, dirty, and painful process as inexperienced muscles wilted under unaccustomed usage leading to inaccurate blows landing on knuckles instead of chisel. Furthermore, each blow shook the whole structure, loosening a hail of dried mud and rusty metal, most of which seemed to fall down one's neck. With items such as the drawgear nut, too big to split this way without spending excessive time, 'Ernie the Burner' was called in to operate. Ernie, his face singed to a ruddy hue by constant radiation from oxy-acetylene flame was a cheerful, if simple, character, always ready to trundle his barrow of gas bottles along, unwind the tangle of rubber tubing, and ignite the burner with a spit and a roar. The first time I watched this I was fascinated as glowing globules of molten metal dripped onto Ernie's ragged overalls, whilst he, like some Indian fire walker seemed totally oblivious. Eventually the offending component dropped off, to lie sizzling in the grease on the pit floor, while Ernie rewound his piping and went off to find something else to amputate. He might have made a competent, if somewhat lethal, surgeon of the old school.

While thus engaged beneath the tenders, the geography, hierarchy, and etiquette of the place was learned. At the north end of the shop, between the two traverser roads which spanned its length, was the tool and oil stores, presided over by a dour character of complexion as oily as his stock in trade. From him was received the basic tool kit, hammer, chisel, ball of cotton waste, and tin of sand soap, the latter a special blend of soft soap and fine sand, made in Swindon's soap works (nearly everything was manufactured on site). Sand soap had an abrasive characteristic, very effective in cleansing grease ingrained into the skin, although hardly the type of product sold in lady's beauty salons. All the above accoutrements were handed out so grudgingly that one might believe the storeman paid for them out of his own pocket, a basic characteristic of all storemen.

Above the stores, and reached by a flight of wooden stairs were the shop offices wherein dwelt the foremen and clerks. Chief foreman in 'B' shed was Bill Bullock, a large man of the old school who wore his pepper and salt trousers at half mast and never sallied forth into the shop without his regulation bowler hat, the badge of office. A pronounced olfactory organ, of pock-marked surface and rubicund hue, earned him the sobriquet 'Strawberry-konk', never of course uttered in his presence. The two under-foremen wore trilbies, and had no outstanding characteristics. Such a lowly creature as an apprentice never came into contact with a foreman, unless guilty of some heinous offence, and my normal contact with authority was the chargehand, Freddie Johns, a cheerful, pipe-smoking character who despite the amount of dirt and grease everywhere invariably maintained his shoes in an immaculate and highly polished state, always recognisable from below.

Each chargehand had a 'box', rather like a sentry box but containing desk and chair, for carrying out routine paper work. For some odd reason, these wooden structures were devoid of windows, and inevitably any chargehand therein incarcerated was thought to be having a snooze. Although not a chargehand, 'B' shed had an incredible character who somehow rated a box, possibly on account of his extreme age. But for the war he would undoubtedly have retired, but as ground man for the overhead crane he was still at work, aged around seventy. Nicknamed 'Thunder' due to past association with an ultra-slow character called 'Lightning', he was a gourmet of sorts. Thunder's box always contained some black pudding, hung until it was green, by which time it was adjudged edible. Furthermore, Thunder ate snails! These were not the *escargot* of French cuisine, lovingly cooked in wine, garlic and butter, but good honest GWR snails, picked off the line, and munched alive between toothless gums with evident relish. Thunder attributed this taste to service in France during the first world war, about which he had a great number of amusing anecdotes. Couched in his rich Wiltshire vernacular, Thunder could entertain for hours, and well I remember a typically indelicate story concerning a lady of easy virtue picked up on leave in Paris. Apparently she was wined and dined to excess, whereupon by the time they got to bed 'Er were fartin' loike a bluddy Gatlin' gun'.

Another curious personality was Jimmy the Nut Man, who presided over the bolt stores and handed out his wares with the same lugubrious reluctance as his colleague in the tool stores. Jimmy was of short stature, sported a pipe smoked upside down, and despite his fairly menial position, a man of evidently right wing politics. Whenever an opportunity arose, he would buttonhole an apprentice and after a general ramble about this and that, exhort them to beware of 'Them ther com*mun*ists', putting accent on the second syllable, as in communal.

As mutual probationer I had Barry Pearce, whose father was an electrician in the works, and from whom I was warned about some of the pranks played on raw apprentices, such as being sent to the stores for a left-handed hammer, or a bucket of steam. Accordingly, when one day the fitter to whom I was allocated told me to go to the stores for a tallow candle, I laughed at him, thinking it to be a leg pull. The more he remonstrated the more I laughed, until more or less dragged there by the scruff of the neck and made to draw out a candle. It turned out to be the standard illumination used inside a tender. Screwed into a $\frac{3}{4}$-inch nut, it was reasonably stable and highly portable, whereas an electric light on a lead was likely to become snagged in the anti-surge baffles which criss-cross a tender tank, and worse, could short out with lethal effect should insulation wear. Thus, lighted like Florence Nightingale, we crawled round dank tender interiors, attending to strainers and level gauges, a claustrophobic task for one affected with that ailment. Occasionally, one would find a fish flapping out the last of its life on the tender floor!

One learned to beware the bowler-hatted apparition of 'Strawberry-konk' as he proceeded on his daily round of the shop. At the warning 'Weigh up, Gaffer's coming', anyone idling grabbed the nearest hammer, leaped into the adjacent pit, and pounded hard on the nearest piece of locomotive or tender. As nearly every component was hammered on and hammered off again, the chance of being queried on such activity was remote. In fact, one of the local jokes was 'If at first you don't succeed, try a bigger hammer!' Crude though this may seem to the lay outsider, it helped to explain why Great Western engines left works with good, tight, motion, and did not emerge with a brand new built-in mechanical knock, as did the poor locomotives thrown together at Crewe or Doncaster.

Lunch time was spent sitting outside in a locomotive cab, watching trains go by while eating sandwiches. Food consumed, a brisk walk down to 'A' shop revealed what engines were ex-works, and more interesting what new engines were under construction. My arrival at Swindon coincided with the appearance of Hawksworth's '1000' class, of which the first five or six had motion stamped with the originally intended 99XX numbers. A photograph was in the local paper before I actually saw no 1000, and was not impressed by the long, single, splasher which looked like some archaic reversion to Crewe practice. The vast double chimney looked more suitable for the 'Queen Mary' and in fact was later replaced by a single chimney, as fitted to the rest of the class. Boiler pressure of

A clean County, 1015, at Acton on a Bristol–Paddington train. These engines had the loudest bark and best acceleration of all GWR 4-6-0 when built.

280 psi was clearly chosen to 'equal' Bulleid's engines, for the next orderly sequence for a GWR locomotive would have been 275 psi, not that 5 psi would have made any difference to the performance in service. A curious machine, virtually a 'Modified Hall' chassis upon which was mounted an LMS 8F boiler with increased pressure. Possibly they were an attempt to produce a two-cylinder equivalent to a 'Castle', but somehow they were not popular. Certainly they had the loudest bark of any GWR locomotive, and were excellent at acceleration, even better than most Great Western locomotives. Not usually known is the fact that in addition to non-standard driving wheels, they also had crankpins one inch longer than standard to take the increased piston thrust, plus valves of longer lap ($1\frac{7}{8}''$) with correspondingly increased travel. All these details were only discovered later, but it is convenient to include them here.

On other days, the forlorn little clutch of engines awaiting repair or scrapping, near the Gloucester junction, was investigated, to see what strange types came to light. In those early days, following war's end, traffic declined to peacetime levels, and large inroads were made into the older pannier tanks, particularly the 17XX, 18XX, and 27XX series suddenly rendered redundant. Over the years many curious oddities appeared on this dump, including 0-4-0ST no 92, officially withdrawn in 1942 but retained complete at Wellington until brought down to Swindon for scrap about 1946. Whilst up at the junction, a daily transfer trip from the siding next to the Gloucester line to the wagon

1009 at Swindon being prepared for test runs, fitted with a temporary stove pipe double chimney to Sam Ell's proportions. In the foreground is the plate framed bogie used under several classes in the past.

works yard north of the station, was well worth seeing and hearing. Motive power was one of the diminutive panniers of 1901 or 2021 classes, with their old cast iron wheels, and the cavalcade left about 1 pm, in a traffic lull. Fifty or sixty wagons were common on this turn, and on one occasion I counted 72. With lots of struggle and slipping, despite the application of avalanches of sand, the little engine slowly dragged the seemingly endless trail of trucks across the main line, with clicking wheels and moaning flanges never drowning out the engine noises, even when it was well out of sight behind the station buildings. Many years later I saw a pathetic travesty of this once awe-inspiring operation – a 204 hp agricultural-tractor-on-flanged-wheels dragging the half a dozen or so wagons which was all a vanquished works on a run down railway system could muster.

Saturday morning was a time for weekend anticipation, with work carried out at noticeably relaxed pace until 11.00 when all hands knocked off for an hour's cleaning up prior to leaving at noon. Soon after 11, Bill Bullock strode out followed, after a decent interval, by the under-foremen. Once clear, a skittle alley was set up on the traverser road, using spring hangers as pins. These were bowled at by wooden blocks which during the war had replaced the rubber and plate sandwiches which cushioned shocks. After several years in service, these wooden blocks seemed to retain energy, absorbed under compression, and when bowled this released itself in very springy bounces. One morning, Strawberry-konk worked later than usual, unnoticed by anybody, and while striding down behind the tenders a particularly bouncy block soared over the top and knocked his bowler off! There was a roar of rage, and within seconds nobody was in sight, but great sounds of energetic hammering miraculously reverberated throughout the shop!

Social life for a probationer apprentice in lodgings was almost non-existent. On weekdays there was a bath and meal, followed by simply listening to the other lodgers recounting their adventures or complaints. Saturday was laundry day, not included in the lodging tariff, and I patronised OON LEE CHINESE LAUNDRY, a steamy little establishment just round the corner. The bundle of dirty apparel was deposited in exchange for a scrap of coloured paper with stamped-on number. Upon presentation a few days later one's laundry was returned after answering the catch question 'Pasellocolla?' First time this was totally incomprehensible – I thought they were speaking Chinese. Vainly I requested my laundry as per paper slip, but eventually was helped by a regular customer who interpreted the 'Chinese' as 'Parcel or collars', without which answer they seemed unable to find the laundry. Today, these little Chinese laundries have disappeared from the scene, replaced by launderettes, but Oon Lee's descendents doubtless make a living in the restaurant trade.

One weekend, I think the first, without much to do, and being by then 'in' the railway locomotive works, I tried out my hand at locomotive design. Reasoning that since Churchward used a common boiler design for his largest express and freight locomotives, then current freight haulage needed an engine with a 'King' boiler. An attempt was then made to scheme out a four-cylinder 4-8-0 using 'King' components (fig 1) soon found out to be impossible! Cylinders, much lower down with 4'7½'' wheels, fouled the bogie, and the calculated tractive effort was over 56000 lb, far too much for the likely adhesion weight. In retrospect, my logic was faulty, for the answer would have been a two-cylinder 2-10-0 with 'King' boiler (fig. 2) not unlike the 2-10-2T with 47XX boiler which unknown to me had already been schemed out at Swindon. Churchward did not use four cylinders on his freight design, but this had escaped me in my initial enthusiasm for the project. Clearly, there was a lot more to locomotive design than could be gleaned in a week or two's probationary apprenticeship, and the subject was dropped for a while. Meanwhile, the probation period passed, and I was pronounced fit to be a full apprentice (I never heard of anybody who did not!), so was given a 'shift' next door to the 'R' shop, to learn turning.

Forty years old and game for anything, grimy Churchward Mogul 6356 helps the summer Saturday passenger rush by hauling a west to north express, seen approaching the Severn tunnel.

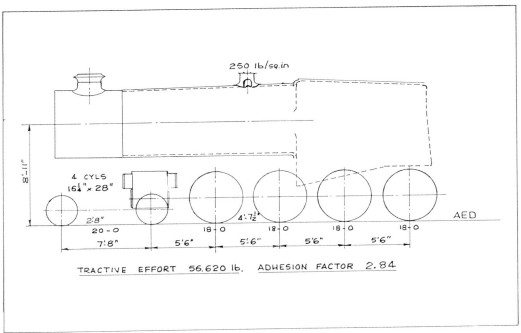

Author's early apprentice scheme for a heavy freight locomotive built of King class components. Excessive tractive effort, inadequate adhesion, and cylinders fouling bogie wheels became so apparent that the scheme was never completed! (Fig 1)

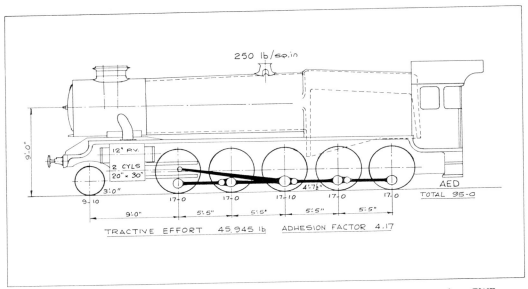

Several years later, the practical way of designing a "King Freight" as a 2-10-0, in more modern GWR idiom, was thought of. Such an engine would probably have included outside Walschaerts motion, as in the 1500 class, and could have been accompanied by a 4-8-0 mixed traffic version, a "super 47XX". (Fig 2)

3

'PRENTICE LAD

The first job, as a real apprentice, was inevitably the 'R' shop, to which I was 'renumbered', reporting thus to their check board. This shop was the old main machine shop, built of local stone in a massive manner, and one of Gooch's original workshops. As contrast to its venerable ancestry, it seemed, more than any other shop, to be populated by apprentices. After initial breaking-in in the 'B' shed, apprentices commenced two years turning training, always starting in the 'Scraggery', a corner of the shop appropriately, at that time, presided over by a chargehand named Harry Turner. Within his domain, the simplest and crudest of machine work was performed, to wit 'nut-scragging'. For the benefit of the uninitiated, millions of hexagon nuts were machine-forged elsewhere in the works, for use all over the system. These were drilled and tapped by slightly more skilful staff, and then had to be faced off, top and bottom, a process known as scragging. The nut was fed onto a threaded mandrel on a rather basic machine, and a simple facing tool run over it, top or bottom as was the case. Here the raw apprentice learned the 'feel' of a machine, cutting steel with hardened steel, was taught some basics on grinding the tool to the requisite cutting angles, and of setting it up to something approaching the optimum operating height. The scragging lathes were simple and robust, as well they had to be, for a totally inept attempt by the apprentice, too fast, tool incorrectly ground and set, resulted in a horrible jam-up, sufficient to bring tears to the eyes of a craftsmen turner!

Apart from his apprentices, Harry had a permanent staff of semi-skilled labour in the shape of several women, remnants of a much larger force of wartime female workers. These ranged from young and pretty to old and grotesque, and included one particularly pretty young lass, well endowed with the bulges which men admire, and whose overall-clad figure, walking, re-sembled two small boys fighting under a blanket. This was a source of fascina-tion to youngsters just beginning to appreciate that there was more to girls than silly giggling at school, and as perhaps the least worldly of my contemporaries, I was delegated to give it a slap next time it undulated past. Smack! I don't know who was most surprised – the recipient of this unwonted aggression, or the aggressor, who discovered for the first time in his life, that lady's bottoms are even softer than they look! Fortunately the girl's initial anger at this impertinence soon subsided, and I was not hauled before higher authority.

Having completed a sojourn in the scraggery without wrecking too many machines, I was moved to the mud plug gang. Now all steam enthusiasts know what a mud plug is, that little tapered, threaded plug with a square end, screwed into strategic locations round the firebox to allow access for washing out and inspection therein. In steam days railways used prodigious quantities of these, and Swindon had a small section of the 'R' shop devoted to their production. Apprentices graduated from the scraggery were initially set the task of turning the tapered contour, then later, when more skilled, of adding the screw thread by means of a tool called a chaser. The whole operation was basically boring, yet needed concentration as failure to extract the chaser in good time jammed up the machine. In the scraggery this was less of a problem, each machine being individually motored, but on the mud plug gang one had really joined the machine shop proper, most of whose machines were then driven by a veritable maze of belting reaching down from overhead drive shafts to the machines below. Any jam up on one machine meant stopping the whole system to repair one belt.

First thing in the morning, after everybody arrived, overalls were changed in to, and many sat on the nearest bench to glance at the glamour girls in the *Daily Mirror*, the normal organ of news dissemination apart from the shifty-eyed radicals who sported the *'Daily Worker'*. A few minutes after starting time the Gaffer would be spotted as he strode in and the nearest man pressed the start button of the electric motor driving his shaft. Wheeeee, it accelerated, followed by further Wheeees down the shop as a fugue of electrical power broke the former relative silence. Overhead shafts were connected to individual machines by woven belting joined by copper stitchwork, each belt, passing over upper and lower pulleys, providing further unsynchronised rhythms, flip flop, flip-te-flop, click clack, click-te-clack as belt joints by the hundred flapped over the metal pulleys which transmitted power to the machines below. From time to time a belt would break, from carelessness or fatigue, whereupon the whole production line had to be stopped while the 'beltie' and his mate arrived to effect repairs, perched up on insecure looking ladders and sweating anxiously away whilst the de-powered machinists below indulged in an orgy of idling and chatting safe in the knowledge that authority was literally powerless to protest. After the offending belt had been repaired, the rhythm resumed, flip flop, flipetty flop, click clack, clickety clack.

About this stage in my term, other apprentices were discovered, leading to discussions on their interests (if any) and outlook on life. Most were trade apprentices, some by choice but many because father was a railway tradesman insisting on son following his footsteps. Some ridiculed us 'premiums' for choosing as a career such a 'dead' industry as the railways. At that time, such

names as Marples and Beeching were unknown, and nobody had any inkling
of the vandalism which was to be wreaked by Beeching under instructions from
his destructive overlord, Marples.

   A greater level of interest was naturally found amongst the premium apprentices, who had opted for the life from outside, and with Swindon boasting
considerable fame in the locomotive world, premiums came not only from all
over the country but all over the world. Some names from early days, still
remembered, are Keith Gourlay and Henry Pearce from near Ormskirk, Lancs,
who might more naturally have graduated via Horwich, Mike Casey, from
Glossop, a 'natural' for Gorton but whose Swindon training has taken him
today to the top mechanical engineering post on British Railways. Alan Clothier was son of a GWR motive power officer in Plymouth, too senior to claim a
free apprenticeship for his son, and more senior, already in the drawing office
was Tony Sterndale, very much the Public School man at the time, but often to
be seen, with camera, recording things going on in the locomotive world. It was
from Keith Gourlay that I bought my first camera, and of these early acquaint-
ances deep friendships sprung up, such that I still regularly correspond with
Henry Pearce and Tony Sterndale, after more than forty years. From these early
days I also well remember Bob Gasper and Keith Hemsley, both from India,
Bob I recall from Jamalpur. For these, and many others, the Swindon apprenticeship was undertaken to obtain a sound grounding in engineering and while
some were railway and locomotive enthusiasts, many were not. Of those who
were enthusiastic, the degree of involvement varied, from those who just knew
that nothing could ever beat a 'Hall' or 'Castle' through those sufficiently
interested to travel abroad to see what was happening overseas. However, in
the ten years spent at Swindon, only one other real locomotive design enthusiast was encountered, that being Tony Sterndale. Two people in ten years. This
possibly explains why, in the course of British locomotive history, so many
indifferent locomotive designs were foisted upon the owning railway. Assuming that the situation I knew at Swindon was fairly normal, and with railway
promotion being very much on a seniority basis, the chances of a keen locomotive designer being placed in charge of that function when really needed are
quite small. The man with the real knowledge and desire may be too old, with
insufficient time to perform his task properly, or too young, needing perhaps
more experience in other aspects of executive life to be entrusted with the top
job. Of the four big names in locomotive mechanical engineering, in Britain,
during the course of the twentieth century, Churchward obtained his chieftain-
ship at just about the right time of life, with the added advantage of being
virtually, but not nominally, in command for several years during which his
early mistakes were 'covered' by the nominal incumbent.

   Gresley took office at an early age, giving time for a cautious start before
rising to great eminence. The two other 'greats' both took executive office late in
their careers. but nevertheless had immense effect on locomotive practice,

these being Stanier (from Swindon) and Bulleid (from Doncaster) both of whom only gained eminence by changing railways after possibly substantial frustration on their home systems. Bearing in mind the above, it is perhaps very understandable that so many British CMEs, especially about the turn of the century, were insufficiently able to direct locomotive design into the channels it should have taken. Even after grouping, Fowler in particular on the LMS, under pressure from Anderson and Symes, weakly permitted undersized machines of indifferent efficiency to be mass produced whilst concurrently, Collett at Swindon only maintained an apparent superiority by producing 'new' classes manufactured from Churchward components, already some twenty years ahead of contemporary practice. After that twenty year lead time had been used up, and Swindon's products compared with those of the other lines following nationalisation, Swindon was found to be wanting in thermal efficiency, on the one hand, and maximum output on the other. Only in starting a train from rest, and accelerating, were Swindon products never really bettered.

During the mud plug career, it became time to enrol at night school (later euphemised as evening classes), at 'The College, Swindon', an educational emporium presided over by Jack Churchman, the Principal. Initial enrolment was in the main building, but as the most junior starter I found that the crowded junior classes were held in assorted children's daytime schoolrooms, sitting in old fashioned desks of a style imagined outgrown. Basic classes, first year, were mathematics, science, and engineering drawing, each taking one evening per week. The day's schedule was thus hard manual work, in the works, from 7.55 to 5.30 pm, dash to lodgings for a quick bath and a meal, ready for studies from 7.00 to 9.30 pm. The two nights weekly not devoted to school could be used for homework, but I, with optimistic unreality, took a further subject making four nights per week at school. This was perhaps not so unwise, apprentice wages were 28 shillings per week gross (about 25/- nett), and lodgings came to 35/-, the shortfall being made up by a £5 per month allowance from my parents, leaving precious little for anything else. There was thus no cash for idle indulgencies, and despite the arousing sense of sexual awakening, in a young, active, and virile male, girl friends were out of the question. Taking a girl to 'the pictures' demanded extensive budgetary planning, and I rather envied the locals, living with parents, who seemed able to achieve such exciting outings with evident ease. Several years later the situation reversed, as I, still a bachelor, enjoyed foreign travel, pub evenings, and adequate female company while those who started early were bogged down with mortgages, whining wives, and screaming brats. Poverty, while young, is a blessing if only one can extrapolate it into the advantages in later life! Few have such wisdom when young, and in my own case it was a 'compulsory wisdom' enforced by the inability to do anything else, for which I will ever be grateful, but can claim no credit. At the time, I was envious!

Ex Rhymney Railway P class, GWR no. 83, in Swindonised condition, stands in Rhymney station attached to an old RR coach.

After a stipulated period I was eligible for travel at privilege rates, about quarter fare, and lost no time taking advantage of this. Having become quite fascinated by my brief glimpse of those Welsh engines, and wanting to see more of them, several Sunday trips were made to Newport, Cardiff, and Barry, to ferret them out. Swindon still worked a 5½ day week, so Sunday day trips were ideal. Travel out was on the 7.50 Swindon to Bristol via Badminton, consisting of two non-corridor coaches hauled almost invariably by one of Swindon's '29s', the lightest of tasks even for so venerable a machine. Bowling through the sleepy, Sunday morning countryside of Wiltshire and Gloucestershire, there seemed little traffic to warrant the train at all. A glimpse of the Midland after Chipping Sodbury, and perhaps a banked freight climbing through the tunnel were the only diversions. To catch the Cardiff connection, one had to detrain at Filton Junction, one of the bleakest and most draughty stations on the Great Western, devoid of such facilities as a tearoom. From here, after a fairly lengthy wait, a Bristol–Cardiff express was caught, and my first experience of this was quite a shock, for the train itself, about eight or ten coaches of respectable main line corridor stock, was hauled by a diminutive 'Dean Goods' 0-6-0. This was regular winter Sunday operation, as maintenance was carried out on the Severn Tunnel during such periods, and the shortest alternative route was via Sharpness and the Severn Bridge, traversing the

Midland line from Westerleigh to Berkeley Road. After climbing the bridge approach, easing slowly across the bridge itself, and regaining the main line at Lydney, the little 0-6-0 really showed its paces as an express engine. In those days, most GWR expresses loped along at a steady 55 mph, and this was well within the capacity of a 'Dean Goods', as I found to my surprise.

Once in South Wales, Sundays were very dead, especially as regards freight traffic, but there were plenty of locomotive sheds to explore, many with varying quantities of those fascinating non-standard Welsh engines. GWR enthusiasts think of Paddington as the hub, or perhaps more realistically as the fulcrum of the system, and the West of England as the main line, but from a traffic point of view, Cardiff was almost certainly the most important centre. Within a twenty-five mile radius of Cardiff there were a score of locomotive sheds, housing a quarter of the railway's locomotives, several important docks, and one of the three main workshops. Nowhere else on the Great Western was such a concentration of activity, and it is surprising how few enthusiasts bothered to visit the area. Apart from the sheer quantities involved, the locomotive variety was quite amazing, from the plethora of Welsh engines in their various stages of Westernisation, most of the standard GWR classes except, in those days, Kings and 47XX, plus a number of GWR classes built especially for South Wales ranging from the little 1101 class dock tanks to the 72XX 2-8-2T. The more I saw of the Welsh locos the less I seemed to know, since there were no easily available published references to them at that time. At one stage, I sent a letter to the Works Manager at Swindon, requesting details of dimensions etc., but received only a typically snooty reply to the effect that he could see no reason how such information could benefit my engineering apprenticeship! Such was the old Great Western.

In July 1946, while still in the 'R' shop, there occurred that great annual event always known as 'Trip', or the works summer holiday. By then it had, I think, expanded to a fortnight's duration but it was still known generally as 'Trip week', this being of long standing when the GWR ran special trains all over the system, conveying workmen and their families to various destinations of their choice. 'Wher be goin' Trip?' was the standard greeting for weeks before the exodus, and the answer was likely to be 'Weston' or 'Weymouth', by far the most popular destinations where the Swindon workman happily went to what, for that period, was effectively Swindon-on-Sea, full of familiar faces. One of these resorts, possibly Weymouth, referred to it as 'Swindon Week'. Something like twenty special trains ran from Swindon over a few hours at the beginning of 'Trip', probably half a dozen each to Weston and Weymouth, a couple to Paddington and South Wales, with others to the Midlands and the North, and of course to Devon and Cornwall. My first 'Trip' was spent in South Wales, ferreting out places such as Danygraig and Burry Port which could not be visited on the standard Sunday visit. Two special memories remain, one of seeing the last Port Talbot 0-8-2T, 1358, arrive at Danygraig shed late afternoon.

Collett 0-6-0 2292 with a surprisingly long train is about to enter Sodbury tunnel, with a 51XX banker shoving hard, when at the optimum moment a 68XX rolls out of the down portal with a westbound train.

3858 en route from Gloucester to Swindon, one of the last 2-8-0 built to this original Churchward design. Note the set of points and crossings in the leading wagon, perhaps going to Swindon works.

It was the only time I saw it in steam, and never discovered what special duty (if any) kept it going for a dozen years after its sisters had been scrapped. The other special memory is of slowly overtaking, just east of Port Talbot, one of the two remaining PTR 0-6-2T, 184 or 188, running along the parallel PTR line towards Tondu. The rest of the trip remains a pleasant haze of odd, sometimes unique, locomotives run to earth in obscure sheds, of travelling on the briskly timed Cardiff Valley passenger trains behind 56XX, Taff 'A' and 'O4' classes, and Rhymney 0-6-2T, and of course the inevitable auto trains, mainly worked by 64XX, a few 48XX, and even an old 3561 class 2-4-0T. Tondu shed had a daily business train to Cardiff worked by a 44XX, smallest of the 2-6-2T, whose little wheels must have revolved very rapidly along the main line, which it traversed with few stops, on what was probably the only express type train ever worked by this class.

After graduating from the mud plug gang, there was a boring interlude on the automatic lathes, making boiler stays and similar components, a period in which apprentices seemed to be used as cheap labour rather than learning much of use, other than patience. Once the material was loaded into the machine, all operations were automatic, all one having then to do being to spot check the products for dimensional accuracy. There was a strong tendency, when on 'automatics' to set the thing going and then wander off to look at more interesting work being performed elsewhere, or to go and chat with the nearest enthusiast-orientated apprentice on the subject of steam.

A more interesting 'R' shop turning job was the manufacture of pistons, carried out by a large and very quiet old fellow called Tom, with an apprentice assistant. Turning the piston rod was fairly tedious, since once on the go, it would take about twenty minutes for the tool to traverse the rod, over three feet long on the engines with 30 inch piston stroke. Tedium could be averted by grinding the tool such that the swarf, or metal shaving, came off in a continuous spiral which could be directed along the shop floor, winding itself steadily along. Somewhere, it would probably hook itself into somebody's overall trousers, after which it would wind itself up like a spring until suddenly excess tension caused it to snap, whipping about like an angry snake, and showering everybody with oily cutting fluid! It was politic to disappear for a while after such a successful prank.

On the subject of disappearing, in the yard between the 'R' and 'G' shops, dating from the original works, was a very primitive form of lavatory having a row of cubicles whose seats were placed over an open drain through which water flowed continuously. The standard prank here was to occupy the up-stream cubicle early, and when several lower down were comfortably occupied by workmen having their early morning session, probably accompanied by a smoke and reading the paper, a crumpled up newspaper would be ignited and floated down the water stream, singeing several bottoms en route. One had to flee rapidly before the enraged owners could dress and pursue!

Returning to the subject of piston manufacture, Swindon pistons were different to most, being hollow castings screwed onto the piston rods with a taper thread. Most railways used a taper face and separate large nut, but the Swindon design allowed a smaller clearance volume to be obtained. The hollow piston had four core holes, used during the casting process, and plugs were screwed into these making them steamtight and also acting as stays. Old Tom usually worked on the piston head, and when the apprentice had made the rod, the two were united. It was an incredibly crude process, which nevertheless worked! The rod was introduced and screwed into the head by hand, as far as it would go, the head being held in the chuck of a large, low speed, lathe. A bracket would then be clamped on to the rod, and supported on a hydraulic ram attached to a pressure gauge, and the lathe set in motion. As the taper thread became tighter and hydraulic pressure increased, old Tom watched carefully and at the appropriate pressure slipped the lathe's driving belt on to the neutral pulley. By such means were manufactured a very effective piston assembly which for some reason other railways were unable to emulate. Perhaps they got too 'scientific' and ignored the Old Tom ingredient.

Other shops worked in during the turning portion of my apprenticeship were the brass shop, opposite the brass foundry, wherein all manner of brass bits and pieces, such as safety valves, clack valves, injector and ejector components etc were manufactured. Brass has quite different machining properties to steel, and new techniques of tool grinding had to be learned. From there, it was a short term in the 'O' shop, or tool room, followed by a fair period in the 'G' shop wherein worked the millwrights. This was the most interesting part of the turning apprenticeship, as everything was a special job rather than production work. The 'G' shop covered all sorts of work, although its main function was maintenance of works machinery. Grafted onto this was any sort of non-standard job unsuitable for the more production orientated machine shops, and these included the little motor tractors used for works transport and more familiar to travellers hauling baggage around Paddington station. All sorts of pumping machinery abounded throughout the GWR, including the massive beam engines used at the Severn tunnel, whose valves and other components were turned in the 'G' shop, which had not only the largest diameter faceplate lathe in the whole works, but also the lathe with the longest bed. It was upon this latter that I saw being set up a large diameter shaft something like thirty feet long, which upon enquiry turned out to be the propellor shaft from one of the company's ships. This took, I think, a couple of weeks to machine, the operator sitting on a seat which moved along with the saddle, where he could keep an eye on things. Of course, an apprentice was never let loose on this sort of job, which needed the most skilled and experienced of turners, the cost of a possible mistake being enormous.

The final 'Turning' shift was to a dank little sub-shop, attached for administrative purposes to the 'P1' shop (boiler mounting) but actually situated in a corner of the main boiler ('V') shop. Here were produced, again on automatics, copper firebox stays about which the less said the better. The chargehand was a gimlet eyed little man who strongly disapproved of his apprentices 'taking a walk', so we had perforce to spend the tedious hours chatting to one another while the automatic lathes churned out copper stays by the million. There was at least one enthusiast apprentice with me for part of the time, which meant we could talk steam, or when stumped, discuss the more arduous subjects being taught at the 'Tech', of which differential and integral calculus was my pet hate, being taught in such a manner that its use was never clear. Trade apprentices had usually dropped out of night school by then, being more interested in girls and football, the latter being somewhat of a religion in Swindon.

The local team was called Swindon Town, invariably known as 'The Town', and from what I could gather was a rather mediocre performer in the third league or division. First thing Monday morning the whole works seemed alive with a verbose and acrimonious post mortem of the previous Saturday's match, who should have done what and when, and who should, or should not, have been selected to play. Bitter recriminations were the order of the day, and well I remember an old workman complaining vehemently, after a lost home game, that 'the other side were playing to win', which I thought was the object of the game! Two of us devised a good leg pull for the Saturday afternoons of home games. All one had to do was to walk in a direction from the County Ground, at about close-of-play time, looking somewhat miserable. Anxious Swindonians who for some reason failed to attend the match, would grab one earnestly by the lapels and beseech 'How'd they get on?' The answer was always something like 'Lost 5–2', causing the enquirer to slink into his house like a whipped puppy, until the football edition of the local paper, printed on pink paper and known as the 'Pink 'un' possibly revealed our deception, unless we had guessed correctly. The local rag was called the Evening Advertiser, known invariably as 'The Adver.', a typical provincial paper full of births, deaths and marriages, but being Swindon, occasionally enlivened by a photograph and description of the latest works product.

VISITS HOME

Subsisting in rather dreary lodgings, visits home were made at roughly monthly intervals, at first to grandfather's abode in Sussex, and later also to Lee, in southeast London, where my parents had settled after the war. The most direct method was simply to catch a train to Paddington, nip across London on the Underground, then continue from Charing Cross either by electric to Lee, or steam to Ticehurst Road in Sussex. For the ordinary traveller that is quite good enough, but in time I tired of the plodding journey to Paddington, in crowded trains timed to do the $77\frac{1}{4}$ miles in two hours (a speed more in line with narrow gauge colonial railways) and even then arriving late.

For the steam enthusiast and budding locomotive engineer there were several alternatives – true they all took longer, but the important factor was the journey rather than the arrival!

Alternative one consisted of taking the early morning train from Swindon Town station (nothing to do with the football team) down the old M&SWJR line to Andover Junction, thence by Southern to Waterloo. These alternative routes, incidentally, only became really worthwhile after the five day week had been introduced, giving Saturday mornings for extra travelling time. The morning train from Swindon to Andover was rostered for a 45XX baby Prairie, and incredible as it may seem, down those long sweeping curves through the Wiltshire Downs, one was more likely to achieve 70 mph behind the little tank than with a 'Castle' en route to Paddington. A very good lesson, big wheels are no advantage if they fail to rotate rapidly, and from those early days I have never been afraid of the idea of smallish wheels for fast work. At Andover, the train to Waterloo usually had a Bulleid Pacific, whose performance was diametrically opposite to that of a GWR 'Castle'. The latter would make a brave and impressive start, stamping away with confident surefooted adhesion, but once out of earshot from the station, notched up and eased off considerably, continuing at plodding gait to the next stop. By contrast, the Bulleid locomotive started off with several violent slips, and after suitable delay got into its stride with offbeat, sneezing, exhaust, but once under way sped uphill and down dale with exhilarating vigour. There was little to choose between overall times, the Bulleid *had* to run fast to regain time lost in starting, and the economics of train dynamics mean that accountants would certainly favour the GWR method. There remained the third alternative – a locomotive which would start in Great Western manner then run like a Bulleid, an unbeatable combination which set my mind into motion.

Meanwhile, there were other delights to be experienced travelling the Southern way, purely sensual delights unconnected with locomotive efficiency, other than as examples of what not to do. By looking out, at Basingstoke, for what was on the next Waterloo local, often nothing of much interest, I was able to sample the Drummond T14 'Paddlebox' 4-6-0, whose main attribute was noise, and the rebuilt N15X 'Remembrance' 4-6-0 whose performance seemed to be in the sturdy, unexciting category, not dissimilar to the Robinson locomotives experienced earlier around Sheffield. Even the sound effects were similar, possibly biassing judgement. When visiting grandfather in Sussex, very much more scope was available, and the first line of attack was the Reading–Redhill line, worked mainly by Maunsell 'Moguls' and in earlier days, before I tried this route, by aged Stirling B1 and F1 4-4-0s of feeble power and large wheels, seemingly totally unsuited to this line with its fairly heavy gradients. In later days, by waiting at Reading until an interesting locomotive appeared, I was able to experience such old 4-4-0s as Drummond L12 and S11s, and Brighton B4X. Of these, the Brighton engine, despite its large boiler and impressive appearance, was the most sluggish of all, due to a poor front end design resembling the equally poor Midland 2P. By contrast, the Brighton's I3 class 4-4-2T, with smaller boiler but quite good cylinder design, was a very lively performer even on stopping trains on heavy gradients, for which its large wheels and limited adhesion seemed unsuitable. One wonders what sort of 4-4-0 the Brighton would have produced had they included I3 cylinders in the B4X design, with its proven K class boiler.

About this period in the author's apprenticeship, several moves occurred whose exact dates are unimportant, but which changed life considerably. The five day week is one aspect, already mentioned, in a positive sense, and there was the formation of a Labour Party government, leading to the nationalisation of British railways, the latter as of 1 January 1948. Up to this time, politics had been ignored as being a rather stupid game suitable only for those with nothing better to think about. Forty years later, the same judgement applies, plus the realisation that stupid politicians with their equally stupid theories are a danger to mankind and cannot be simply ignored. The first political reality encountered by the author was the British National Health scheme. Up to then, health had been covered by the benevolent GWR sick fund, costing a few pennies a week, and administered by a relative handful of dedicated and efficient company clerical staff. This excellent organisation was perforce absorbed by the National Health scheme which soon betrayed its Socialist failings by becoming a vast bureaucracy, providing less health at something like five times the cost of the former GWR company set-up. About the only people within this 'health' bureaucracy who failed to benefit were the essential personnel, such as doctors and nurses, always behind the parasites when it came to pay and conditions of service.

Nationalisation of the railways was another thing. I had joined the Great Western with the thought, or ambition, of eventually becoming its Chief Mechanical Engineer. With four railways merged into one, this ambition was reduced by 75 percent in theory, but with the evident bias towards the LMS (the biggest and worst) of the four private companies, this ambition was even more reduced. On December 31st 1947, at home with the family, I went to Paddington to see the last GWR departure (11.50 pm, South Wales) and the first BR train 12.10, Birmingham, somehow imagining miraculous changes taking place between one and the other. Quite ridiculous, of course, as the engine, stock, and staff were still Great Western when booked on duty. Despite the massive following for the GWR, there were very few gathered at Paddington to see the last Great Western train leave, no official send-off, and I think only one photographer, probably P. J. T. Reed who was certainly there.

Somewhere around this period there occurred, for the last time, a sort of 'Rag Week', rather as practised in university cities, but at Swindon carried out by railway apprentices, student nurses, and young teachers. Swindon being on the main line to South Wales made it a popular place for student nurses (mainly

Irish) and newly graduated teachers (mostly Welsh) who found it conveniently situated for getting home at holiday times. There was thus a strong tendency for Swindon's premium apprentices, once able to host girl friends, to find themselves one from this Celtic fringe, while the Swindonians proper kept to themselves. The 'Rag Week' was geared to collect monies for hospitals, very deserving in the old days, but when such activities became a bureaucratic sinecure, the incentive to help disappeared overnight.

Rag Week itself was fun. Several of us found an old barrel organ somewhere, and dressed as 'tramps' went round 'busking' in the streets and particularly to pubs. I was not quite 18 years old at the time, but nobody seemed to query my strictly illegal appearance in various pubs, wherein I was weaned onto draught beer. About this time I moved residence into the Toc H hostel in High Street, already having a large proportion of Railway types, in a club-like atmosphere I found very suitable. Conditions were fairly spartan, with refectory type dining room, large general lounge amply provided with leather armchairs, and a quiet room for studying. Ample hot water was available from a coke-fired boiler in the cellar, and each inhabitant had to take a week's turn in stoking it. Needless to say, the steam experts from the works proved less adept at maintaining hot water temperature than the bank clerks!

Permanent staff were limited to a housekeeper and cook, both resident, and possibly a non-resident housemaid. The housekeeper was a prim and chronically virginal old maid, former matron at a girl's school, and tending to treat all, young and old, as naughty schoolgirls – especially when we arrived from the pub after meal time! The cook was young, plump, and pretty, but had a non-resident boy friend. With a Labour government in power, rationing was still in force (it had been discontinued in France and even Germany!), and each denizen had two small jars containing butter and sugar rations, usually insufficient to last the required week. The hostel was run by an honorary warden, who, when I joined was Llew Edwards, GWR draughtsman, keen rugby player, and territorial army officer – a totally extrovert character. Across the road was the 'Bell' hotel, a fine old coaching house whose landlord, Sidney, was proud of his draught Bass, invariably maintained in immaculate condition.

Within this genial atmosphere, I found a quiet fellow resident, Tony Sterndale, with steam locomotive ideas close to my own. He was interested in Welsh locomotives, and having a camera and considerable skill thereof, had photographed many of them. Furthermore, he was keen on locomotive design, including the study of overseas practice, and like me tended to dabble in design possibilities within the confines of the British loading gauge. His designs, at the time, were rather ahead of mine, but then he was five years my senior, and had more time to think about things!

Just before joining the Toc H hostel, while still in my old 'digs', I set to scheming out a mixed traffic 2-8-2T for the Welsh valleys, this being worked out in reasonable detail, although very GWR in concept. The idea was to run an accelerated suburban service up the valleys with a locomotive capable also of handling heavier freight trains. A diagram of this is illustrated. Fairly soon afterwards, reading some article on Welsh Nationalism, I envisaged a sort of 'South Wales Railway' starting at Cardiff, running all services with tank engines for which the main line was very suitable, with passenger trains reversing at Swansea and Carmarthen. Very rough sketches were done for three main classes to handle the main traffic, but these sketches have disappeared over the years and are remembered as a 4-6-4T passenger engine with about 6′ 0″ wheels, a 2-10-4T for heavy freight, 4′ 6″ wheels using the same boiler design, and the general purpose 2-8-2T with 5′ 0″ wheels. About that time, my 'turning' career ended and I was sent back to the 'B' shed, to start at the bottom again, as it were, as a fitter apprentice.

4

FITTER

Returning to the 'B' shed after two years' absence, I found myself on locomotive rather than tender work, which was far more interesting. Even though only the smaller types were repaired in that shop, it was a good feeling to be scrambling about real locomotives, for the first time during my apprenticeship. Manufacturing components is all very well, but nothing like being engaged on the real thing, even if it was only a 'Bulldog' or a pannier tank! One of the first things learned was that inside cylinders and motion really are a bloody nuisance, even to me then young, lithe, and slim, a claim few who know me today may regard as credible. A crank axle, two connecting rods, and four eccentrics with attendant Stephenson valve gear are more than enough to cram in the four feet between plate frames, without having also to insinuate a human being to put them all together. Certainly, I was already predisposed to outside Walschaerts valve gear, but working on these inside cylinder engines changed a preference to a determined conviction. Three cylinders instead of four, where two could not be sufficient, also made a great deal of sense, and I could sympathise with the philosophy behind Holcroft/Gresley conjugated motion, although the acoustic results therefrom showed the application to be at fault.

It was also discovered that GWR small engines, looking so much part of a family outwardly, differed considerably internally. This was highlighted by a fitter who referred to a standard 0-4-2T as a 'Wolverhampton engine', bewildering to me as it was built at Swindon and allocated somewhere quite irrelevant. To him, as a fitter, it was the motion design which counted. 'Swindon' designs, such as Dean Goods, 22XX, and the 57XX Panniers had crossheads with upper and lower slidebars, rather similar to what may be easily observed on outside cylinder engines. By contrast, the 0-4-2T, together with the 54XX, 64XX, and 74XX (plus the later 16XX) pannier tanks had underslung crossheads with multiple slidebars copied directly from the old '517' class 0-4-2T built at Wolverhampton in 1868. There was virtually nothing standard between the two series as regards motion work. Churchward would have 'done his nut' at such archaic construction, and given the remit to produce new tank engines for shunting

Neat and pretty, Collett's branch line 0-4-2T was basically an Armstrong 517 class in all major details. Churchward, surely, would have added superheater and piston valves at the very minimum.

and light passenger work, would almost certainly have come up designs only (instead of five) based on the more modern 45XX con

Working underneath an engine is always a frightening experience novice. Tangled up amongst the valve gear, twisted and contorted into a ballet-like posture in order to hammer a cotter pin into a valve spindle, one has the vague background worry that were the locomotive to be moved by accident, there is no avenue of rapid escape. It took ten minutes to worm yourself into the position, and a few degrees of rotation of wheels and motion could totally close the escape route! Fortunately one's mind was usually too preoccupied with fitting those damned bits and pieces to think much about escape. However, one wonders how anybody could deliberately design a motion so difficult to assemble, dismantle, and maintain – all the more so on a railway system where a draughtsman was not employed who had not been through a five year workshop apprenticeship and studied part time for his National and Higher National Certificates in Mechanical Engineering. Industry today is inured to the 'draughtsman' provided with an 'instant' course which teaches him to draw with the pointed end of the pencil, with little idea as to how it is to be manufactured and assembled. In the Victorian era, when inside cylinder locomotives were designed, difficulty was considered a virtue, and obstacles placed against ready access to locomotive valvery and feminine pudenda alike produced a generation or two of determined and ingenious men able to conquer hot continents and cold, continent females with equal ruthlessness.

Another initially frightening experience is wheeling an engine. Crouched in the pit beneath, along with several other men, each ready to slide an axlebox between its hornguides as overhead the crane grinds and rattles, relentlessly lowering the locomotive down upon one's very head. Indeed, apart from feeding the axlebox into its appointed space one had to keep an eye open for protruding details which *could* press down upon one. Imagination boggled at the thought of a chain breaking, sending the whole lot crashing down, but this never happened to my knowledge. The worst mishap, which probably happens to every new apprentice, is failure to guide the box in properly, causing it to tilt and jam across the horns. WHOA! to the crane driver's ground assistant, and umpteen tons of locomotive had to be lifted, then lowered and tried again. There used to be a Swindon song, sung to I forget what tune, called the 'Crane Driver's Lament'. Words were:

Down a bit, down a bit, not too far, WHOA!
Up a bit, up a bit, not too far, WHOA!

These words were repeated endlessly, making it a sort of engineering version of 'Lloyd George knew my father'.

After a few months on actual locomotives, it was back to components, the next shift being to the rods and motion gang in the 'AM' shop, the machine section of Churchward's massive 'A' shop complex. Compared to the shops worked in up to then, all part of the original works, built in stone, and exuding a rather dingy atmosphere, the 'A' shop was light and airy. Being 'open plan', as it were, it had no dark corners and recesses within which, in many of the older shops, lurked strange characters with stranger idiosyncracies, such as 'Thunder' already mentioned. The chief foreman, Mr Millard, presided over a gathering of under-foremen, each with his group of chargehands, under whom came various tradesmen, apprentices, and labourers. I do not know how many men were employed within the 'A' shop, doubtless well over a thousand, yet railway practice called the man in overall charge a mere foreman! In most places one tenth the size, outside the railway, he would be called at least works manager, or even works director.

Rods and motion was a clean job compared with working on and underneath locomotives themselves. It was largely a matter of cleaning off accumulated rust and grime, examining for cracks, pressing in new bushes and checking centre to centre distances by trammel. One interesting thing noted was that one could *never* trust the engine number stamped on a piece of motion. With Swindon's standardisation, components were applied willy-nilly to the first suitable locomotive, and whereas at one time numbers had been crossed out and new ones applied, this was rarely done in my time. I remember working on a connecting rod for a 'County Tank', the last of which had been withdrawn ten years before I joined the GWR. Presumably, when such locomotives were withdrawn, any standard components in good condition were simply returned to the spare parts pool.

Whilst in the 'AM' shop I also spent some time on the axle box gang, fitting the brass inserts and liners which made such a satisfactory design, by then also exported to the LMS by Stanier, revolutionising their hotbox problem. Somewhere around this time, having been 'nationalised', there occurred the famous exchange trials between locomotives of the four grouped railways, in which the GWR locomotives made a poor showing in efficiency, due to their smaller superheaters, unchanged from Churchward's days, when lubricants were less developed. The advantages of higher superheat had been well demonstrated during the war, by LMS class 8F, WD 'Austerity' 2-8-0, and the American 'S160' class which had been used on loan. F. W. Hawksworth had appreciated this and initiated the use of higher superheat with three row applications on 'Modified Halls', 'Counties', and 'Castles', introduced 1945–46. Four-row installations were fitted to 5049 in 1947, and ordered for a 'King' whose boiler was thus equipped in GWR days although the locomotive, 6022, was not outshopped until February 1948, by then BR (WR). For some reason, the latest Swindon techniques were not put to test on these trials, although later on, with improved draughting as developed by Sam Ell, efficiency figures of similar order to the LMS and LNER contestants were obtained.

More visible was the range of experimental liveries applied to locomotives and coaching stock, unfortunately before much in the way of colour photogra-

Eighty of Stanier's class 8F were built at Swindon from 1943 to 1945. Much later, 48412, back on its original home ground, clanks through Acton with a goods for Paddington.

phy was common. It is no mere GWR prejudice that judged 'Castles' in LNER light green to be unsatisfactory – there was simply insufficient contrast between the polished brasswork and the background. Conversely, the 'Kings' in the darker blue livery looked really superb to this author, although traditionalists objected as a matter of habit. Similarly, the GWR green, later adopted for passenger locomotives by BR, looked somewhat drab *without* the accompanying polished brasswork. The LNWR lined black also sat uncomfortably on some engines. Suitable for designs with large cab panels, some engines with shortish cabs, notably Maunsell 2-6-0 on the Southern, looked distinctly peculiar in this style.

As for the passenger coach livery, the 'plum and split milk' livery was terrible. Enthusiasts referred to this as 'blood & custard' but Swindon's nickname was 'puce and puke'. Chocolate and cream, as adopted by both the GWR and the Pullman Company has a lot going for it and in the author's travels round the world he has seen it happily used in Rhodesia (currently, Zimbabwe) and in Malaya, looking as smart in 'darkest Africa' and tropical Asia as on the Cornish Riviera.

Incidentally, the last 'Trip fortnight' under GWR auspices, in 1947, was spent exploring Lancashire and Yorkshire in some detail, travelling up GWR via Birkenhead, whose locomotive shed produced a couple of rare vintage locomotives of the 1901 and 2021 class, of which the shed had many. One was a

A typical locomotive from Scotland, sturdily built but not very efficient. Nevertheless these Pickersgill 0-6-0 outlived the more modern WD 2-10-0, seen dumped in the background.

saddle tank, and the other a pannier having a domeless boiler with raised Belpaire firebox. I never saw either again, and both were presumably cut up at Wolverhampton. The main part of the trip was a fairly solid bash with few highlights, but a visit to Horwich produced a run in steam railcar 10600, in which the front of the coach rode just like a locomotive footplate. One could understand why these contrivances were replaced by push-pull trains with normal locomotives. The Hughes 4-6-0 were still working passenger trains between Manchester and Blackpool, and I waited at Preston until one came along, heading west. Just before departure, what should come in on the next line but the last 'Claughton', 6004, giving the choice of runs behind two rare classes. I stuck with the Hughes, and later regretted this as several were still at work and the run could have been repeated, not that it was very exciting. On the other hand, I did not see the 'Claughton' again, and thereby missed a unique opportunity.

While on the subject of 'Trips', the 1948 fortnight was spent in Scotland, notable in being my first visit north of the border, and the last major holiday spent in Britain. There were still a lot of Scottish locomotives at work, mainly 0-6-0, 4-4-0, and similar smaller types, but I managed to see a few of the more interesting survivors, and even to manage a few runs. With typical LMS operating, the run north was behind a 'Duchess' to Carlisle, where the big engine was taken off and a class 5 substituted for the run to Glasgow, over Beattock. At this place, a Pickersgill 4-6-2T came on as banker, so I forsook my usual front compartment position and galloped down the platform to the rear position, a rather interesting open coach of unknown origin, with two large droplights per compartment, enabling one to lean well out to look at, and listen to, the banker. A good strong engine! Somewhere up the bank, I suppose near Greskine, there was an adverse signal and the class 5 eased up, the driver probably hoping to avoid a stop. Sensing a drop in speed, the banker's driver opened up flat out and nearly pushed the whole caboodle past the signal!

On this first Scottish trip, runs were obtained behind several 'Caley' 4-4-0s, on stopping trains of course, and a '60' class 4-6-0, but none were impressive. The Highland was not visited beyond Inverness, but I managed to *see* the last 'Clan' and 'Loch' classes, both out of steam. The following year, 1949, a fellow apprentice John Godfrey and I made a massive continuous bash to Scotland on August bank holiday, the forerunner of the really intensive *BASH* which became standard operation as steam declined in later years. We set off via King's Cross on Friday night, on the through coaches to Fort William, and I remember getting some heavenly fresh coffee at Waverley station. Our coaches were detached at Cowlairs, and we ran behind a quite new K1 to Fort William, and were delighted to find a K4 on the Mallaig connection, one of our hoped-for locomotives. From Mallaig we took a MacBrayne's steamer to the Kyle, a lovely journey through the Isles of Western Scotland, and from Kyle to Dingwall a class 5 took us with great competence over the lovely scenic line, an experience I believe is again available. All this in 24 hours after leaving Swindon! At Dingwall we had something to eat, and caught the 'Drunk's special', leaving soon after closing time, all stations to Tain, hauled by a Caley 4-4-0. It was then late Saturday night, we remained on the train and slept the night in the coaches. Sunday was spent getting to Dornoch. No public transport ran on the Sabbath until late evening, when there was a 'bus. Enquiry revealed that there was a ferry from Tain to Dornoch, and we walked down a long spit of land to the ferry terminus, a bleak spot with a box containing a large flag which one had to wave to attract the attention of the ferryman, resident the other side. We waved and waved until our arms ached, but evidently the ferryman was at the kirk and didna' worrk on the Sabbath. Eventually we gave up, walked the considerable distance back down the spit to Tain, and started hitch-hiking to Bonar Bridge.

Well, there was precious little traffic, none of which stopped, including a minister of religion (probably Presbyterian) who ignored two weary hikers trudging northwards – evidently helping fellow men was something to be preached from the pulpit but not put into practice! We walked all the way to Bonar Bridge, reached late afternoon, and were attracted by the scent of fresh bread at an outlying cottage. By then we were famished, but had a tin of corned beef for such an emergency. Knocked at the cottage door, opened by a dear old lady, who we asked for bread. 'We don't give food to tramps' was the response, whereupon we produced money and offered to buy. That was different, and having established that we were not tramps, and could pay, we were given a lovely fresh loaf free of charge, the old dears being far better proponents of their religion than the minister thereof! They might have been horrified by our subsequent actions, whereby we withdrew to a decently secluded spot, opened the beef tin, tore bread and meat in rough halves, and devoured the lot like a pair of hyena trying to exist during a trade union strike by the lion family. Soon after this, a motor was heard, and it was the evening 'bus, which we happily caught to Dornoch, where a good repast of fish and chips was bedded down onto the corned beef and bread. Unfortunately, the Dornoch hotels seemed all of rather high standard, beyond our means, so we retired to the station to sleep in the branch line coach, only to find it totally locked. Disaster – so was the waiting room! The only thing open was a goods guards van, on whose hard benches we tried to sleep, waking up frequently to run up and down the platform to warm up. A long, long, and cold night, supposedly in summer. To add insult to injury, the first morning train was run too late to connect with the northbound main line service, so we failed to ride the Dornoch 'Puggie' and had to use the local 'bus. This Scottish local 'bus performed all sorts of services, delivering parcels, mail, and apparently anything, and we were most impressed by the really *bonnie* conductress, although inhibited by her ability to heave loaded milk churns onto the 'bus. At The Mound Junction we asked for a glass of water and ended up with a full breakfast of bacon, eggs, and fresh oatcakes, produced by the stationmaster's wife who again refused payment. Evidently the myth of Scots meanness is restricted in practice to their religious ministers! Our free breakfast was delivered to the Ladies Waiting Room which, in 1949, still boasted, largely unworn, Highland Railway linoleum on the floor.

   Soon after breakfast, there was a tinkle-tankle, tinkle-tankle of a class 5 rolling in, and we embarked on the train to Wick. At some stage, an old Highland 'Ben' was taken on as pilot for a while, and we detrained at Georgemas Junction. Swindon Public Library had a superb collection of omnibus timetables, and we had determined that one could detrain at Georgemas, catch the train to Thurso, Britain's most northerly station, proceed by 'bus to Wick, then return by the first train south. Furthermore, it worked. The Thurso branch was also worked by a Highland 'Ben' class 4-4-0, and on the southbound run from Wick we had dinner in a marvellous old dining car which somehow seemed higher from the ground than lesser rolling stock, and in which all tables seated two only, in heavy, wooden chairs, loose on the floor. Somehow one got the impression that the Highland section did things on a grander scale than was practised even in southern Scotland, let alone those inferior places below Hadrian's Wall. The journey back to Swindon remains a haze of LMS fusty carriages, probably best forgotten, until Euston was reached at some ungodly hour.

Returning to workaday matters, another move took me into the 'P1', boiler mounting, shop, situated across the Rodbourne Road from the main ('V') boiler shop. In the P1, boilers manufactured or repaired in the V shop were fitted with all the components not included in the basic boiler structure, that is regulators, top feed, superheaters (if any) lubricators, and sundry other details. Each boiler, once completed, was tested under full steam pressure, and a Standard 15 (1000 class) boiler was sited at the northeast corner for this purpose. Obviously, the boiler used had to be capable of supplying the highest steam pressure in use on the railway, and before the 1000 class was introduced, a spare 'King' boiler was presumably installed. On a winter's day, the P1 shop always seemed full of steam and vapour from this live boiler, probably accounting for the fact that several 'characters' lurked within this mysterious atmosphere. From time to time, when a boiler had been tested, its regulator would be opened to both test its operation and release the steam contained therein. What a noise – high pressure steam released to atmosphere makes a very explosive detonation, no form of baffle being employed, and for several minutes afterwards, swirling dust and vapour circulated the shop. Today this would probably be regarded as unhealthy, but I never heard of any suffering therefrom.

As mentioned above, there were several characters in the P1. One was Jack Thomas, an immense Welshman from the Taff Vale, who could fit a Melesco superheater header single handed! Normally this was a three man job, positioned as it was with no access for lifting by crane. Two men would lift the thing, heaving mightily, while a third nutted the studs on the front tubeplate. Jack could lift it himself, resting it on his vast beer belly while he fitted the nuts himself! Of course, such an effort sweated out several gallons of the local Arkell's Ale, easily replaced after work! An opposite personality was a wizened little fitter, name forgotten, whose 'tool kit' comprised a single outsize spanner and a collection of washers used to make up the difference between spanner gap and actual size of nut! Nuts tightened this way had to be re-done by somebody properly equipped, but I suspect the old chap was nearing retiring age and thus tolerated. Another jolly character saw the similarity between the 'Swindon' type superheater header, with its row of nuts, and the 'stops' on a church organ, and could sometimes be heard singing lustily, seated on a plank wedged across the smokebox, while manipulating the 'stops' on the header.

For most of my P1 sojourn I worked with Jack Stewart, the trade union shop steward, quite unlike most of his breed. Those encountered before and afterwards seemed to be neurotic and unpleasantly puritanical trouble stirrers, prone to address everybody as 'brother', one step away from the communistic 'comrade'. It certainly seemed that those who were skilled did the work, while the others ran the trade unions – the craftsmen and the crafty! Jack, as mentioned, was totally different to his 'brothers', being an outgoing and jolly character seemingly without a care in the world. During the war he had been a warrant officer in the army, stationed in the Middle East, and was full of hilarious stories of episodes concerning British soldiery and the 'Wogs', always ready to exchange their 'sisters' or a case of local beer for some coveted army stores.

Rodbourne Road separated the P1 from the main boiler shop and boilers were transferred beneath the road via an underground passage with a hydraulic lift each end. There was also a sloping walkway for pedestrian traffic, and for some obscure reason, the blacksmith was located in the V shop. He was needed for adjusting regulator rods, which passed right through the boiler from the cab handle to the regulator in the smokebox. The rod was rarely right for the assembled boiler, and since the rolled and riveted platework of a locomotive boiler cannot be manufactured to tight tolerances, each regulator rod had to be fitted to its parent boiler. Usually it had to be 'drawn' (lengthened), 'jumped' (shortened), or have the angle of the operating crank altered. The only way was to assemble the rod in the boiler, try it out, then remove it, trundle it under Rodbourne Road on a barrow to the smith, whose actions were guided by such cryptic chalked instructions as 'jump $^3/_4$', or 'draw $^1/_4$' chalked on. Sometimes the same rod needed two or three trips to the blacksmith to get it right, a tedious process. On the other hand, once correct, it could hardly get out of adjustment in service, being a solid chunk of metal with no loose components.

Boilermaking itself was a separate trade, not included in my curriculum, and seen from the outside was more of an art than a science. The complex shapes of a Swindon firebox, tapered from front to rear, and with a contour composed mainly of various convex and concave curves, would baffle most production engineers today. At Swindon they were produced on massive plate rollers operated by men who, with a chalk mark here and there produced the final result almost by sleight-of-hand! So confident were they, that the pilot holes for the stays were drilled when plates were flat, and those on outer and inner fireboxes always lined up when the boxes were assembled! Even the crane men, classed as labourers, possessed uncanny skills. Calculating the centre of gravity of such a boiler would be a daunting exercise, involving reams of calculation leading probably to a wrong answer. Yet these crane men always lifted boilers with a single sling round the barrel, at optimum position, and I never saw one lifted without it being perfectly balanced at first attempt.

From the comparative crudities of boilermounting I moved to the R shop yet again, where Tom Marshman, JP, presided over the safety valve gang. Tom was a shortish man with round, solemn face, beaky nose and spectacles, inevitably earning him the nickname 'The Owl', the appropriateness of which was enhanced by his wearing a dust jacket rather than overalls. Work on this gang involved some highly skilled fitting, each fitter or apprentice having to assemble the various components, scrape and grind the valve and valve seats into a perfect metal-to-metal fit, and finally to adjust the direct loaded springs to the correct pressure. Most time consuming was the scraping process, the final fit having to be perfect. Normal production was one safety valve per day, but my first one took a week. The slightest imperfection, even a hair sized nick, meant a leaky valve, and there was no way one could fiddle it through the system. Having, hopefully, produced a perfect job, one mounted it on the hydraulic test rig and adjusted springs to correct pressure. Tom would then be called from his box to test it, pumping away solemnly with eyes on the pressure gauge. As described, a slight nick in the brass surface would allow water through, usually in the form of a fine jet.

This would be noted, and Tom Marshman, JP, delivered his verdict – 'pisser'. When one had a pisser, the whole valve had to be dismantled and work started again. Having got it right, distances (to one hundredth of an inch) were measured between the cross bars and the collars on the columns. Ferrules were then made to these sizes, stamped with the dimensions, and assembled into the valve. Tom would then test again, and if satisfactory, enter into the safety valve register. Each valve had its own number, and at each overhaul this was noted together with adjusted pressure and the length of ferrules fitted. This was a safety measure, such that if a valve was tampered with by shed staff, resulting in a mishap, components could be checked against the register afterwards.

After my round of the main fitting shops, there was a further spell in the Millwrights (G) shop, again spent on most interesting work. For a while I became a motor mechanic, on the little tractors used at major stations and on

One time Swindon works shunter 1369 finds refuge at Wadebridge, Cornwall; rather appropriate as the engines were a second development of basically similar engines built for the Cornwall Mineral Railway in 1873.

Former Barry Railway class B1 272 as works shunter, Swindon, 1950. Still lettered GWR and with shed code denoting Cardiff Valleys, Barry.

the works internal transport. At this stage it may be appropriate to say a little about this organisation. Heavy work, such as the movement of locomotives, boilers, and similar equipment, was done on rail, using a variety of works shunters for locomotive, carriage, and wagon works. With the variety of power available, each had its own specialities. Carriage works shunting tended to be fairly light, using light panniers especially of the '1901' class, together with, while they lasted, some of the old '517' class 0-4-2T of which I particularly remember 1436 which retained inside bearings to the trailing axle until scrapped. The wagon works had particularly sharp curves for which Swindon shed retained three 1366 class outside cylinder pannier tanks and ex-BPGV 0-6-0ST 2195, formerly *Cwm Mawr*.

The locomotive works had two sources of works shunters. There were capital stock engines from Swindon shed, usually standard 0-6-0PT or 45XX, used on any duties involving movement outside works precincts. There were also purely internal shunters, based inside the works, and invariably comprising withdrawn tank engines with still some life in them. When I first started at Swindon, these were usually the older panniers, such as 17XX, 18XX, or 27XX, often with open back cabs. When the ex-Barry 0-6-2T started to come to Swindon for scrap, these were pounced upon with joy by the works shunting crews, having far better cabs, roomier, and more enclosed, than the ancient 0-6-0PT. For several years the old Barrys ruled the shunting roost, and were so much liked that at one stage an attempt was made to have No 207 repaired in B shed. However, somebody forgot to make sure the staff knew it was a fiddle and there were some bleak responses when costs were booked against a locomotive which officially did not exist! Later on, both Taff Vale 'A' and '04' classes were used on the works shunt, but none of the Rhymney engines were similarly employed, perhaps being too large.

In addition to rail usage, there was an extensive road system for lighter components, using trailers hauled by the little tractor units upon which I worked in G shop. This system was well organised, with trailers allocated to specific routes, whose identities were painted on. Keeping trailers to specific routes minimised situations where one might suffer a dearth of trailers where wanted simultaneously with a surplus somewhere else. There were also a few agricultural type tractors fitted with buffer beams fore and aft, used for moving and placing one or two rail wagons. Finally, one should mention the ENPARTS wagons, the code shortened from 'Engine Parts'. These were vacuum fitted fast freight vans used to convey new or repaired components from Swindon and other major workshops direct to the using depot. They usually ran on regular parcels or passenger trains, ensuring minimum delays to locomotives out of service awaiting parts. I am sure no other British railway was so well organised in this respect.

Another G shop task was crane maintenance, and on this I worked with an odd fellow called Jessie, a member of one of the breakaway religious groups

Ex Taff Vale class 04 207 was the second 207 used as works shunter, the first being ex-Barry Railway B class. This 0-6-2T is almost totally Swindonised above the running plate plus other details such as coupling rods, buffers, cab footsteps etc.

who worshipped in corrugated iron chapels scattered throughout Swindon. Jessie was an utterly sincere adherent to his faith, to the point of being a complete fatalist. Working on an overhead crane, he would balance himself on an outrightly dangerous perch, perhaps a plank cantilevered over thin air, violently swinging a heavy hammer for the task in hand, confident that if God did not want him to fall off, he would not! Mutually co-existing on the same gang was a crude fellow whose mode of speech went, typically, 'Go to the fucking stores and get a fucking five eighths ring spanner to get this fucking nut off' Such were the contrasts in character in what, to the outside eye, were a homogenous mass of overall-clad workmen. Nevertheless, such outwardly rough manifestations so typical in a masculine society often concealed characters who were kind and loving to their wives and families, and even to the shop cats kept throughout the works as rodent exterminators. These cats were fed regularly by the men, and the poor animals' furs were invariably matted and tangled from stroking by kind but greasy hands.

Pump maintenance was another G shop responsibility, and one of the most interesting jobs I experienced, which took me back to the dawn of the Industrial Revolution, was to work for a week on the ancient canal pumps at Crofton, near Grafton. These were on the Kennet and Avon canal, purchased by the GWR to forestall competition, but compelled to remain open for irrigation purposes. As such, minimal expenditure was made for maintenance, and these old pumps were of the Watt beam type, dating back to the early nineteenth century. There was a probably apocryphal story of the beams being cast locally 'in the fields'. Working pressure was about two or three pounds per square inch, just sufficient to fill the power cylinder with steam, which was then condensed by water sprays, the resulting vacuum providing the pumping effort. The cylinders themselves were immense, something like five or six feet in diameter and about eight feet piston stroke. The pump house was of two or three stories – one had to climb a flight of steps to get from one end of the power cylinder to the other, with similar arrangements for the pump cylinder, situated wholly or partly underground in a dank cellar. Movement was very slow and stately, perhaps twenty strokes per minute, and the various valves for steam, cooling water, etc, were actuated by a seemingly complicated system of trips and levers.

Our job was to repack the pump valves, carried out deep in the subterranean workings. Even refitting covers to these valve chambers was a long and tedious task involving yards and yards of rough stringy packing, liberally covered in graphite, wound round the studs upon which one could seemingly tighten the nuts for ever without reaching total tightness. The Crofton pump exercise was a most pleasant interlude away from the normal day 'inside', the local term used for anybody employed in the railway works. In fact, the first time I heard a woman say her husband was 'inside' I imagined him to be in prison, and was amazed she was so open about it!

Four of us were engaged on the Crofton job, Stan, a young chargehand, a fitter and a labourer, neither of whose names I remember, and myself as apprentice. We assembled daily at Swindon Town station and rode the Andover local to Savernake, where we detrained and walked along the line to the pumphouse. Lunch was a cheese roll or two and a pint of bitter at the local, canalside, pub, a delightful place with stone walls, thatched roof, and flagstone floors, whose scrubbed wooden bench decor was totally unspoiled by any suggestion of the depraved plastic-and-chrome age yet to be perpetrated on the human race. At knocking-off time, we caught the branch auto train from Savernake Low Level to Marlborough, where there was a pub on the platform and a substantial wait for the Swindon connection. Stan and I, not being (then) great beer drinkers, had a quick pint and then cycled back to Swindon on our bicycles which we had taken down in the guard's van of the morning train. The fitter and his mate took the heaven-sent opportunity of a good booze-up while waiting, without much their respective wives could say upon eventual arrival home!

Incidentally, at Swindon Town station, the combined vagaries of a sparse branchline service and peculiar British licensing laws ensured that, with one or two daily exceptions, when there was a train the platform pub was shut, and when the pub was open there were no trains! Thus the pub's real *raison d'être*, that of refreshing travellers was almost completely negated, and it became just another local pub, known colloquially as the 'Ghost Train'. The landlord, or licensee, was a jovial country squire type whose twin passions in life were the maintenance, in superb condition, of his vintage supercharged Bentley, of immense engine capacity, and of his straight-from-the-wood Draught Bass. Later on, in my draughtsman days, I spent New Year's Eve in this unreal establishment, with a deserted station outside, while some ancient character played music on a set of bells, never seen (or rather, heard) before or since. With me was my then Welsh girl friend and a young Birmingham university engineering student doing his vacation work 'inside', and who was incredibly embarrassed when the girl friend had to use the platform 'gents' because the 'ladies' was locked! He was so afraid of being 'caught' at the urinal that more went down his trousers than down the drain, which must have ensured a very uncomfortable walk back to his lodgings.

Whilst on the subject of Swindon pubs, there were about half a dozen whose names were directly concerned with the railway, as befitting a railway town, some in so subtle a manner as to be lost to the casual imbiber. Outside Swindon Junction station was the Great Western Hotel, a commercial travellers' refuge which in later days, when I visited Swindon on business, served such delicacies as scampi and escargot, unheard of when I lived in Swindon. In Newport Street, Old Town, was the 'Railway Hotel', an otherwise undistinguished hostelry whose sign was a rather well executed painting of an old GWR 2-2-2 express locomotive. Along Faringdon Street, close to the works, was the 'Locomotive', decorated in later days, inappropriately, by Stephenson's 'Rocket' rather than an indigenous product, and further along the same street was the 'Rolling Mills', obviously works-inspired, and the 'Sir Daniel' whose origins would be totally opaque to anyone unfamiliar with early Great Western history. Closest to the works main entrance, and used extensively for office parties and other unofficial thrashes, was the 'Gluepot' untypically allied with the carriage rather than the locomotive works. Somewhat out of context, but to complete the picture, some time in the 1960s, visiting Swindon on business, I was shocked to find, in a brand new housing estate, a brand new 'pub' of totally plastic and chrome decor, complete with canned musak and instant pressurised 'beer'. It was called the 'Steam Train' and outside had a vague neon outline of a GWR 4-6-0 and some coaches. A total travesty – such a place should be named and be-signed with something appropriate to the diesel age!

MORE DESIGNS

About this time, my pastime of design doodling gelled around a couple of projects, one of which was a locomotive which could start like a Great Western machine and run like a Bulleid Pacific. Another thing which had interested me was the perennially fascinating concept of a steam tank engine to equal electric traction, as once attempted by the Great Eastern with their 0-10-0T 'Decapod'. The suburban scheme was started first, and a study of passenger timetables

Standard 2-6-2T 6132 takes empty stock past Kensington Gasworks.

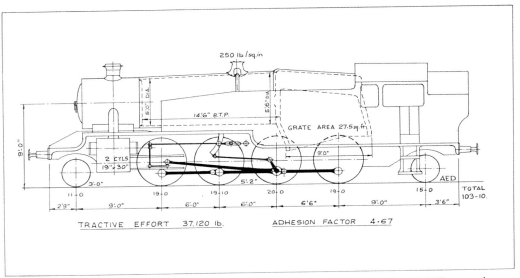

Steam suburban tanks had always fascinated the author, leading to this scheme for a 2-8-2T to equal Southern Electric schedules with eight coach trains. By the time it was worked out, the Southern had advanced to ten-coach trains, making it obsolete! (Fig 3)

showed that in general, GWR suburban services, hauled by 51XX, 56XX, and 61XX tank engines achieved overall speeds comparable with those of Southern's electrics, the GWR locomotives usually having loads of about five coaches totalling around 150 tons. The standard Southern train had been eight coaches, and to compete with this, the two-cylinder 2-8-2T shown in figure 3 would have been about equal to the task. However, the Southern had just upped its standard peak hour trains to ten coaches, immediately outclassing the 2-8-2T.

First attempt was a larger 2-8-2T, with overall size and proportions not dissimilar to the immense Cossart valve geared 2-8-2T built for the Northern railway of France, whose description was read in a copy of 'The Locomotive' magazine. I had started to take a distinct interest in Continental practice, or such as could be gleaned from British publications, seeing in some locomotives the bases of design which could be applied to British practice. My large 2-8-2T, featuring 3 cylinders 19" × 24" and Lemâitre blastpipe, was Bulleid inspired and even had BFB wheels 5' 6" diameter, larger than the French locomotive and showing a conservative leaning towards the 'proper' wheel size for a British suburban locomotive. With 275 psi boiler pressure tractive effort worked out at 46,000 lb which, with a 22 ton axle load gave an adhesion factor of 4.28, decidedly on the low side for duties needing sure-footed adhesion. Thompson's class L1 2-6-4T had a similar factor, and were distinctly slippery customers! Furthermore, while the nominal tractive effort was 24% more than the earlier 2-8-2T, adhesion weight was but 10% extra, limiting the real effectiveness of the design under all but ideal conditions.

While this was being pondered upon, the tank engine's main components (in typical Swindon manner) were worked into the main line mixed traffic 4-8-0, to start in GWR fashion and run like a Bulleid (fig.4). This of course was a narrow firebox machine, like the corresponding tank engine, with a boiler of distinctly Swindon proportions although larger than that of the 'King', and having a modified safety valve and top feed assembly containing pop valves. These had reduced height compared with the GWR direct-loaded valves, enabling a larger boiler, of higher pitch, to be accomodated within the loading gauge. This was particularly necessary as one had then to think in terms of the wider BR spectrum, rather than just the GWR with its generous loading gauge.

It may be thought rather conservatively Great Western to retain a narrow firebox for such a main line locomotive, and no doubt there was a residue of such conservatism in my mind at the time. All the other former main line companies had adopted wide fireboxes for their largest locomotives, Swindon being the sole exception. However, there was some narrow firebox support from France, where on the Northern railway, Collin's 'Super Pacifics' had narrow fireboxes with 37.6 sq ft grate area, these boilers being also used on the corresponding 2-10-0 freight engines perpetuated post-war in the SNCF class 150P. Furthermore, Chapelon's brilliant 4-8-0s with their well publicised performances were also narrow firebox engines with 40 sq ft grate area in a box whose *inside* length of 12' 1½" was greater than the outside length of a 'King' firebox.

Then there was the starting factor – a locomotive with trailing coupled wheels is more surefooted than one with bogies fore and aft. There are two reasons for this. Firstly, the force at the drawbar exerts a leverage at the rear of a loco- motive, tending to depress the rear, loading the trailing axle and easing the weight on the front bogie or pony truck. With a locomotive such as a 4-6-2, it is the trailing truck which takes this extra load whereas with a 4-8-0 the extra is on a coupled axle, thereby increasing adhesion. The second point in favour relates to trackwork around busy junctions and termini, where locomotives do most of their starting. At such places there are many visibly 'soft' spots, with track insufficiently supported, and a locomotive with carrying wheels at each end can get 'suspended' on these, partially unloading the coupled wheels, with corresponding loss of adhesion. Thus the choice of a narrow firebox 4-8-0, to give the Swindon-type surefooted starting had more behind it than mere conservatism, and seemed to be in line with the practice of the great Chapelon himself, although without compounding or poppet valves. Figure 4 shows this proposed locomotive.

The suburban engine was then tackled again, and the large rear overhang (inspired as possible by the French engine) prompted a remark by somebody that it should be a 2-8-4T. This would not assist the tractive deficiency, but an extra pair of coupled wheels would. Hence it was re-schemed as a 2-10-2T, with 5' 0" wheels as being quite big enough for suburban work, providing several bonuses – more tractive effort at starting, far higher adhesion factor, and even a

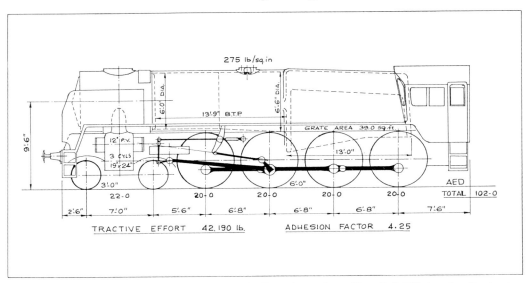

Author's scheme for a locomotive to "start like a GWR engine and run like a Bulleid". Ample adhesion to effect the starting, three cylinders, short stroke, and Lemâitre exhaust for the fast running. Even with hindsight, it would probably have been rather a useful machine. (Fig 4)

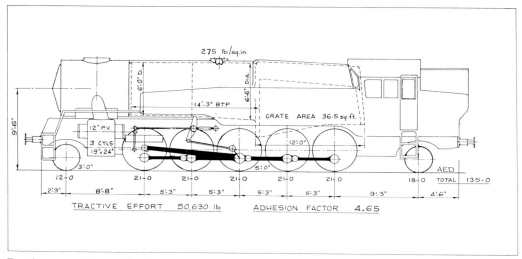

To achieve what figure 3 had been outclassed by, figure 4's components worked into a 2-10-2T to run ten coach trains at Southern Electric schedules. (Fig 5)

slight reduction in axle loading. This final solution is shown in figure 5. Incidentally, while working out the main proportions of this engine I was drawn towards the claim that the Great Eastern 'Decapod' 0-10-0T could accelerate a 300 ton train to 30 mph in 30 seconds. With the knowledge available to me at the time this seemed an unlikely happening as it would need a constant accelerating force equal to the nominal tractive effort of the engine, making no allowance for friction and other resistances. Furthermore, this unsuperheated, slide valve engine would then be producing 3000 horsepower by the time it attained 30 mph! In fact, under ideal conditions, the GER loco would have needed over a minute to attain 30 mph, and this old Great Eastern claim must be seen as a big confidence trick, doubtless well-meaning, but never substantiated since it was physically impossible!

FIRST TIME OVERSEAS

Studying overseas practice on paper was all very well, but there is nothing like seeing it yourself, first hand. Apart from collecting copies of 'The Locomotive' and the 'Railway Gazette', to both of which I subscribed regularly, I had managed to pick up one or two French books especially 'La Machine Locomotive' by E. Sauvage and A. Chapelon, perusal of which had both fired my imagination and caused me to brush up my rusty schoolboy French. Then the 'Railway Gazette' published a large article on the SNCF complete with a list of workshops, and having run out of new places to visit within Britain (other than Ireland, a technically uninteresting backwater) there germinated the idea – 'why not visit France?' Apart from the Chapelon compounds, there were the post-war American built class 141R some of which included features I was eager to look at, cast steel beds, roller bearings, mechanical stokers, etc. There was no way I could afford to visit the USA itself, anxious as I was to experience their enormous locomotives, but in France something of American practice, more up to date than the wartime 2-8-0s, could be seen. Planning the trip round the French workshop list proved difficult since I could not find out where half of them were! A trip to Thomas Cook's in London was of no help either, since many works were in suburbs of major towns and cities. Sotteville, a major miss, was excluded because nobody knew it was in Rouen. I suppose, with similar lack of information, a Frenchman would be unable to find Gorton or Stratford, although he might well have travelled to the *wrong* Stratford and mystified the denizens thereof by asking for the locomotive works! Certainly he would have been unable to discover the whereabouts of Stafford Road, but might have hopefully visited Stafford and been similarly mystified by the inclusion of Bagnall's as a major BR workshop!

Having worked out as good an itinerary as possible, the works manager, C. T. Roberts, was approached to try and obtain some sort of authorisation from the SNCF, for these visits. Unknown to me, he was rather a Francophile, and seemed delighted that one of his apprentices was willing to 'give up' his holiday to tramp around French railway workshops. The requisite authorisation was obtained, together with privilege ticket forms for the rail journeys, and come July 1949 I was off on this great adventure.

It is difficult to recreate the excitement and even shock of one's first trip abroad, especially when travelling alone by boat and train as did I. Since then I have travelled round the world, to many strange, uncivilised, and even hostile places, but none have ever generated the excited anticipation of the unknown as that initial, mundane, everyday Channel crossing, emergence from Britain's womb into the Rest-of-the-World. From the moment the Channel packet berthed at Calais it was very much another world. My limited French, carefully mis-enunciated word for word, and syllable by syllable was no match for the verbal avalanche of French 'as she is spoke', and neither could understand the other! The burly *porteurs* with their blue shirts, brass badges, and *espadrilles* were frankly intimidating as they scowled through fierce visages complete with regulation two-day beard and half a cigarette, floating in a haze of garlic and Gauloises! However, I struggled down the gangplank, trying hard to look used to this sort of thing, through the *Douane* and onto the station, where platforms were called *quais*, something I thought limited to marine berths.

The first engine seen was a chunky and rather ugly 0-8-0T, class 040TG, which amazed me by having outside Gooch valve gear. This survival from the earliest Swindon days had long since disappeared from GWR locomotive practice, and the only Gooch gear still working was on the enormous single cylinder stationary engines which powered Swindon's rolling mills. More amazing was the fact that this French loco was built in the 1930s, although a

French Nord locomotive class 040TG had Swindon connotations in possessing Gooch valve gear. Built from 1930 to 1933, they were probably the last ever built with this motion, long since vanished from GWR motive power.

pure development of much older machines. At the head of the main Paris boat train was, as expected, a Chapelon Pacific of class 231E, examined closely before departure. Mechanically, it was hardly impressive, everything possible being adjustable by a thousand-and-one wedges, shims, and set screws which in Britain would all have worked loose and fallen off in no time. The *mecanicien* was going through his routine of tapping, tightening, and oiling, as so necessary with such a complex piece of machinery.

Climbing aboard the train, it was soon departure time, and with a silly squeal on the high pitched whistle (even worse than the LNER type) she eased off with much hissing of cylinder cocks, and rumbled over the dock lines to Calais Ville where Gallic hordes invaded the train for the run to Paris. The three hour run was not so exhilarating as I had been led to believe, probably because I had no idea of the gradients being ascended while the uncanny silence of the compound ahead gave the impression of going downhill all the time! Later, when I realised what they were actually doing, as opposed to what they sounded to be doing, it was realised what great engines they were. Traffic seemed light by British standards, but then, trains were heavier. Accelerating from the stop at Amiens we were overtaken at first by a huge train of bogie hopper wagons, loaded with coal, headed by a massive 150P compound 2-10-0, running as sweetly as a sewing machine, without a clank or a wheeze. Now here was a real visible contrast with a British coal train, a string of badly sprung matchboxes on wheels, headed by a banging and clanging 0-6-0 or 2-8-0, perhaps half the load running at half the speed, with twice the effort! From Creil onwards we encountered the impressive 141TC class 2-8-2T, with fascinating Cossart valve gear, again effortlessly accelerating push-and-pull suburban trains of over 300 tons weight, complete with air-operated doors as seen only on the Under-

Chapelon's rebuilt Pacifics of Paris–Orleans origin were the final development of the two PO Atlantics which became GWR 103 and 104. Sold to the C. F. du Nord, 231E25 speeds through northern France in 1959.

ground and similar services in Britain. Here it was all done with steam, the sort of services and the sort of steam that I had been dreaming of for Britain.

In those days, British magazines published very little on foreign railway systems, especially the enthusiast publications. One heard about the latest American or Continental machine from time to time, but nothing of the relics which, like Britain's, also survived. Impressions gained were that everything was massive and modern, but as an enthusiast as well as a budding engineer, I was delighted to discover the quaint and ancient lurking in dark corners here and there.

Undoubtedly the most advanced and powerful suburban tank engines ever built-141TC42 departs Gare du Nord, Paris on the dot at 9.00.

At the Gare du Nord were some old slide valve 4-6-4T which worked lighter suburban trains from the Gare Annexe, while empty stock work was mainly in the hands of some Canadian 2-8-2T, later discovered to be rebuilt from World War I 2-8-0 tender engines. There were plenty of class 230D, modernised compound 4-6-0, a mixed traffic contemporary of the former 'Atlantic' express locomotives, and the sort of thing which would have become the GWR 68XX class had Churchward decided that compounds were the way to go. First place on my itinerary was La Chapelle depot in Paris, to where I walked next morning, and was greeted by the *Chef du depôt*. Still struggling to express myself in inadequate schoolboy French, some papers were brought into the office by an exceptionally well bosomed Parisienne. The foreman greeted her with a tweak of her aggressively proud nipple, and then introduced me. I stood there mute and embarrassed, not knowing whether I was supposed to do the same, blushed fiercely, and chickened out by shaking hands, to their great amusement.

Down in the depot I was surprised to find, derelict, an old de Glehn compound 4-4-0, still with its pre-SNCF number, which was rather like going to Old

France's ultimate express passenger steam locomotive, compound Hudson 232U1 eases out of Gare du Nord with a rather nondescript train to the Belgian border.

Oak Common in 1949 and finding a 'Badminton' class behind the shed! There was a two cylinder 4-4-4T, class 222TA as shed boiler, and a very well proportioned simple expansion 4-6-0, described to me as *Allemagne*, a word not then in my French vocabulary. So ignorant was I of Continental practice that I was unaware that here was one of the World's classics in steam, the Prussian P8 *mädchen für alles*! The most outstanding find was 'Hudson' 232U1, brand new, and a complete surprise as no inkling of its existence had filtered through to the British press. I explored her thoroughly, and made sketches of some of the unusual mechanical features, as shown in the later close up photograph of the motion arrangement.

In 1949, all main lines into Paris were steam, except those from the South-west, and the major stations of the Nord, Est, Lyon, and Ouest (St Lazare) were totally steam except for some third rail electric suburbans at the latter, and the inevitable railcar on some duties. There was also the all-steam Bastille station, discovered only on a later visit. Each station, as in London, originated with a former separate railway, locomotive types and classes were different in each,

The motion of 232U1 with such modern ideas as roller bearing rollers in place of die blocks on the expansion link and radius rod. Yet French tradition dies hard, as witness the complicated, cottered, arrangement on the roller bearing return crank!

other than the 141R Americans which swarmed everywhere. The Nord had its Chapelon and indigenous Pacifics, the seven pre-war Hudsons of classes 232R and 232S, plus other types already described. Next door was the Gare de l'Est, largest of the Paris termini, with yet again a completely different range of power. Top link were the 241A Belpaire boilered compound 4-8-2 of very impressive appearance, some 141P post war 2-8-2, while lighter services worked elsewhere by Pacifics were operated by large 4-6-0 of class 230K. Suburban work was handled by smaller, older, 141TB 2-8-2T with two cylinders, plus later 141TC with three cylinders on heavier duties. Empty stock and shunting was handled by ex-German 0-8-0 well tanks class 040TX. St Lazare had its own varieties of Pacific, of which the 231G were probably the best looking French Pacifics. Yet another old 2-8-2T appeared on suburbans, plus some 3-cylinder machines built to the Est design. The PLM at the Gare du Lyon, the old *ligne imperial*, while it remained faithful to compounding, used a simpler system with only two sets of valve gear for the four cylinders. Various 4-6-2, 2-8-2, and 4-8-2 comprised their mainline classes, and alone in Paris, even their suburban engines were compounds, mainly 4-8-4T with two alternate wheel sizes, some of each with either piston or poppet valves. There were also some older compound 4-6-4T for lighter trains. It was all extremely interesting, surrounded by new locomotive types at every turn, rather like those wartime evacuation days five years beforehand.

Next stage of the journey was from Paris to Strasbourg, behind one of the superb-looking Est 241A locos heading about eighteen heavy continental coaches with which it kept up a steady 100 to 110 km/h. Around Noisy-le-Sec, with its vast, smouldering, roundhouse, several heavy 2-10-2T were noted on transfer freights, and once past there, with head out of window, an extraordinary looking locomotive was noted approaching on the adjacent track. I decided to note the number and check the identity afterwards, if possible. What a number it was, 031 130 TA 19, taking some concentration to remember, leaving just enough time to note that it was some kind of articulated tank engine.

Along the main line, American 141R class thundered past, their loud, thin, abrasive exhaust contrasting with the hush-hush of the native compounds. Strange that so voluble a race as the French should produce such deathly quiet steam power, while the staid, quiet British built locomotives which clashed, banged, and roared along in a thoroughly extrovert manner.

Between Nancy (where a large Est 4-4-0 was seen on shed) and Strasbourg, a series of flyovers changed the four track line from left to right hand running, and the rather flat plains of northern France started to fold into the pleasant hills of the Vosges. Architecture, both general and railway, changed abruptly into the Teutonic, and all sorts of neat looking simple expansion types began to appear, later identified as well known Prussian classes, for we were now in the territory of Alsace-Lorraine, which has changed hands twice in the railway period of history, background information only subsequently assimilated. One started to wonder at the standard of teaching suffered by the average British scholar, during which both history and geography are taught as incredibly boring subjects, whereas here I was, travelling through a fascinating geographical region, steeped in history, having been taught nothing of either! Somewhere along the line we were put into a loop to allow the Paris–Strasbourg 'flyer' (for want of a better word) to overtake. This was a train of lightweight coaches, about four or five, mounted on ten-wheeled rubber tyred, bogies, with steel flanges to steer through the pointwork. And what was on the front of this – some sort of internal combustion contrivance of appropriate 'modernity'? Not on your life. These high speed trains were hauled by the old 230K class de Glehn 4-6-0, the largest and heaviest French 4-6-0s, but nevertheless dating back to 1905 and built until 1925. These had been 'transformed' between 1932 and 1947 with advanced superheaters and exhaust systems, increased boiler pressure (256 psi) and improved valvery, with low pressure valves 350 mm ($13\frac{3}{4}''$) diameter. At $82\frac{1}{2}$ long tons, they were about the same weight as a

The 141R class in France were the nearest big American steam. 141R 1311, one of the last built, featured cast steel bed, roller bearings, and Boxpok driving and coupled wheels, all thoroughly American.

rebuilt 'Royal Scot', but had a larger grate area (GWR 'King' size), and large wheels 6' $10\frac{1}{4}''$ diameter, nominal, sounding rather North Easternish. Very interesting that these old locomotives had been chosen to power this top speed, prestige, train, which they handled most competently. Those used on this train were given outlandish styling, distinguishing them from their rather staid looking contemporaries, but certainly they were flyers. Imagine the GWR, about 1947, introducing a high speed train and running it with a souped up Churchward 'Star', for that was the equivalent! Before leaving this subject, the acoustic effects of such a remarkable train are equally remarkable. Flashing by with the usual silent exhaust of a French compound, one heard first the 'diddly diddly dum' of locomotive and tender wheels encountering the local point and crossing installation followed by a high pitched 'wheeeeeeeeeee' as the rubber tyred coaches traversed the steel railtops.

Arriving at Strasbourg, an impressive station in the German style, I encountered for the first time, modern German locomotives. These I found most impressive, the lighter 2-10-0 of class 50 (150Z in French numeration) and the vast three-cylinder machines of class 44 (150X). Coming from a railway where

The German 44 class 3-cylinder 2-10-0, first seen in France in 1949 surprised the Swindon trained author with their mastery over the heaviest trains. 95 tons of adhesion of course helps. . . .

highly competent train starting was an accepted normality, the 44 class was extremely impressive even to me. I watched one start a train, estimated at about 2,000 tons, stopped at a signal on one curve of a triangular junction. The line was obviously uphill, gradient unknown. One could imagine the Midland trying it with triple-headed 4Fs, with a couple of 'Jinties' as bankers, or the LNER emulating a modern day 'Pop concert' with two or three Gresley geared, syncopating, monsters, clashing and banging as they slithered round the bend. By contrast, the 44 class just eased this massive load up and around this difficult start, no slip, no fuss, giving the impression that one could have hooked another thousand tons behind without creating any problem. These big 2-10-0s were also impressive in their mechanical integrity, rolling into Strasbourg station with international trains from Kehl, just across the Rhine, the only sound heard, as they coasted into the station, was the click of wheel tyres on rail joints. A British freight loco would roll under the arched roof with a deafening Bangle Bongle, Bangle Bongle of loose axleboxes and rodding, totally absent in these superb locomotives. As a result, I went to France to investigate French and American practice, and quite unexpectedly returned most impressed by

German practice! Sound, simple, locomotives, very accessible for maintenance, yet with an effectiveness and efficiency comparable with the French compounds.

Two incidents after this stand out as being worth recording in this French holiday narrative, one being where, near Perigeaux in the south of France, after inspecting a not very interesting locomotive works, I ambled out to inspect a long line of derelict machines dumped in some nearby sidings, looking for possible 'gems'. Most of the derelicts were class 140G, rather dreary 2-8-0 of World War I vintage, built to the British loading gauge but as far as is known, never run in Britain. While plodding through this dump I heard a loud thrashing noise, as could only come from a saturated, slide valve, locomotive working hard. Dashing across to the main line I encountered such a sight as may have been painted by Monet in the previous century! A train of flat roofed, four wheel carriages of ancient design rolled by, headed by a 'Forquenot' 2-4-2 tender locomotive with tall chimney, outside cylinders and valve gear, totally out of place in the mid twentieth century! Later, I saw several more of these machines, classes 121A and 121B, with different wheel sizes, usually simmering behind remote sheds awaiting the call when the railcar's battery went flat. Evidently, what I saw was such an occasion, a wonderful trip into the backwoods of time.

The other experience worth recording was my one and only ride behind a 240P, the short lived yet famous Chapelon 4-8-0 which managed to cram a quart into a pint pot – with disastrous results to the pot! I arrived from Nevers at Dijon late evening, having spent most of the £14 which incredibly, by dint of sleeping mainly on trains, park benches, and even once in a field, had lasted for about twelve days. As wages staff on BR, my privilege tickets were limited to third class (not that I could have afforded second), and I sat waiting at Dijon station for a train to Paris hauled by a 240P. That evening I ambled round the depot, which reminded me of York, a cluster of roundhouses. Instead of being crammed with B16s, Dijon was full of huge 4-8-2, 4-8-0, 2-8-2 and lesser breeds of motive power. 4-8-0 were all the 240P class, but there were several varieties of 4-8-2, some old bullet-nosed 241A, out of use, the rebuilt 241D forming the majority, a few post war 241P, most of which were used then between Lyon and Marseilles, and both the odd engines, the solitary 241C and 241E. After dozing fitfully on a platform bench, I awoke in time for the amazing rush of expresses which left for Paris between the small hours and dawn. These came from assorted places in the south of France, from Switzerland, and beyond, forming almost a suburban service with about twenty trains to Paris in three or four hours. Many were top link expresses 'Rapides' with first and second class accomodation only, and these seemed to draw the 240P class, leaving 241D for the lesser trains. As dawn approached, I began to wonder whether I would manage a 240P run, but one of the last trains in the service had the magic combination of 240P at the head end plus third class accomodation.

The previous train had thirteen coaches and a 241D, and we followed about fifteen minutes behind with a 240P on sixteen. Third class was right at the front, and the first compartment was empty, to my satisfaction. The load was thus about 650 tons, and we accelerated well up the 1 in 125 gradient to such an extent that we soon caught up the older (and heavier) locomotive with its lighter load. After each delay, maximum power was put on until shut down for the next check, and it was the only French compound I heard making significant noise, a harsh thrash from the double Kylchap exhaust. Certainly, the 240P could produce the power, but I am doubtful of their alleged economy figures because after the summit the whole of the compartment was thick with unburned char which also took about a week to get out of my hair. I understand they were very heavy on maintenance, and the following year, 1950, travelling the same route, by then electrified, all were out of use, even though but ten years old. Other modern steam had been dispersed to various areas for continued use, but the sad evidence is that these superb power producers were simply uneconomic, certainly in maintenance and probably in fuel costs.

As a rather interesting postscript, I have subsequently experienced even better performance behind South Africa's 'Red Devil' class 26 4-8-4 which, with two simple expansion cylinders, and lacking the 240P's high pressure, poppet valves, and compounding, produces significantly more power from a similar weight of locomotive. Moreover, the class 26 has a robust cast steel bed, and substantial grate area, both lacking in the 240P, showing that even the legendary best of 1940 had been bettered by 1980, and that steam development had continued.

This trip to France had proved thoroughly interesting, informative, and educative, by far the best locomotive experience to date. I had gone with an open mind, to study French and American practice, and ended up being most impressed by the German engines seen, which appeared to combine French standards of efficiency with American standards of robust construction and accessibility. Similarly, from an enthusiast level, what set out as an engineering know-how exercise, sowed the seeds of an interest in overseas locomotive history, for how can one see and experience such locomotives without wanting to know more about them? And if France had so much to offer, what about all the other countries in Europe? Thus one trip had widened my horizons from the British Isles to the rest of the world.

Soon after returning from France, the fitting stage of the apprenticeship ended, and the final phase as an Erector commenced.

5

ERECTOR

'Erecting' is simply the assembly of locomotives from their component parts, and apart from the smaller engines dealt with in the 'B' shed, already experienced, most of this work was done in the AE shop, ie the part of the A shop complex devoted to erecting. So large was the A shop, virtually a works within a works, that it was subdivided into an AM machine section, AW wheel shop, and AV boiler shop, while the locomotive test plant was also within its four walls. The main shop occupied an area about 1000 feet long by 700 feet wide and contained two traverser roads each serving pits on either side. In very round figures, it had an approximate capacity to build 150 and repair two thousand locomotives annually, the repairs being roughly equally divided between heavy, and intermediate or light. At the time I entered there was a campaign going on to speed up actual time in the shop, and I think a heavy repair took just about two weeks during which the locomotive would be completely stripped down, components repaired or exchanged, and the whole thing re-assembled, valves set, steamed, weighed, and delivered back to the operating staff. Boilers took longer to overhaul than the engine portion, and were always exchanged on a heavy repair. During intermediate and light repairs, boilers usually stayed in the frames.

What happened was that locomotives were delivered to the small yard opposite the main offices, by the Gloucester line junction, then moved to the sidings outside the A shop, beside the main line. Initial inspection took place here, and older locos for scrap were weeded out and dumped in the 'Con Yard', the most westerly part of the works area, backing on to the old MSWJR line from Cheltenham. This name originated in the 1890s, when the broad gauge was being abolished, the area then being the 'Concentration yard' for broad gauge locomotives. Within the Con yard was the C shop, where locos were actually cut up, a fascinating place to pay one's last respects to a favourite engine. Outside was a stack of numberplates from scrapped locomotives, some from well before my time at Swindon, including the miniature size plates from works crane tank 1299.

Locomotives to be repaired were marked with splashes of paint denoting

A "panned" photo captures the speed of a Churchward Mogul near Kemble heading a heavy vacuum fitted bogie wagon freight, very untypical for Britain.

components to be repaired or scrapped, and those allocated to the A shop were shunted onto the traverser and winched onto the stripping pits, inevitably the first task for the apprentice erector, who moved round the shop in the same order as a locomotive being repaired. Work on the stripping pits was very dirty, as earlier experienced in the B shed, and it took but a day or so to strip a locomotive down to its bare frames. This way, one obtained a very good idea about the anatomy of the various classes, as all passed through these pits in order of arrival, and indeed continued through the shop, irrespective of class. Next to the stripping pits was the 'bosh', a heated tank of some mixture in which all greasy components were dumped, in trays, for degreasing. There was also a larger receptacle in which the whole frame was wheeled for similar treatment by sprays, such that after the stripping pit, heavy repairs continued on quite clean locomotives. Those for intermediate and light repairs, with boilers on, were too big to fit into the spray area.

Next stage was the frame gang, where the Zeiss optical lining up apparatus was used to accurately line up cylinder centres and hornblocks, the latter both longitudinally and laterally. No such apparatus was available in the B shed, where this operation was carried out by the time honoured method of stretching a piece of string through the cylinder bore. Frame gang work was quite hard, with a lot of hand grinding of hardened hornblocks which were out of line. After that came the cylinder gang, where cylinder and piston valve liners were either bored out to the next size, or replaced if worn to the scrapping limit. Several things were learned here, of interest to enthusiasts, who often argue at great length about the nominal dimensions of locomotives, and the nominal tractive effort figures derived therefrom. Cylinder diameters, and of course piston valve liners, are not fixed dimensions but increase with wear. When a locomotive enters works, this wear is taken up by boring out to the next standard dimension, and new valves and pistons, with suitably enlarged rings, fitted to match. When the liners have been bored out to the maximum possible size, such that they are too thin for further machining, they are replaced by new ones to the original nominal size. The most extreme case I came upon was a 'Mogul' whose nominally $18^{1/2}$ inch cylinders had become $19^{1/4}$ inches, but this may have been a result of deferred wartime maintenance. Assuming it also had minimum wheel diameter due to wheel wear, of say 5' 6", then the tractive effort calculated from these actual dimensions works out to over 28,000 lb, instead of the nominal 25,670 lb, a considerable increase! This shows that pedantic arguments based on nominal sizes are quite meaningless. Similarly, quoted weights expressed to the nearest hundredweight are so much hogwash, and are usually the actual weight of the prototype locomotive in whatever condition it happens to be weighed. Steel plates, which comprise much of a locomotive's metal content, have a rolling tolerance of 5 percent, from maximum to minimum, making a possible 5 tons on a 100 ton locomotive. Furthermore, locomotives, like humans, 'put on weight' as they age, as various details found weak are strengthened by various methods, a rib here, web there, thicker material somewhere else, all small but adding up to a ton or two in the end. Even successive layers of paint must have some effect on the total!

Something learned on the cylinder gang was that a group of locomotives had different valve sizes than those always quoted as the invariable standard. These were 'Halls' from 5921 to 6900, 68XX, 78XX, and the 29XX with outside steam pipes. Instead of the Churchward 10" valves with $1\frac{5}{8}$" steam lap, these had 9" valves with $1\frac{3}{4}$" steam lap, same as the King class. Why this was done defies reason, as one cancels out the other change in dimension, unless some bright spark used it as a means of increasing quantities (and reducing prices) on the otherwise special components for the Kings. The chargehand on the cylinder gang perforce had to maintain a register of these dimensions, and in 1950 when I was on his gang, policy was to replace these 9-inch valves (or whatever size they had become over the years) with standard 10 inch units retaining the longer lap and travel, as were fitted new to Halls and Modified Halls from 6901 onwards. A fascinating little bit of history, quite invisible externally, and therefore generally unknown.

Another bit of 'invisible' modification was to the cylinder casting design. Churchward's cylinders were very well designed, with straight, direct ports, as were only adopted much later by other British railway companies. The steam chests were cylindrical, just large enough to fit the valve liners into, this also being normal practice. During the late 1920s, or perhaps the 1930s, André Chapelon in France made a statement that to lessen pressure drop when valves opened to admission, steam chest volume should equal cylinder volume, an empirical proportion impossible to conveniently achieve but offering an ideal to

While on a track testing jaunt with Bob Hancock, 2937 was shot at Newport before embarking on a test run to Hereford.

Swindon out shopped 6848 in the early 1960s in fully lined out green livery, but it was soon vandalised to make way for politically inspired diesels.

aim for. Evidently someone at Swindon picked up this bit of wisdom, for about that time GWR cylinders were redesigned with a 'bellied out' section between the valve liners, increasing volume by, one imagines, at least fifty percent, a useful and easily incorporated design feature missed by BR's Derby engineers when they designed the standard locomotive range. Probably it happened just after Stanier's departure, or he would have used it on LMS locomotives.

Production arrangements at Swindon were well organised, when one considers how little time was spent overhauling a locomotive. For example, once the wheels were dropped they were sent over to the AW shop for turning, retyring if necessary, and axlebox journals machined. Once the new journal diameter was known, the axlebox gang in the AM shop bored out a set of boxes to suit, and within about five or six working days of the engine entering for stripping, wheels and axleboxes were delivered to the AE shop for mating together, and frames dropped into place over them. Rather amusingly, the fitter who fitted axleboxes always assumed they would be too tight, and went over the carefully machined whitemetal surface with a scraper before even trying to bed them onto the journal. All this, including fitting a new or replacement boiler took place on the east side of the main traverser road, such that locos had boilers and coupled wheels in position ready to roll across the traverser to the west side where motion, bogies, and other items were fitted, painting carried out, and valves set.

At the north end of this west side was the new work gang, where frames were set up (after having been fitted with horn guides etc in W shop), where frame plates were cut and slotted. Boilers were mounted, engines wheeled, motion fitted etc until they were in a comparable state to a newly overhauled locomotive, whereupon new and old took turns at the valve setting and painting sections at the bottom of the shop, nearest the head foreman's elevated office.

The assembly gang I was allocated to was headed by Stan Lewington who had a reputation for being a tartar and slave driver, although never giving me any trouble, perhaps because I was keen and interested, and got on with the job. The final assembly of a locomotive was, to me, the most interesting part of the works experience, for one began to see why certain parts were made in a particular manner, and, equally how things could be better arranged! Great Western (that is, Churchward) practice was good in many ways, but there is nothing like trying to fit a difficult component on a humid June afternoon to instil into a prospective designer's mind that a better way could, and *should* be devised!

The standard two cylinder locomotives, despite having inside valve gear, were not difficult to get at, as there was ample room between the two sets of valve gear, and none of the components were unduly heavy to handle. Perhaps the most awkward item was the steam chest front cover, tucked under that bit of curved running plate angle, with its support plate, making actuation of a spanner surprisingly difficult. Churchward knew what he was doing in his original designs, without the curved end, and I fancy both the LMS and LNER locomotives provided similar problems, judging by their later designs with gaps in the running plate for easy access to valves. Castles and Stars were bad, just where one wanted to be was a massive casting, known as the 'cage' bracing the frames between the outside cylinders and acting as general support and motion bracket for the inside motion. How some of the larger and older fitters got into it I do not know, it was bad enough for me as a young, lithe, apprentice. During my period on 'Lewington's', I had the interest and misfortune to work on no 4000, by then generally rebuilt as a 'Castle', but still retaining a cage of different form as doubtless associated with the original 'scissors' valve gear. One really needed to be a monkey to climb around inside that one and get things done properly. Funnily enough, the 'Kings', probably due to the greater distance between axles, were far easier to get into than the smaller 4-cylinder types. This class also had a speciality. Due to the long firebox, the plate frames were not braced for a corresponding length, and the presence of the ashpan precluded any cross staying of normal type. To alleviate this, the two trailing

During electrification from Euston, London–Birmingham trains were concentrated on the former GWR route; 6006 *King George 1* passes Park Royal and the Guinness brewery siding with a Birmingham train.

The GWR vacuum brake pump, although efficient, was a pain to set up, almost invariably needing bracket holes welding up and redrilling. Those on the 28XX class were among the most accessible as shown here. Note the small crosshead and slide bar for the valve spindle, unique to these 2-8-0s.

hornstays included lugs between which was pinned a solid cross stay from one to the other, its shape leading to the inevitable nickname of the 'hambone'.

Perhaps the worst job on these four-cylinder locos was hammering in the cotters on the inside crossheads. To do this, a staging was set up outside the loco, and balanced partly on this, and partly on the running plate stood the hammer man, equipped with a 14 lb sledge hammer. A sett, about three feet long was led down to the cotter itself, and guided into place by the man beneath. We could not see one another and worked by sound – a bellow of rage from below meant that the sett was not properly in place when struck! Despite this possibility of injury, my fitter preferred to be below, leaving me to do the nominally harder job, and I became quite adept, and well muscled, by practice on 'Castle' cotters. At about this time, Swindon had its annual 'mop' fair, a relic of medieval times, held in the High Street, closed to traffic for the occasion. One of the inevitable sideshows comprised a wooden block one had to hit with a mallet, sending a pointer up a vertical runner with a bell on top. If one rang the bell, a prize was won, usually something quite useless such as a goldfish in a jar. Well in training on four-cylinder overhauls I had a go and nearly knocked the bell off with the first stroke of the permitted three. The disgruntled attendant grudgingly gave me a paltry prize and refused to let me even have the other two strikes, let alone continue with another round!

A difficult smallish component was the vacuum pump, mounted on a bracket by fitted bolts, ie bolts which were a tight fit in the hole, preventing sloppiness and misalignment of the pump. Invariably the thing did not line up properly at first try, so the bolt holes in the bracket had to be welded up, marked out, and drilled again, usually an awkward job. Illustrated is the arrangement on a '28' from which it can be seen that with the pump casting mounted inside the support bracket, the only way of marking out and drilling the holes was also from inside. Of course, the wheels would not be in at the time, but it was a tight, dark, place to work. Worse were the 4-6-0s, where the whole thing was tucked up underneath the running plate valance. No wonder that the Southern and the LMS, both of whom tried vacuum pumps, gave them up as a bad job.

Despite Lewington's alleged severity, there was occasionally some fun on his gang. Each fitter was allocated a particular locomotive to complete, assisted by a labourer and an apprentice. There was a tradition that should a fitter make a detected mistake, an old umbrella was unfolded and placed over the chimney of 'his' engine, alerting anybody to come and jeer until the error was rectified. During my term, a practical joke was played on my mate while fitting the connecting rod on, I think, a 'Hall'. Due to the running plate overhead there was no way such a rod could be lifted by crane, and it was too heavy for the three man team, so others were called in to help. By tradition the locomotive's fitter was at the big end, and screwed on the cap, fitted cotter etc. On this occasion, the men at the front of the locomotive guided the small end above the top slide bar instead of between the bars where it should have been! Up went the umbrella, and the poor chap could do nothing until his mates helped take it apart again, only after all possible had come to see and jeer! The instant design thought in my mind was a hole in the running plate through which one could lift the rod by crane. Later on, watching the BR Standards being built at Swindon, I noticed that the main connecting rods still had to be lifted by hand, using half a dozen men.

Valve setting was effected on a special rig at the south end of the shop, with small powered rollers to rotate wheels to the desired quarters. Four-cylinder engines needed at least the leading coupling rods in place, so that inside and outside valves and pistons were correctly set, but on two cylinder engines the job could be done prior to fitting coupling rods although this rarely happened as one would then need to remove connecting rods to get at them. Inside cylinder engines, such as 56XX, were often valve set before fitting coupling rods, for obvious reasons. I had only a short sojourn on valve setting, being overtaken by events in the shape of trade union activity. However, I did enjoy helping with one locomotive, and accompanying it on the trial run down to

5691 from Abercynon after a rare overhaul at Swindon in the mid 1960s; Welsh valley 56XX were usually overhauled at Caerphilly. Their inside motion was a devil to get at!

Dauntsey on a pleasant sunny day. Engines on trial were obviously a nuisance to operators, since they hauled no loads, and we were stuck in the siding at Dauntsey for some time as there was a procession of trains to pass first. The driver knew somewhere where mushrooms could be gathered, and went off to collect them, returning with his hat full plus very wet feet from the marshy ground where such delicacies thrive. Removing his shoes, he hung the wet socks over the firehole to dry, without putting anything heavy on to hold them. Meanwhile, the fireman, noting a drop in pressure turned the blower on, neatly sucking the driver's socks into the fire! He was not amused, but we were.

Then came trade union trouble. Although a 'closed shop', with tradesmen having to join a union, apprentices were excluded during the course of their training. For some reason, the union, whose shop steward in AE was a particularly unpleasant type, decided to make a stand to try and force apprentices to conform. Several did so, but I refused and was made a test case. Possibly the union radicals disliked me because I read the 'Daily Telegraph' instead of the 'Daily Worker' a decision not so much political but due to the fact that when reporting railway happenings, the 'Telegraph' usually got details reasonably correct whereas other papers perpetrated the most appalling howlers. I figured that a paper which could correctly report things I knew about, probably also correctly reported other matters. Anyhow, I was 'sent to Coventry' (a dreadful,

LMS, stronghold). Since valve setting is very much a team job, and the men were instructed by their union not to work with me, I was transferred to the new work gang, where a batch of 1600 class small panniers were being built as a final flowering of nineteenth century Wolverhampton practice. I erected one of these almost single handed, fitting on all sorts of smaller bits and pieces, but every time something too big came up, I had to disappear while several others did the job without me in attendance. This irked the union, and eventually they called a strike, affecting the whole AE shop. It was midsummer, I think June, hot and humid, and I was struck with the attitude of the workmen, many of whom I had worked with in my rounds of the shop. Sitting on the benches, on strike, there was no hostility towards me whatever. 'Don't join the union, Dusty, its too bloody hot to work anyway' was a typical remark. I began to see that trade unions, far from being the least bit democratic, were petty tyrannies, usually of the competent by the incompetent.

   Of course, works management could not tolerate this situation, so I was transferred to the material testing house, not under union intimidation, and where I spent the remaining few months of my apprenticeship in an almost academic atmosphere with little to do and plenty of time to do it. Not being one to idle, I brought in my instruments and started doodling locomotive designs, now in the firm's time. However, it was time for 'Trip', and having seen those German engines on my French trip, I decided to include that country. Discovering that Swindon public library (a superb institution) kept a copy of *Cook's Continental Railway and Shipping Timetable*, several lunch breaks were spent poring over this fascinating publication, planning a route. Having been to France, it was clearly advantageous to enter Europe by either Belgium or Holland, and having purchased a good book on Dutch locomotives (*'Onze Nederlandse Locomotiven'*), while knowing little about Belgium, the obvious course was to travel via Ostend.

ABROAD AGAIN

Another locomotive which fascinated me was the streamlined Algerian Garratt, with Cossart valve gear. I had seen, and been unimpressed, by the Midland Garratts but realised that there must be more to the breed than the Midland made of them or they would not be so popular. Having already encountered Cossart valve gear in Paris, that feature was seen as being a sound, everyday, engineering possibility, being employed in suburban service, probably the railway duty demanding the utmost in reliability. What *Cook's* showed me was that in my two week holiday period, I could cross Dover–Ostend, see something of Belgium, cross into Germany and head south to Italy and Sicily, where a ship could be caught from Palermo to Tunis. One could then travel along the North African coast via Algeria to Morocco, returning via Spain. For some odd reason, it could not be done in the opposite direction without needing extra time. 'Priv' forms for the rail journeys were obtained, and the only unknown factor was the cost of the two trans-Mediterranean transits.

Belgium was quite interesting from an enthusiast viewpoint, but had little of engineering note. I saw outside framed, inside cylinder 0-6-0PT, looking like very boxy and misshapen GWR engines, Caledonian-type 4-4-0, 0-6-0, and 4-4-2T, French compound 4-6-0, lots of Prussian types, including the elegant class S10 four-cylinder 4-6-0 and an S10^2 3-cylinder version, using Holcroft's originally proposed conjugate valve gear. Native types seemed very heavy, and not particularly effective relative to their size, especially the four-cylinder simple 'Pacifics'. I had a run also behind one of the unique streamlined 'Atlantics', with inside cylinders and bar frames, like nothing else built anywhere. American types were there in plenty ranging from squat little Baldwin 2-6-2ST which seemed only able to creep about, to modern, post-war mixed traffic 2-8-0, class 29, built mainly in Canada. They ran very well, despite smallish (5 foot) wheels, and by setting the trailing wheels back, a decent sized wide firebox was accomodated over the wheels. Valve gear was elegant and well laid out and they set thoughts in motion.

Travel to Germany was a nightmare, on the 'Nord Express'. My priv. ticket order was made out from Brussels to Cologne, but once on the train was horrified to discover the ticket read 'Köln'. Was I booked to the wrong place? Would I be thrown off the train, very crowded, in the middle of the night? Of course, nothing like this happened, as I discovered that Köln is the correct German spelling for what the French and English call 'Cologne'. I was only really assured of this by seeing, on the station end, a large advertisement with the familiar '4711' logo, and 'Kölnische Wasser'! An old saying claims that ignorance is bliss, but travelling alone in totally alien places, it can be a worrying nuisance!

Köln Hauptbahnhof in 1950 was totally steam and very busy. There were the expected 01 and 03 Pacifics, of which I had found published descriptions, plus three-cylinder versions of each, new to me. In the dark of the small hours it was fascinating to find electric lights under the running plates enabling the motion to be examined as well as in daylight. Access to the three-cylinder engines was unbelievably simple – bar frames being shallower the way in was over the top, and of course there was only one set of motion. What a delight compared with the cramped cage of a 'Castle'. Another elegant three-cylinder type seen at Köln was the class 39 passenger 2-8-2 with all cylinders driving the second axle and valve gear actuated from the third. Each valve had independent Walschaerts gear, but that of the centre valve was actuated from a double return crank on the left hand side. The only thing between the frames was the big end, as with a Gresley engine, but the method of actuating the centre valve was far more positive. One had only to hear that beautiful even exhaust beat to know everything was just perfect. Another remarkable type, of which only one was seen, was the class 62, 4-6-4T with wide firebox over quite large (5' 9") coupled

The German 62 class 4-6-4T seen at Köln in 1950 has a wide firebox over the top of fairly large driving wheels, giving the author ideas for a wide firebox 4-8-0 for Britain.

wheels, together with all supplies in a massive back tank, preventing loss of adhesion as coal and water was used up. Altogether, those few pre-dawn hours spent on Köln's platforms taught me a lot about good locomotive engineering practice, strongly augmenting the previous year's impressions that German engines were superbly designed.

The next new country encountered was Italy, where quite the opposite prevailed. One might imagine that a race who could breed names like Maserati and Alfa-Romeo, with their ability to produce super fast motor cars, might also espouse good locomotive engineers. No! Italian steam designs, quite impressive from a distance, made even Midland locomotives sprightly by comparison. Hopelessly inadequate valves and steam ports, four cylinders sharing two small valves with crossed ports (as was actually copied by Derby for the Lickey banker, in an incredible situation where the World was scoured for the worst possible practice to copy), meant that Italian locomotives were just sluggish plodders. It was interesting to note, in my journey down that boot shaped peninsula, that some modern and sprightly machines, to wit Stanier 8F 2-8-0, and USA wartime 2-8-2, were all dumped out of use. One imagines that they frightened the life out of FS drivers, by rapidly accelerating when regulators were opened, being perhaps regarded thus as dangerous! Many of the US Army S160 class were seen in use, these also being sprightly by Italian standards, but being numerous they had to be retained, possibly by being somehow hobbled to keep them within local non-performance levels.

The final stage of the southbound journey consisted of crossing to Sicily on a train ferry, all in glorious sunshine, a delightful experience. Once on the island, at Messina, the inevitable Latin chaos and confusion reigned while the train was shunted off the ferry and assembled in the station, and I walked to the front to note a sluggish 685 class 2-6-2 at the head end. Just before departure it became obvious that we were to have a banker, so back down the length of the train to find the Italian version of the Lickey Banker, as seen by my still unworldly eyes, a four-cylinder 0-10-0. So, I positioned myself in the back compartment to absorb this experience. Sound effects were quite mystifying as the train set off. The four cylinder 2-6-2, with quite large wheels, was puffing faster than the small wheeled 0-10-0, which made no sense at all. Luckily the last coach had a vestibule door with windows, and by peering out it was seen that this curious 0-10-0 was a compound, with two high pressure cylinders one side and two low the other, using a single piston valve for each pair of cylinders. The result was a four-cylinder locomotive which made but two exhaust beats per wheel revolution, in total contrast to Southern's Lord Nelsons which made eight. It started to become clear that there was no such thing as 'Continental' practice, as glibly quoted by those who had never left the comfortable confines of Wiltshire's steam capital. There were those German and French locomotives from which much could be learned, but down in the boot of Italy, motive power would have greatly benefited from consultancy by the CME of even such a minor Welsh railway as the Taff Vale.

At Palermo, the whole planned trip came to an abrupt end. Cost of the passage to Tunis was totally beyond my means, leading to a quick scuttle back up Italy, at full fare, across the south of France to Perpignan where I picked up my originally proposed route through Spain, and from where I had privilege ticket forms. At Perpignan was a little railway, the C.de F Perpignan Oriental, sounding like something heading towards exotic places, but which had a delightful 0-4-4-0T Mallet in use, the first such articulated I recall seeing. The route had been chosen to include the Béziers–Neussargues line, reputedly worked by the ex-Midi 4-8-0T, a rare breed in anybody's book. Initially I was disappointed to find the line electrified, yet some of these 240TA were in steam on shed. Then one came in piloting an electric, off the branch, and I discovered some traffic remained steam worked and managed to get a run behind one to Sévérac, on a local passenger train. Possibly they worked some of the branches off that line, utilising a local passenger to run to and from the main shed for washouts, etc. That was the last highlight of the trip, after which it was a solid bash back to Swindon.

TEST HOUSE

The material test house was a quiet little enclave, behind the G shop, presided over by a foreman under whom were one or two men only. It was a coveted move to finish one's apprenticeship on, especially if timed to coincide with the final examinations for the Higher National Certificate, since there was little to do and one could spend the time 'swotting'. In my case, I was too late for this, so time was spent on locomotive design.

Main daily duties for the apprentice comprised walking, twice daily, to a couple of places in the works, and collecting water samples to be tested for hardness etc. As I recall, we did not even do the testing ourselves, but sent them over to the chemical laboratory. There was a long tensile machine upon which were tested to destruction samples of chains and cables supplied from outside, such occupying perhaps an hour or two each week, while samples of incoming steel etc were tested for tensile and bending strength, again only occasionally. One wore ordinary clothes instead of overalls, and in general felt very civilised!

Following my second continental trip, with so much new absorbed, and so much time to spare, drawing instruments were brought into work and several ideas worked on. A streamlined 4-8-4T version of the three-cylinder 4-8-0 was schemed out, with casing based on those Algerian Garratts I had failed to see, but the main idea demanding attention was the use of bar frames and wide fireboxes.

First attempt was to revamp the two-cylinder 2-8-2T with these features, which proved quite easy, hardly surprising in retrospect as British Railways subsequently built their superb class 9F with wide fireboxes over 5 foot coupled wheels. The next stage was a lightweight 4-8-0 for secondary lines, about $15\frac{1}{2}$ ton axle load and 5' 3" wheels, which went together well. Again, couple up the trailing bogie wheels and the whole thing was not unlike the later 9F. The problems started when larger locomotives for mixed traffic duties on main lines were attempted. Larger wheels, and larger boilers, all crammed together within the same loading gauge. Those extra few inches of the GWR loading gauge would have been very useful, but I set myself the target of not exceeding 13 feet total height. Evenly spaced coupled wheels, as used on the smaller engines, made it virtually impossible to fit in an adequate firebox and, equally important, an adequate ashpan. Both the American-built 29 class in Belgium, and the German 62 class 4-6-4T had trailing coupled wheels set back for this reason, and about the most satisfactory of the various schemes is shown in figure 6. Of course, one can argue that a 2-8-2 is a better solution, but some residual GWR prejudice against trailing trucks, probably inherited from dis-

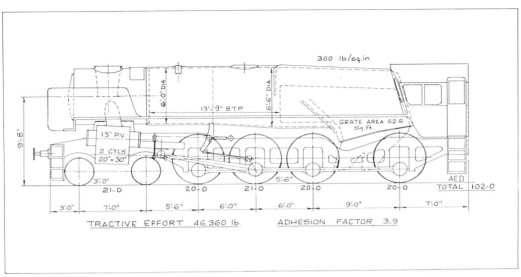

A good look at Belgian and German locomotives in 1950 showed how bar frames and wide fireboxes could be accomodated without a trailing truck, an inbred Swindon inhibition. Roller bearings throughout, including crankpins, are included in this scheme for an ultra rugged mixed traffic 4-8-0 within the British loading gauge. (Fig 6)

cussions about 'The Great Bear' preconditioned me towards a 4-8-0 which in any case was a more interesting and challenging design project.

A QUICKIE IN PARIS

By autumn the shadow of looming National Service was getting dense, and I was rather anxious to see more of that French articulated encountered in 1949, realising that two years in the army might preclude any such visits. Thus, on the last few days of civil and civilised existence I took two days or three days off to go and look for it/them. Being seen on the main line near Noisy-le-Sec, where there was a large locomotive depot, first stage was to go and see the foreman there. No, he had some splendid 3-cylinder 2-10-2T, but no articulateds. In fact it took some time to get him to understand what I was looking for, until a rough sketch and the engine number were written down. Sudden enlightenment! Yes, he knew what they were and where they lived, and on request wrote down the depot name. In the very flowery calligraphy so common in France, it looked like 'Boligny' and seemed to be quite close. Nobody at Noisy station had heard of it, so back into Paris to study one of those rather fine maps found in all main line termini and most Metro stations. There was no 'Boligny', but there was a place called Bobigny, not far from Noisy, but with no railway station, nor even any indication of having railway importance. It was also difficult of access, involving one Metro trip to an obscure terminus, followed by two rides in those delightfully archaic Paris buses, with open back platforms and waving, rather phallic, direction indicators. The area penetrated seemed largely undeveloped and I began to feel that the trip was a wild goose chase when a railway was crossed over and there was a marshalling yard and locomotive depot! In British terms, it was rather like trying to find Toton shed and yard, with nothing more than the name to go on.

The sun was out, nice late afternoon light, and several of these beasts were in the yard, so I managed to photograph one of each TA and TB versions. I hung around hoping for an action shot, but dusk soon came and it was back to Paris for the morning train to Calais and home. What is most remarkable is that there were many of these engines, I think at least sixty, first built in 1905 and lasting until 1950 centred latterly on Paris. Yet action photographs of them are extremely rare, even albums by well known French photographers lacking such shots. I should have stayed an extra day and arrived similarly late for the army, some did with the most feeble excuses, and no punishment. So ended my formal apprenticeship, starting on the Great Western Railway and finishing under the still quite young British Railways. It was known that a series of standard locomotives were in the offing, and that some lightweight 4-6-0 would be built at Swindon, but apart from that available information was remarkably thin. However much the subsequent designs reeked of LMS practice, a goodly degree of Swindon non-communication seemed to have found its way into BR headquarters, unlike later days when diesels were heralded with much hoo-hah and masculine bovine manure!

LNER LOCOMOTIVES

During apprenticeship days, as has already been recounted, thorough exploration had been made of Britain, plus a start made on the Continent. Something has been said of how both the Southern Railway and its Bulleid locomotives had been found impressive, while the LMS system remained largely unimpressive, its best features being the Stanier locomotives although these were mainly too small for the heaviest duties on Britain's largest railway, roughly two and a half times the size of the Great Western. Compared with GWR's thirty 'Kings', as top express power, the LMS would seem to have needed about eighty Stanier Pacifics, while their most numerous express class, the 'Jubilees' were of only the capacity of a Churchward 'Star'.

By comparison, the LNER was appreciated in having a 'big engine' policy, but the three hundred-odd Gresley Pacifics and V2s were mechanically unimpressive with their clanking and banging progress, missing and off-beat exhausts, and violent slipping at starting. One could appreciate Thompson's B1 and K1 designs, composed entirely of Gresley components more logically assembled, but his L1 2-6-4T were again very slippery, particularly disastrous in a suburban engine, and should have been 2-8-2T. As for his 'Pacifics', again the philosophy behind them was appreciated, but the execution clearly, and visibly, faulty.

What were really appreciated were the Peppercorn class A1 Pacifics, whereby the mainly Gresley components were reassembled in a more harmonious manner. It was an education to stand on Finsbury Park platform and watch a procession of northbound expresses climbing from King's Cross. Gresley engines roared up under a vertical column of smoke, the hop, skip-and-a-jump exhaust betraying the fact that only two and a half cylinders were working. By comparison, the Peppercorns purred up, faster, with all three cylinders fully operative, while the double Kylchap system allowed a freer and quieter exhaust. At that time, I considered them the best express locomotives in Britain, an opinion largely unchanged today.

Outside framed 0-6-0PT 1287 built in 1878 as a saddle tank was withdrawn in 1939, then reinstated due to the war. Latterly stationary boiler at Leamington, finally scrapped at Swindon in 1952.

A much Swindonised Cambrian 0-6-0, at Swindon for scrap. To some it is barely distinguishable from a Dean Goods. The repositioned balance weight on the main driving wheels showed that a standard GWR crank axle had been fitted.

Swindon's C shop was the dismal place where locomotives were cut up. 0-6-2T 33, ex-Rhymney Railway class M, awaits the torch, while the remains of a 3150 class 2-6-2T are in the foreground.

6

ARMY DAYS

Throughout the apprenticeship period there hung the shadow of National Service. One had to register at 17 years old for normal call up at 18, but those still studying during an apprenticeship were allowed deferment until 21 years of age. After the war, as peace descended, this service was soon reduced to one and a half years, and extrapolation of the trend pointed to a substantial shortening, or even abolishment by 1950, when my apprenticeship was due to finish.

The Korean war changed all that, and it was back to two years by 1950.

One possibility was to join the merchant navy as a junior engineering officer, but to totally avoid the army one had to stay there for five years. Several of my fellow apprentices did just that and enjoyed the life, whose attractions to me were the possibilities of seeing far places and the locomotives used therein. The main disadvantage would have been separation from locomotive engineering during that period, coupled to the possibility of being unable to rejoin the railway, so this was reluctantly abandoned. Another alternative was to join the army on a three-year short service commission, although this again meant actually resigning from the railway. Three years as an officer sounded better than two years in the ranks, and I went to the local recruiting office to enquire, but was told to apply to the War Office in London. This seemed unlikely for a junior officer's position, although later I discovered he was right, and I resigned myself to the normal routine.

Returning from the quick trip to Paris, a final thrash was held at the Bell Hotel in Swindon, consuming vast quantities of draught Bass, and having a beard ceremoniously hacked off by a contingent of local nurses. They may have, in sober state, been adept at removing pubic hair prior to an operation, but in our mutual insobriety they made a good mess of my face, removing bits of skin and leaving tufts of residual hair! Having been ordered to report to the REME (Royal Electrical and Mechanical Engineers) camp at Blandford, I set off next morning from Swindon Town station. The father and mother of all hangovers was soon blown away as the little 'forty-five' tank sped across the Wiltshire downs, and on a beautiful autumn morning the prospects of two years in the army seemed not bad at all. It would be a change, and there was still the prospect of an overseas posting with new locomotives to see.

At Andover Junction the Southern train to the west arrived in a haze of that railway's characteristic antiseptic smell, and a green coach next to the engine was boarded. It was the expected Bulleid Pacific, and after the regulation violent slips slowly accelerated up the gradient – snaffle clank, snuffle bonk, snaffle clank, snuffle bonk. Another change at Templecombe, to a train of drab maroon coaches hauled by a Stanier class 5 which rolled into the station with a deafening Tangle Tongle from loose axleboxes and motion. Civilisation ended at Blandford, and the final few miles from station to camp were in a Bedford truck whose whining differential and buzzing tyres were in contrast to the autumnal stillness of bucolic Dorset.

Once inside the camp it was a different world entirely. Fresh paint, white-wash, and polished brass were everywhere, quite alien to a locomotive works graduate, but doubtless as dear to the commanding officer as a gleamingly painted and polished 'King' was to Swindon's works manager. Lots of funny little men strutted about in teddy bear uniforms surmounted by grotesque berets, the whole aspect looking like a mass of clockwork Charlie Chaplins. In charge of each group was a corporal or sergeant squawking totally incomprehensible commands in what seemed another language, soon to be assimilated.

We bewildered civilians were entered up, numbered, led through a labyrinth of stores and issued with strange items of clothing and equipment. Huts and beds were allocated after which it was down to the cookhouse for our first army meal. Behind a long counter of unappetising foodstuffs lined up a selection of the scruffiest and most moronic individuals scraped up in the National Service net, while at the entrance stood a corporal bawling 'only one plate, yer in the army now, roight!?' Upon this chipped and cracked plate (the army's passion for spotless cleanliness extending not to its cookhouses) were dumped limp haddock, soggy potatoes, a chunk of rock hard pastry, wash of watery custard and dollop of strawberry jam. Into a pint mug was squirted some brown fluid, euphemised as tea, and at the exit stood another corporal bawling 'Yew stupid, 'orrible little men, whoi didn't yer take tew plates!?'

The first evening was spent polishing boots and brasswork, and coating an assortment of belts and straps with a filthy green mud the army called 'blanco'. I cursed myself for not joining the merchant navy, where the worst may have been some initial seasickness.

The next few days were spent learning the army's extraordinary language and funny little ways. All NCOs seemed to have what could be called an Aldershot accent, made up from the worst of Cockney, Brummie, and Scouse accents, and one learned to comprehend and act upon strange commands such as 'Git fell in. Zywere! Faster next time, roight? Boi the roight, quiiiiick, AA! As a squad shambled along, more or less in step, the NCO would try and time sinister and dexter footsteps with his chant of 'Ep oi ep oi ep oi'. Every start, stop, or change of direction had to be undertaken with petulant stamps of the feet worthy of a bad tempered schoolgirl, and it all seemed childishly illogical. Much appreciated were occasional rests for lectures when one learned which end of the gun the bullet hole was, and more up the army's alley, how it could be cleaned and polished.

Assorted intelligence and educational tests of remarkable ease and simplicity weeded out a batch of us then sent to Honiton, Devon, as 'potential officers'. For the first time in years I had been away from railways and steam locomotives for two weeks, a seeming eternity, and it was a much appreciated interlude to be dragged back to Templecombe by a constipated Derby 4-4-0, then whisked down to Honiton by a Bulleid Pacific. As a potential officer, the army first wanted to weed out those lacking resolve and determination, this process starting at Honiton station where we had to shoulder our packs and kitbags, then run 'at the double' to camp. For the first month we were buggered and chivvied about mercilessly, and a couple of men went 'N.D' or Non-Desirous of continuing the training, being then returned to Blandford.

Our squad comprised mainly 21 year olds, with an apprenticeship or university behind them, and were collectively more mature and immune to NCO terrorism than the usual 18 year old intake. As a result we had an unusually low 'N.D.' rate and equally, being less easily moulded into the army's peculiar little ways, an equally high proportion including myself, failed to become officers. Nevertheless, Honiton was much better than Blandford, for one thing the food was reasonably edible with usually several choices of main course. My hut happened to be at the edge of camp, beside the Southern main line, and in off duty moments one could savour trains climbing the bank, headed by snuffling Bulleid boxes, brash cocksure S15s, or gentle T9 4-4-0s.

An early attempt to obtain 'ND' candidates was a cross-country run up Gittisham hill, in full battle order, an exhausting ordeal. What sustained the others I know not, but I kept going by imagining myself as some vast 2-12-2T, with ample boiler power, tackling loads and gradients as never before! Our platoon officer was a pleasant, National Service, second lieutenant, betraying his civilian outlook by the provision of positive incentive. We soon found that most of the more strenuous exercises finished at the 'Hare and Hounds', a pub situated at a remote Devonshire crossroads and the best performers were treated to a pint on the King's Commission. I seemed always to be one of the also rans, having to buy my own beer, no mean expense when pay had reverted to that of a first year apprentice of five years past.

Midway through the course, we had our first '48 hour pass', and I went home to see my parents in London. En route, at Basingstoke, was spotted a Drummond T14 4-6-0, the last I ever saw in steam, and that weekend coincided with the last run in regular service of an Ivatt C1 Atlantic, which I saw off in thick fog at Kings Cross. At home was a large parcel containing the 1947 'Locomotive Cyclopedia', and as its thousand plus pages were too much to absorb in a weekend, I took it back to camp and spent several spare moments studying the final flowering of American steam practice, as detailed therein. Inspired by these, I started out to sketch my own range of BR standard locomotives, and coincidentally also included eleven types, but here the similarity ended, although the overall appearance was not dissimilar. Like the BR types, mine were mainly 'mixed traffic', but included some purely freight and shunting classes, whereas the eventual BR standards were more clearly passenger orientated. Also, mine were more evenly divided between the upper and lower power categories, unlike BR's Derby-inspired range, with seven out of the eleven original classes in the Midland power groups 2, 3 and 4. Being a little uncertain of bar frames still, mine also had plate frames, but were uniformly drawn with wide fireboxes and, strangely, with the 28″ piston stroke used on the larger BR types. Brief details as originally sketched out in an army barrack room were:

Type	Wheel diameter	Axle load (tons)	Grate area (sq ft)	TE @ 85% (lb)
4-8-0	5′6″	18½	49	43,000
4-8-4T	5′6″	20	49	43,000
2-10-0	5′0″	18	49	50,000
2-12-2T	4′6″	18	49	55,000
4-8-0	5′6″	17	36	35,000
2-8-2T	5′0″	18½	36	35,000
2-6-0	5′0″	17	26	25,000
2-6-2T	5′0″	18	26	25,000
0-10-0T	4′6″	18	26	35,000
2-6-2T	5′0″	14	20	20,000
0-8-0T	4′6″	14	20	28,000

Four interchangeable boiler types, three wheel diameters for the whole range, and four cylinder sizes, from 17″ × 28″ to 20″ × 28″ covering the whole series, certainly standardised with more discipline than the Derby group. No express passenger type was included, and the obvious 4-6-2, when later tried out, would not fit the fairly short largest boiler, the only possible alternative, other than a non-standard boiler, was a 2-6-4, another rare type.

Meanwhile, Christmas came and went, with more welcome leave, and we went to Barton Stacey, near Andover, for investigation by WOSB (War Office Selection Board). When results were known, the three youngest, untrained, but *least committed* were given commissions in this technical corps, while those with engineering degrees, certificates, etc, were returned as corporal fodder for the remaining 21 months of army life. Three of us were posted to the Ordnance Depot at Bicester, Oxfordshire, perhaps the worst military slum in Britain, a sea of mud supporting hundreds of Nissen huts, like a regiment of evil, overgrown, slugs. We arrived after dark and reported to a company officer who seemed surprised at our appearance – possibly we could have taken a day or two off with nobody the wiser, this being the start of becoming an 'old soldier', successfully defying the system without detection. Booked in we were distributed amongst those dreadful huts which in that cold midwinter were appalling residences. Cold seeped up from the raw concrete floors and icy winds howled through the ill-fitting ends and doors. A central pot stove roasted those nearest, leaving the remainder to freeze. Wash houses and latrines were scattered here and there, often a couple of hundred yards from one's hut, and it was not unusual for soldiers with full bladders on a wet and windy night, to simply lean out and piddle unhygienically onto the grass, rather than make an uncomfortable journey to the dank, appointed place.

Railway-wise, the town of Bicester was served by two lines, the GWR Old Oak to Banbury cut-off, and the LMS (formerly LNWR) branch from Bletchley to Oxford. The camp was four miles outside town, and served by a military branch off the LMS line. The army loco shed (another Nissen hut) was just behind our quarters, and had an allocation of about eight or nine WD 'Austerity' 0-6-0ST, whose deep, choked, booming exhaust was frequently heard. Apart from the freight duties relevant to an Ordnance Depot, there were also passenger trains, run mainly for civilian staff working in the camp but living in town, or connecting with LMS local trains. This train ran in every morning, returning late afternoon, and comprised a wonderful assortment of old LMS coaches, including some from such railways as the North Stafford, and the Tilbury line, as well as others with no identification. At weekends, a leave train ran to Oxford for main line connections, but this was of main line BR (LMR) rolling stock. Presumably the LMS, and later BR, refused to allow army coaches onto the main line, for fear of a blanco infested axle box seizing up at speed and bringing the whole railway to a grinding halt.

Travel on the 'Bicester Bullet', as it was known, was fun. The saddle tanks choked themselves to death at about 15 mph, by which speed the exhaust became a continuous, wet, vomiting roar. Track maintenance was dreadful, and even the fiercest sergeant-major could not make the sleepers stand still in line as the train rolled over them. Accordingly, the train lurched, swayed, rocked, creaked, and groaned, constantly on the fringe of derailment. Those who have written in wonderment of riding slow, rough, trains, on the 60 cm gauge in the Balkans or Iberia have no idea of the competing standards attained by the Bicester Bullet. Only the goats were missing, and the meanest Serbian peasant probably lived more comfortably than we soldiers in that Oxfordshire swamp. Being a workshop rather than a training camp, weekends were usually free after midday Saturday, when I usually made my way back to Swindon, to talk steam with old cronies, and to horrify those more junior about what to expect when called up. Being still on the railway's books, I remained eligible for privilege tickets, and could travel cheaply.

My first stay at Bicester was of mercifully short duration, and I was posted again to Arborfield, near Reading. Yet another pleasant journey at Army expense, on three of the four former railway systems, LMS to Oxford, GWR thence to Reading, and Southern to Wokingham. While changing trains (and stations) at Reading, an early 'Britannia' was seen passing through light engine, possibly for trial purposes, the first BR standard loco seen. I was certainly impressed by the general proportions and detailing, although to me it was an express passenger engine rather than mixed traffic.

Arborfield, where I took an electronic course on the stabilisers used on Centurion tanks, was by far the best posting encountered in my service career. The barracks were permanent, brick built, and generally modern, and the whole morale was decidedly better than at Bicester. Even food was good, and full dining halls contrasted with the miserable facilities at Bicester, wherein fed only those with no money to eat out. Life at Arborfield was more in the nature of a college than an army camp, and apart from morning muster parade we simply studied by day and amused ourselves by night. Evenings were often spent at Wokingham, perhaps swimming in the summer, followed by a pint or two at the 'Three Frogs' or the 'Olde Rose', our favourite local pubs. One crony had a three wheel Morgan motor car, and of three who were 'mates', on several occasions we pooled resources to find we just had enough for a pint each plus half a gallon of petrol for the Morgan. Situated about half way between Swindon and my parents in London, weekends were usually spent at one place or the other.

Easter 1951 saw courses stopping for a week, and I betook myself off on a trip to Germany, travelling as far south as Nürnburg, where the local *Eisenbahndirektor*, having been to Swindon before the war, treated me very well indeed, showed me around, took me to dine with his wife and family, and lent me his locomotive diagram book. This I spent nearly all night copying out, giving as it did details of the bewildering number of locomotive classes to be then found in Germany. One locomotive in the dump, which I did not identify for years, was an old Russian Ov class compound 0-8-0, presumably converted to standard gauge in Poland, and finding its way west in the war. Apparently I had only just missed seeing the huge Bavarian 0-8-8-0T Mallets which had been banking at Hof just beforehand.

Nürnburg, despite overhead wires and bright red diesels, operated plenty of steam. Haughty 01 Pacifics with booming exhausts hoisted trains to Frankfurt, while elegant compound Bavarian examples ran expresses east to Regensburg and Passau. The ubiquitous 50 class 2-10-0 were seen on everything from mainline freights to local passenger trains, while the massive 44 class handled the heaviest traffic. Station pilots were a mixture of old Bavarian 0-6-2T and 0-8-0T and there were the inevitable P8 4-6-0. On the return trip I detrained at Laufach, where banking was seen on the way out, and watched in awe eastbound freight bellowing up the hill with 3-cylinder 2-10-2s of class 45 at the head end, banked by 2-10-2T class 95. That evening, at Würtzburg, a train arrived from Ulm behind one of the neat, ex-Württemburg State Railways Pacifics, the only one I ever saw.

Back at Arborfield, the course finished, and I went on to another at Bordon, a wooden hutted camp, quite comfortable, and served by the Longmoor Military Railway, close to our barracks. Access to civilisation was by the Southern's branch from Bentley, worked by an M7 0-4-4T and push-pull unit. After completing this course it was back to Bicester for the remainder of my time, and after working on the shop floor for a while, on anti-aircraft guns, a chance encounter with a technical warrant officer showed I could draw, and they needed a draughtsman. This was superb, the job was a sinecure and the main regular duty seemed to be producing the seating plan for the weekly officer's mess formal dinner. There were but occasional technical duties, and much time to myself. I was sent for a basic draughtsman's trade test, very easy and about the standard of a first year apprentice at Swindon. After a specified minimum time, the grade two test was taken, again easily passed, and finally the grade one, entitling me to an extra ten shillings per day pay, about the same as a corporal. As 'chief draughtsman' of a small office (with one subordinate) lance corporal rank was allowed, but at a mere six pence per day, with all sorts of extra duties such as fire piquet commander, I preferred to remain rankless.

With so much time to spare, I started on quite detailed design work on my BR standard locomotive range, working out cylinder and valve layouts, boiler details with A/S ratios etc, thoroughly amusing myself and putting National Service to some personal use. By that time, I was also becoming an Old Soldier, and put on 'fatigues' for a couple of days, for some trifling offence against military paranoia, I was detailed to clean out the company office. In the course of this, the duty system was discovered, a card index of all personnel in either numerical or alphabetical order, I forget which, with marker cards for duties. The marker was moved up every day, and the next batch of names rostered on the order board. So easy, I just removed my card and destroyed it, the system being such as to preclude discovery. On another occasion, a staff sergeant whose job included regular inspection of certain stores held in other depots around the complex, needed a lackey to help with the donkey work. I was handy and available, so detailed for this duty lasting, I think, two or three weeks. As the S/S liked to start early I was excused parades to accompany him, and likewise issued with an army bicycle, to be drawn from the quartermaster every Monday and returned Friday or Saturday. The final 'perk' was a gate pass valid for entry and exit from all depots in the area, rather a flimsy slip of paper but undated.

After the inspection tour was over, the S/S simply dismissed me one day with instructions to return to my old duties. Guessing that he had not bothered to tell anybody else, I found that the instruction that I could be excused parades had not been countermanded. Neither had the quartermaster been advised that the bicycle was no longer required, so I continued to draw it each Monday, returning it in immaculate condition each weekend. He might complain to authority about the condition some bikes were handed in, but not Durrant's! Thus, while the others awoke early, went on parade, and were marched the quite considerable distance to the Central Workshops, I arose at a slightly more gentlemanly hour, cycled to work, and entered using the gate pass, kept in immaculate condition to conceal its lack of expiry date. Mondays to Thursdays I returned right time, but on Fridays, to use the current term, I 'skived off' early, returned bike, and headed off to Bicester WR station to catch a special army leave train, just too early to catch using the correct methods. For some reason, the REME prided itself on being not only a technical corps, but also 'jolly good soldiers', meaning that we were the last to leave on Saturday mornings, all very well for the privileged officers, but not for the National Service 'squaddie'. Thus, I bypassed this system for the rest of my service days. Had there been a mean minded person in the hut, I could have been reported, but we all took the attitude that anybody who could get away with anything which might offend authority was slightly heroic. There were, for example, 'sportsmen' excused parade for training (usually in bed) who nobody would dream of squealing on. Wednesday in the army is sports afternoon, just as doctors always play golf on Wednesdays. Those not named for some kind of organised sport were usually rounded up for useful activities, such as mowing the lawns of the officer's mess, this being possibly an incentive to take an interest in organised games. As the user of an army bike, of decidedly unsporting character, Wednesday afternoons found me declaring my sport as 'Cycling, Sir'. Trundling out of camp on this lumbering machine, before authority rounded up stragglers in the huts, I usually made for one of the two local lines, watched trains for the afternoon, and returned after a pint or two in a country pub. All much better than mowing lawns or sweating away at some army sports event.

Meanwhile, on weekends to London, I found that the army leave train which could just be caught on Saturdays was an interesting operation being the return working of the Friday night fast freight from Paddington Goods to Birmingham, usually headed by a 4700 class large wheeled 2-8-0. During my apprenticeship I had never known much about this class, and cannot remember working on one, although from a fitter's viewpoint it would be little different from a 43XX Mogul. Seen as a dead loco ex-works they looked slightly 'wrong', with too much smokebox, but in fact were a remarkable concept, by Churchward, years ahead of his time even just before retirement. The boiler was the basis of that used later by the 'Kings', slightly longer in barrel and firebox, whilst overall they were Britain's largest and most powerful mixed traffic locomotives from 1921 until Gresley produced his V2 class in 1935. Under Churchward, they would certainly have been multiplied and probably developed, but cautious Collett and his henchmen seemed afraid of the concept. Travelling fairly regularly behind a 47, I began to see their worth, recognised so

Churchward's very imperial mixed traffic 2-8-0, probably the best ever Swindon loco, but illogical timidity restricted the 47s to only nine locomotives.

much later in that though they were numerically a very 'non-standard' class in the days when Beeching's accountants were wreaking illogical havoc on the motive power fleet, these engines were amongst the last GWR class to remain intact. They ran fast, climbed well, and rode well, a superb locomotive. One could always tell when some inferior locomotive, such as a 'Hall' or 'Castle' was on that leave train.

The magic 'D-day' of demobilisation approached in 1952, and with typically army incongruity, I was demobilised at Aldershot, a depot at which I had at no time served during the two year career! All the kit had to be lugged across country, by at least four train journeys, and dumped into some army stores with the identical junk as carried in the quartermaster's emporium in Bicester. I suppose, even in the army, there are accountants who control that sort of mismanagement.

There was some 'Demob leave' to be taken before re-entry into civilian life, spent firstly in visiting Swindon, having an interview with Gilbert Scholes, Chief Draughtsman, and securing entry to that hallowed place, the drawing office. With the remainder, I ventured further East, to Jugoslavia, a fascinating adventure, involving the use of a visa for entry, made via Trieste at the border post of Poggiarale Campagna. Although not strictly behind the 'Iron Curtain', since Tito had broken with the Moscow Mob, here was another country indeed. Even the border area, set within the *Karst* formation was rocky and bleak, and once across the border the train was surrounded and inundated with grey uniformed police with red star cap badges. Wagons bearing the strange insignia JDZ – J Д Ж filled the sidings and on a branch train to Gorizia was a tall, gaunt, 2-6-2T, class 17, of Hungarian origin, my first Eastern European locomotive.

As far as Sezana the train was electric hauled, using clearly Italian types identical with those on the Trieste side of the border, but from there onwards to Ljubljana, motive power was a handsome 2-8-2 of class 06. Ljubljana itself was a fascinating place, large, busy, with an amazing variety of locomotives, mostly of quite bizarre appearance, even to me with some previous continental experience. Platforms were rail level, and people seemed to walk all over the place without hindrance, so I did the same and wandered through the locomotive shed, right opposite the station. No problems.

For the first time I became aware of that strange beast, the two-cylinder compound, with normal size cylinder one side and vast low pressure unit the other. Nothing to be learned there, even if it seemed attractive, there was no way one could get a cylinder 35 inches diameter into the British loading gauge. Of more interest were class 10, ex Austrian 4-8-0 with wide fireboxes over coupled wheels, just as I had been trying out in Swindon test house. Very interesting to examine them in the flesh, as it were, and see how it was done, although they were smaller engines than I envisaged, and built within a far more generous loading gauge. Later, at Zagreb, I was to encounter the Hungarian version, JDZ class 11, a very elegantly detailed engine. Locomotives with strange, humpy looking, boilers, turned out to have Brotan water tube fireboxes. These had been described in the British press but never given any indication of success nor quantities built. Here, many locomotives had such boilers some clearly having been in service for thirty or forty years, a most interesting piece of locomotive information.

Just before dusk there came from the east the sound of a three-cylinder locomotive worked hard, and there was a lengthy train pounding through the station headed by a Prussian class G12 2-10-0, with conjugated valve gear but remarkably even beat. Worked hard? It seemed to be nearly in mid gear but nothing was obstructing the exhaust flow! In the station restaurant I was presented with a typed menu comprising totally incomprehensible words. Some of the food being consumed at adjacent tables looked pretty unappetising, and the waiter and I were totally unable to communicate verbally. So, I looked at the prices, chose something in the middle range, and was relieved when it turned up as ham and eggs!

All I did was to travel along the main line to Beograd (Belgrade), returning the same route, but seeing plenty of interest. On the way back, at Zapresić, just east of Zagreb, was a dump of locomotives containing a large, Brotan boilered, wide firebox 4-6-0, and a 2-6-6-0 Mallet. I immediately detrained and seeing some suspicious looking police, wandered through the village and made my way eventually to the dump. However, I had been spotted as clearly non-Jugoslav, and just lifting my camera to the 4-6-0 heard a shout and there were two police running towards me, one with drawn pistol! Clicked shutter, and put camera down. They escorted me to the station but clearly did not really know what to do. I asked to speak to the British Consulate (!) and eventually they put me through to the French Consulate in Zagreb who said I should get on the first train out of Jugoslavia, as I was doing anyhow. He then repeated this to the police, in Serbo Croat, and they happily let me board the next main line train West. I failed to photograph the Mallet, but several years later tracked them down and got them in action, so nothing was lost!

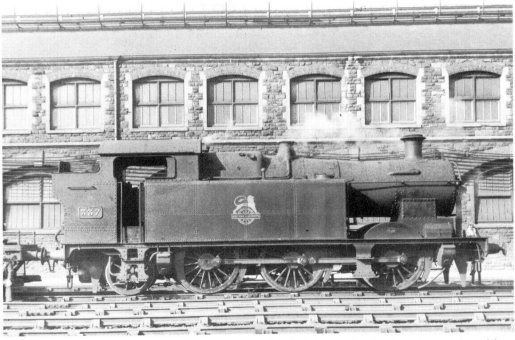

Taff Vale's final loco class, the A 0-6-2T, sadly relegated to Swindon works shunter, after withdrawal from regular service. Behind is the works foundry, a by no means poor example of Victorian industrial architecture.

After the Welsh engines had gone, Swindon works shunting crews had to make do with the cramped cabs of older standard panniers. 8738, near the works turntable, has a welded lower patch on the tank side, with original rivetted upper portion.

7

DRAUGHTSMAN

Returning from my 'demob leave' to Jugoslavia, there came the great day when I entered that holy of holies, the drawing office. During the entire workshop apprenticeship, some of the older hands, hearing some official name, would remark; 'Ar, clever young chap, used to work along of Oi; went up to the Drorin' Office'. So was born the legend of high endeavour, fairly soon lost once employed there. Swindon drawing office occupied the top floor of the CME's office block, quite distinct from the works manager's quarters behind the R shop. The CME block was L shaped, and the locomotive section occupied the long leg parallel to the Bristol main line with Gilbert Scholes, as chief draughtsman, at the station end and Wally Harland, assistant chief on the locomotive side, at the head of the office. The other leg, pointing towards Gloucester and overlooking the running shed, was the Carriage and Wagon section, with its own sub-chief at its extremity. In the corner, where met the two main offices was the general section dealing with pumps, cranes, turntables and all manner of non-rolling stock oddments, and onto which raw draughtsmen were invariably started. Thus commenced in effect a second apprenticeship, learning a new set of rules, fresh working etiquette, and the more gentlemanly way of office life as opposed to the rough and tumble of workshop routine.

Like many others, I started on the survey gang, a rather surprising appendage of the CME's responsibilities, seemingly clashing with those of the chief civil engineer. However, the CME was responsible for trackwork within the workshops, for instance, which sometimes needed their layout revising to meet new requirements, together with building and similar plans within the works. Outside there were locomotive water supplies whose pipelines and pumping stations came under the CME, while another outside job was lining up the race rail of turntables, using a dumpy level.

Roy West and Viv Roberts were two draughtsmen who comprised the regular staff of the survey section, aided and abetted by whichever new draughtsman was being indoctrinated into office life. From the lofty elevation of the drawing office, much could be seen, although the coveted window positions were held by those of senior service. Those on the south side of the

119

locomotive section overlooked the Bristol and South Wales main line with its
constant parade of trains. In the foreground, works shunters puffed up and
down, while across the main line, beyond the carriage shops, the drab grey
slated roofs of New Swindon climbed towards the Old Town and its church
spire on top the hill. The north side of the office, housing the outdoor running
and boiler sections overlooked the Gloucester line and running shed with the
latter's constant activity. East side of the carriage section surveyed the pano-
rama of the Gloucester line curving into Swindon Junction station but those on
the west side saw nothing but the drab roof of adjacent B shed. All these
assorted views were denied us denizens of the survey section, except of course
when walking up or down the office for various reasons.

However lowly my position was in the office hierarchy, it was a good step up
in status compared with being a workshop apprentice. Amongst the 'staff'
privileges were an increased number of free passes annually and, better still,
free passes on the continent. Not only could I explore Europe for nothing, but
second class too – no more the squalor of Balkan third class, trying desperately
to sleep in the discomfort of a crowded, wooden seated, four-wheeler! No
more, either, the need to rise early to commence work at 7.40 in the bitter cold
and murky darkness of an English winter's morn, although it soon became just
as difficult to get there by 8.30! No more 'checking in', one simply signed the
attendance register, but at the appointed hour, Sam Trollop, the registrar, ruled
a red line to separate latecomers from punctual arrivals.

Life in the survey section was pleasant enough, even though initial tasks
comprised mundane duties such as colouring prints with various shades of
wash, rather ridiculous after five years of increasingly advanced engineering
drawing at night school. However, that was the way it had always been done
and that was that. The regular trips 'outstation' to various depots were fascinating to me, involving journeys by steam train, often to a steam depot, although I
can understand Viv Roberts' lack of enthusiasm, perhaps working for hours
lining up a turntable, at some bleak outdoor location, in the middle of January.

Talking of mid-January, it was at such a period that half a dozen of us at the
Toc H hostel decided to take a Sunday walk along the Ridgeway, the old Roman
road from Avebury to Uffington, which section was convenient of access. We
dressed quite lightly on the theory that activity would generate heat, and took a
bus to Avebury, well laden with about half a loaf of sandwiches each for fuel. At
the rate we squandered energy on the dual tasks of perambulation and keeping
warm these were gone by mid morning and we were getting hungry. At some
remote crossroads there was a pub, complete with log fire which thawed us out
somewhat while we stoked up on pub sandwiches and draught beer. After that
it was out again onto the downs and into the darkening afternoon with pockets
of snow in the shade and mud where sunshine had melted it. In the gathering
gloom, close to Uffington, we took the wrong track, keeping to the upper
Ridgeway proper instead of the low track to the village, eventually having to

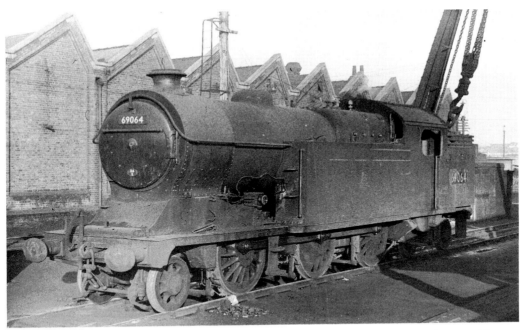

In 1952 Neasden shed was Western Region property and while working here to line up the turntable race rail, Robinson 2-6-4T 69064 was photographed one freezing December day.

squish across a very soggy and newly ploughed field to gain the village lights below. Somewhere in the middle of this we found a goat, broken loose from its moorings, and trailing about three yards of rope, a lethal wild animal which divided its attentions between trying to butt us and running round in circles with the evident intention of lassooing our legs with literally the end of its tether! It was pitch black when we reached the village and although there was half an hour before the last local train to Swindon, we had only the most vague idea of where lay the station. One local encountered gave us typical directions from a countryman who had lived there all his life – 'Ar, straight on here, then turn left at widow Brown's house, carry on past Fred Jones' place, then . . . ' That we *furriners* knew nothing of the village's inhabitants would have been incomprehensible to that worthy Moonraker but luckily a couple of passing trains audibly orientated us and we arrived on the platform in good time. A quick train run to Swindon, twenty minutes brisker walk up the hill to Old Town, and it was not much past opening time when we thankfully entered the portals of the 'Bell' with its cheery log fire and superb supplies of draught Bass.

Back to the office on Monday morning, perhaps another 'outstation' trip to enliven life and expand experience. Life on a nationalised railway was enmeshed in bureaucracy, some of it having perhaps been inherited or developed from former company practice. There were expenses paid at flat rates, irrespective of whether or not they covered the actual expenditure. Two bob was paid for catching a train before 8.00 a.m, and a further florin for arrival after 6.00 p.m. I think each two hour period each way provided another couple of shillings, and on day trips there was a lunch allowance, quite inadequate, which one claimed but took sandwiches. Morning trains to Didcot or Bristol each departed about 7.50, thus paying for the first pint later in the day. With luck and good planning one need not be actually out of pocket after a day outstation, although the overnight and dinner allowances were disgracefully inadequate. A small mini-perk was 'OCS tea'. Travelling OCS, or 'On Company Service', a term still used long after the former companies became 'Regions', tea at station buffets was available a penny less than the public price. All was delightfully informal, one simply ordered 'OCS' from the tea lady, and there it was. An outsider might possibly try it on, but somehow a railwayman, even when clad in an ordinary suit, was always recognisable as such to another railwayman, and a phoney OCS order would probably be spotted immediately.

When travelling with a superior grade of officer, entitled to First Class passes, we hoi polloi also travelled First so that he could keep an eye on his minions without suffering the indignity of slumming it in the Thirds. First Class free passes were like charms. Rarely clipped or even looked at by ticket inspectors, they were badges of superior status calculated to inspire awe upon lesser breeds below. Well I remember having to visit London as dogsbody for my section leader and getting that magic white rectangle of pasteboard. It was during the 'Prom' season at the Albert Hall, and since my ticket remained virginal and unsullied it was used for several extra journeys before expiry date, to attend some of the concerts. It was said that one could probably travel from Birkenhead to Penzance on an outdated First class pass from Swindon to Chiseldon, since nobody would examine it *en route*!

One of the characters in the DO was a large and important looking draughts-man known as Big Ben, still, like myself, a grade 'A' draughtsman despite many years service. Ben always dressed in bowler hat, pin striped trousers, furled umbrella and rolled copy of *The Times*, giving the impression of a Brigadier retired to an important position on the Stock Exchange. Ben always entered and left a train through a First Class doorway, but slunk along the corridors to his seat in the Thirds. He was banned from using the telephone after making some very important and equally costly mis-decision in an extremely authoritative tone of voice, such was his frustrated managerial status! Each tea break, Ben would let his hair down by tossing his empty cup over the trusses supporting the roof, usually failing to catch it, with disastrous results to the cup. Somebody discovered that Ben's bowler was in fact a couple of sizes too large, and that he stuffed the rim with newspaper to make it fit. Accordingly, several of us chipped in to buy a new bowler of the same brand but two sizes smaller, for a practical joke. When Ben strode through the office for his morning session in the 'Gents', the new bowler was substituted for the old, after stuffing the same newspaper into the lining. When he set off for lunch, this new combination sat on top of his head instead of fitting, and after much puzzled pantomine, he eventually discarded the newspapers and went off with the new hat. After lunch, Ben departed for his post – lunch session, so the original hat was resubstituted on the hook, *sans* paper. When he donned it at home time, it fell over his ears. We kept this up for a week, injuring ourselves with suppressed mirth, and Ben never caught on, evidently believing that head and/or hat was mysteriously expanding and contracting for some totally un-known reason.

After several months on the survey section I asked for transfer to the loco-motive section, a request granted almost immediately, fortunately, as this was where my interests lay. I thus came under the eagle eye of Walter (known as Wally) Harland, assistant chief draughtsman on the loco side, a smallish Welshman from the old Taff Vale Railway, entirely devoid of any sense of humour. My immediate section leader was Roland Low, a delightfully urbane and pleasant fellow, while second in command on the section was Peter Kembrey, a rare species in those days being in possession of a university degree. There were two loco sections, the other being headed by Arthur Sly, well known to me as a former night school teacher, many draughtsmen taking on this additional chore to supplement their meagre incomes. Arthur's assist-ant was Ken Dadge, whose flowing moustache gave the impression of ex-fighter pilot turned publican, while another senior type was Les Slade, a quiet religious man.

As a new boy, I was allocated a board in the centre of three rows, junior status being emphasised by having no window position. As compensation (possibly?) I was adjacent to the small group of lady tracers, headed by Maureen Downey, a fairly recent innovation in a previously all male establishment. Of Maureen's staff, I well remember Anne, of voluptuous and eye-catching figure, and pretty Pat Williams, probably of Welsh descent, whose dark eyes and hair combined with snub, freckled nose knocked me into the proverbial cocked hat, such that I felt like a foolish schoolboy instead of a mature adult!

Across the way was the boiler section, headed by F. M. Limpus, together with 'Captain' Holloway who had been commissioned in the 1914–18 war, let nobody forget. Also on that side was Jack Pready, and dear old Harry Flewellen who drew locomotive diagrams and was custodian of the three volume office set of the diagram book. The diagram book assumed some strange form of religious significance at Swindon, and one needed a definite reason before being allowed to consult its sacred pages. Maybe it was just Harry. From time to time books held by people such as loco foremen and divisional staff came in for updating, by removal of obsolete diagrams and inserting new. Several times, being interested in history, I asked for the discards, but such requests were always refused and I saw this delightful material being torn into shreds, to my horror. This was all part of the old Swindon *marque* of secrecy, carried to extreme, not dissimilar to paranoia surrounding Mecca for Islamic states, and 'security' for Russia and its unfortunate followers. In more reasonable countries, worldwide, diagram books have been happily provided simply for the asking when one's real interest in their locomotives has been revealed.

Several other draughtsmen, fellows in the same job, are recalled, Alan Moore, Nobby Clarke, John Collier, George Palfreyman, Alan Peck, all senior to me, and I apologise to those whose names have been forgotten over thirty-odd years of varied employment and duties. Clerical work for the whole drawing office was carried out by Gordon Thorp and his lady assistant, situated in a little hutch of an office behind Wally Harland's desk. Gordon was a cheerful character, never flustered, even when presented with requests for free passes and privilege tickets for obscure places in Eastern Europe and Turkey, some of whose spellings made even Welsh seem civilised!

Initial tasks on the loco section were of course simple and menial, but better jobs started to come my way once basic competence was acknowledged. One was issued with a sketch book, a very well produced article of cartridge paper, hard bound in black cover embossed with BR (WR), of size about 5" × 8", perhaps 120 pages, suitable for carrying in a largish pocket. There was also a calculation book into which any sort of calculation had to be entered, such that it could be exhumed and re-checked in the event of some resultant disaster. An early exercise was the calculation of the clearance between a wheelset of standard profile and rails of standard gauge and new profile. This with the various radii and angles involved was a most complicated calculation, carried out with five figure logarithmic tables, and in retrospect was probably a task set every new boy to test his mathematical and trigonometrical competence. I am sure that a major railway, if it really wanted to know the answer would hardly trust calculation to a brand new junior draughtsman, whilst the use of nominal dimensions devoid of a wide range of accumulative tolerances rendered the final result academic in the extreme. Perhaps I revealed my naïvety by not airing this reality, but it seemed a nicely important job, though nothing seemed to be done with the results when finished.

Initial tasks were naturally of the simplest nature, design or redesign of smallish components, few of which I now recall. What is well remembered is the excellent communication between drawing office workshops, and users. Swindon may have been lacking in its communication with the outer world but internal cooperation was first class. Having completed a job to the section leader's initial satisfaction, one was then instructed to go and see whichever section of the works was involved and discuss with foreman or chargehand any possible difficulties which might be encountered in manufacture or modification. Being fresh from the shops, I was still fairly *au fait* with such procedures, but one may imagine that after several years in the office, more senior draughtsmen lost touch to some extent, making such cross checking doubly valuable.

A considerable amount of junior work was initiated from suggestions usually from footplate staff, as to how something could be improved. Such suggestions, unless quite ridiculous, were seriously investigated, and junior draughtsmen usually had the task of going outstation to have a look, especially where the locomotive classes involved were not to be found at Swindon shed. Many were the pleasant outstation trips thus enjoyed, often armed with foot-plate pass, together with strict instructions not to 'abuse' this item. I normally interpreted this liberally, considering it useful experience to ride the cabs to and from the job in hand rather than sitting comfortably in a coach compartment until strictly necessary. Some of my colleagues tended to dismiss all 'footplate' proposals as devoid of any basis, probably to save themselves the task of redesigning something, but I certainly tried hard to find and eradicate any problems encountered. In one case, this proved impossible. A complaint, probably from a passenger, was that trains hauled by 64XX pannier tanks in South Wales generated excessive fore-and-aft oscillation, to the point of dis-comfort. I spent a day riding auto trains, standing next to the loco and watching buffers and couplings through the end windows, without finding the slightest evidence to support the complaint. These were really quite sweet running little engines, hardly large nor powerful enough to upset a passenger's equilibrium.

What I suspect is that an engine number or numbers had been confused, and that the real culprit was a 66XX instead of 64XX, both series being common in South Wales. Now the 56XX and 66XX with Stroudley crank setting, having connecting and coupling cranks in phase (easily distinguished by the very large balance weights on main driving wheels) were certainly prone to this problem. Well I remember an early morning train out of Cardiff, Sundays only, double headed up the Rhymney valley by two such engines, about a dozen coaches, later split into two trains for day trippers back down the valley to Barry and perhaps Penarth. Travelling one Sunday behind such a doubleheader, each with Stroudley cranks, the fore-and-aft was extremely pronounced when both locos became synchronised and while to me it was an interesting phenomenon, perhaps some Welshman, stomach queasy after too much Hancock's Ale the night before, decided to complain and woozily got the wrong engine number. We were not shown the original correspondence in such cases, increasing the possibility of getting the wrong story.

An amusing incident was when I was deputed to travel to Gloucester to inspect a War Department 2-8-0 as it had been decided that those on the Western Region should be fitted with GWR type ATC apparatus. Drawings available of the cab showed the possible positions to be somewhat restricted, and in any case we were unsure whether, in wartime conditions, things may have been altered but unrecorded. The best way was to look, Swindon had none, but one was stopped at Gloucester, available for inspection. It seemed to me that the best way of trying out possible alternatives was by physical trial and error, and as an actual ATC cab apparatus was very heavy to cart around, I made a cardboard mock up to the major dimensions, the final result looking rather like a cuckoo clock, so a suitable flap and cuckoo were quickly added just

The soul of the South Wales Railway – 0-6-2T 6624 climbs through Bargoed on coal empties on a wet, murky and inhospitable day.

Clanking through Port Talbot is Swindonised Austerity 90179 with local clack valves, top feed cover, plus a fire iron tunnel similar to that on the 2884 class, but on the right hand side as these locos had left hand drive.

for fun. Everybody thought it rather hilarious, except Wally Harland, who totally failed to appreciate how a little levity lubricates the asperities of the daily grind. The 'cuckoo clock' proved ideal, and rapidly showed the best place to install the real apparatus.

A fairly minor job with long reaching consequences was that of fitting manganese liners to the horn faces of GWR type axleboxes. Manganese steel becomes work hardened, and after a little initial wear has a smooth glassy surface which does not wear at all in service. Initial applications were with roller bearing axleboxes, but later it was realised that the same technique could be used on whitemetal boxes. All this was discovered by the LMS, and with the exchange of information possible due to nationalisation (one of the very few advantages of such a merger) it was decided to apply it on the Western. From a draughtsman's viewpoint it was a boringly simple task – the LMS design was simply copied with dimensional changes to suit GWR boxes. However, the reasons for certain practices were queried as a matter of interest, and the answers stuck in my mind. Some 35 years later, by then an employee of SKF, I

was involved with the Rhodesian/Zimbabwean decision to refurbish 87 Garratts for further use, to escape the difficult and costly oil supply situation for
diesel traction. All these Garratts were to be fitted with roller bearings on their
driving and coupled axles (bogie boxes were already so fitted), and as SKF's
railway technical manager in southern Africa I was called in for advice. A BR
feature found necessary was a hole (or holes) in each liner, plug welded to box
and hornblock, preventing the liner from 'popping' when fitted, leading to
fracture of peripheral welds and displacement or loss of liner(s). Bulawayo
refused to accept that this could happen, so after installation without plug
welded holes, they started to fall off in service. Final result comprised replacement to the original LMS design with plug welded centre holes. One wonders
whether, had the coincidence of my earlier involvement with such an installation not occurred, there might remain a serious problem – no real credit to
myself, I merely passed on somebody else's solution to the same problem,
otherwise forgotten over a long period of steam development stagnation.

An interesting project which in the event did not happen, was a proposal to
fit the 47XX large wheeled 2-8-0 with screw reverse. These engines were
favourites of mine, and seemed the correct way to develop a large mixed traffic
locomotive, rather than the 4-6-0 type which Collett, far less adventurous than
Churchward, decided upon. The fact that they were considered for such
modification in the mid-1950s spoke well of their usefulness, and it was indeed
in those later days that they started to be used more frequently for passenger
work, which probably initiated the call for screw reverse. One gets the impression that the timid types who succeeded the master were in fact rather afraid of
Churchward's *magnum opus*. They were officially limited to 60 mph, a restriction placed on no other locomotives with 5' 8" wheels, which were known
to achieve 80 mph on occasions. It could not have been their weight, substantially less than a 'King', and little more than a 'Castle'. They also had route
restrictions which could not have been for just the long coupled wheelbase, for
the 2-8-0T mineral engines with identical wheelbase were not so restricted, and
were of virtually identical weight as the 47XX without tender. I made a point of
asking several senior people in the design and motive power sections *why* they
were so restricted, but quite simply nobody knew. One can imagine the later
and somewhat larger 'King' boiler, made using the same flanging blocks as the
47XX boiler, being applied to a developed version with leading bogie, a sort of
4750 class which would have put the GWR very much in the forefront of large
mixed traffic locomotives. As happened, it was Gresley who developed the
large wheeled, eight-coupled type in Great Britain, with his P2 class, and who
later miniaturised this into the generally successful, if rather slippery, V2 class.

Returning to the task in hand, a modification job of this nature requires much
background 'research', unlike a totally new design with which one starts with
the traditionally clean sheet of paper. Standard office equipment at Swindon in
those days was a large drawing board of the old type, almost flat, over which

draughtsmen contorted themselves in various inelegant positions while concentrating on some detail at the far end of the paper. A tee square and set squares were used to get the verticals and horizontals right, and the draughtsman's posterior was perched on a tall stool similar to those found today in bars, although in those days, one *stood* at the bar, perversely demanding a pint pot with handle then gripping it on the plain side! The lady tracers alone were equipped with modern pantograph draughting machines denied those of us to whom an antiquated drawing board was a step up in status from the workshop hammer and chisel.

Beside the board was a large reference bench, upon which one laid the various drawings relevant to the job in hand. On a fairly major modification job as I was given, it is quite amazing how many such reference drawings are needed. The frame, to which it had to be anchored, cab, standard reversing screw and details, existing lever reverse to get the position right, – all these can be imagined, but in fact each major sub assembly comprised several drawings of details etc., all of which have to be correctly interpreted. The draughtsman's nightmare is a summons to the workshops to view two or more expensively manufactured components which fail to fit together. People who only deal with figures or correspondence, like accountants and clerks, have no idea of the ordeal faced in such a situation. Paperwork itself is rectified (and this includes engineering drawings) far more easily than a large and intimidating chunk of metal surrounded by the derisive and accusative men who have laboriously fabricated the ill fitting components 'correctly' to *your* drawings! The several years I spent at various drawing boards were, fortunately, fraught with only minor mishaps, but I sometimes wonder, had the go-ahead been given to modify the 47s as drawn, whether the whole lot would have mated as smoothly as planned.

During the course of the above job, I was impressed by how little the drawings of 47XX components had been altered over the years. Most Swindon office reference drawings, mounted on linen, were a rainbow of coloured alterations showing improvements effected and weaknesses hopefully eradicated. 'Altered in green, 5.7.23'. 'Altered in red, 7.6.25'. etcetera, provided a complete history of what was altered when. Some drawings with numerous amendments taxed the draughtsman's ingenuity in finding suitable new ink colours, resulting in carefully drawn details and dimensions in mauve, indigo, purple, pink, or puce! The 47XX drawings were largely free from such rainbow alterations, remaining as drawn, being fully satisfactory. This was almost the last fairly major alteration proposed for a GWR locomotive type, and I was sad it was never carried out.

About the same time, new chimneys were drawn up, by Alan Clothier, to suit the 'Improved draught' arrangement as devised by Sam Ell and his team in the testing section. These new chimneys were slightly curved in contour throughout, as opposed to the normal GWR chimney with cylindrical centre

Mentioned in the text, and shown here is the Crewe remedy for loose outside cylinders, with a block welded to the frames and a wedge hammered between this and the cylinder flange. Note also the strengthening webs on the bogie frame of this King.

section, and were applied to Halls, 68XX and 78XX classes. Alan's initial scheme had a sharper central radius than the finalised job, and he was un-impressed when I remarked that it looked rather like a Rhymney Railway chimney!

Higher superheat was by then a generally approved principle with four-row apparatus eventually fitted to all the 'Kings'. Lesser breeds had three-row apparatus, the last 41XX had increased superheat, and drawings were pre-pared for a standard 4 boiler with increased superheat, but I do not think this was ever applied. The number 4 boiler was used mainly on the 'Moguls' and the eight-coupled tank engines. A modification applied to the 'Kings' was incor-porated to counter loose outside cylinders. The LM Region 'Princess Royal' class, based on the 'Kings' and with similar cylinder arrangement also suffered from this ailment and Crewe devised a remedy in the form of strips welded onto the frames close to the cylinder fixing flanges. A wedge was driven into the remaining gap until well tight, and the whole lot then welded up solid. With the inter-regional cooperation engendered by nationalisation this information was passed onto Swindon, who then applied it to the 'Kings'. While I was at Swindon there was talk of fitting 'Kings' with roller bearing axleboxes, and I understand that five locomotive sets were subsequently ordered but never fitted due to the onset of mass dieselisation. This was probably the last major modification considered for GWR designs.

BR STANDARDS

Work in the Locomotive drawing office became increasingly connected with the BR standard locos, and of course the same affected also the Carriage and Wagon sides. Swindon drawings tended to be of any size as convenient to the job in hand, were devoid of any outline margin, and were numbered in a heap from 1 upwards. With the BR setup, drawings were to certain standard sizes, with standard outline rectangles and equally standard 'boxes' containing drawing number, date, draughtsman's initials and other relevant data. Drawing numbers commenced with SC, SL, or SW, denoting standard carriages, locomotives, or wagons respectively, after which was a code for the originating drawing office, DE for Derby, SW for Swindon etc, rather like a GWR shed code! Thus SL/SW/1234 denoted a locomotive drawing originating from Swindon. Where relevant, each regional drawing office possessed copy transparencies of other office's drawings, leading to a bureaucratic situation whereby if, say, Derby modified a drawing, prints of the new version were sent to all other offices, who in turn had to alter their own transparencies to suit. As designs firmed and were put into production, a real chore was keeping these things up to date, a job more suited to a technical clerk than a draughtsman. I used to get bored to tears on such work, especially as Swindon practice included a cloth-mounted shop copy which also had to be altered. Frustrated from real design work, I tended to sketch on the shop copies the sort of locomotive I thought should have been in production, and Roland Low, with an amused glint in his eyes, eventually requested me to desist from decorating detail drawings of little class 3 locomotives with sketches of vast 4-10-0s and 2-12-2Ts which I thought more worthy of consideration than the Derby-inhibited small engines upon which BR were so keen.

Of the BR standard classes, the first built at Swindon were the class 4 4-6-0, a lightweight design of roughly compatible capacity as the native GWR 78XX. The BR design used a boiler based on Stanier's LMS 2-6-4T and this had a larger firebox and potentially greater steaming capacity than the '78'. The complementary tank version, the 80XX, had Brighton as the design centre, and was basically the Fairburn version of LM's 2-6-4T but with a delightful bit of Bulleid in that the tank and cab contours matched Bulleid's carriage profile! Quite logical, a passenger tank engine matching the vehicles it hauled, but I sometimes wonder how such a final fling from Brighton escaped censorship from the staid Midland hierarchy at Derby. For some unexplained reason, the LMS 3000

Swindon built BR Standard class 4 retained such Churchward features as the Brooks type boiler, long travel, long lap valves and straight-ported cylinders. The double chimney was a Swindon modification to the original design.

The BR class 3 tank and tender locos, built and designed at Swindon, had a modified Swindon No. 2 boiler. Despite having the same cylinder, wheel, boiler pressure and tractive effort figures, they were given lighter loadings than the rebuilt Taff Vale A class, in South Wales.

Rebuilt Taff Vale A 351, which retains the original cab and round topped Kitson style tanks, at Barry. Fast, powerful on gradients and superb accelerators, they also had a very sharp bark.

class 2-6-0 was also perpetuated as the BR class 76000, with purely cosmetic alterations. Only Derby could condone two tender engine designs of class 4 capacity, the largest their little minds could imagine!

Swindon's rôle as a parent design office was limited to the class 3 2-6-0 and corresponding 2-6-2T, a rather insulting slight. These were really the LMS 3000 class with a modified Swindon number 2 boiler (as in 51XX, 56XX, etc) reducing weight by a minor degree. There was probably no really valid reason for building such machines in the 1950s other than the inbred Derby inhibition that power classes 2, 3, and 4 should be the basis of locomotive population. Indeed, it is perhaps surprising that there were no BR standards of classes 0 and 1, such was the Midland dominance. When the class 3 2-6-0 was designed at Swindon, somebody went haywire in elevating the running plate to a height unprecedented on other BR standards, making a very 'leggy' looking engine. An empirical rule which seems to work is that the running plate should approximately bisect the height from rail to top of boiler. A study of 'good-looking' designs tends to confirm this hypothesis, with small engines having high running plates looking as wrong as large engines with low 'plates. The twenty 77XXX built were all so leggy, but the tank version was more correctly proportioned. Somebody must have noticed this, for the design was redrawn, and a proposed further five engines, 77020–24, were ordered with a lower running plate conforming to the 82000 tank version. A diagram was drawn, but in the event the construction of these locomotives was cancelled.

Britain's Best Locomotives were built at Swindon. This is no Great Western jingoism but refers to the fact that Swindon participated in the construction of the superb 9F 2-10-0s. Like Maunsell's 'Schools' class 4-4-0, the 9Fs were an amalgam of existing standard components blended in such a way that the final result was better than any of the component donors. I was quite excited as drawings of this magnificent design started filtering through to Swindon for production – the whole concept seemed just right and there was some interesting frame detailing rendering the frame design part way to the welded I section developed in Germany. Bulleid-trained engineers at Brighton evolved a very clever cross-balancing system for the driving and coupled wheels, and this was probably the cause of their ability to run very fast and with remarkable smoothness. Somewhere along the line there were reactionary forces who thought it should be a 2-8-2 of class 8, but I thought it was the 'Britannia' which should have been a 2-8-2, with say 5' 8" wheels, making it more of a mixed traffic and less an express passenger engine. E. S. Cox has published a diagram of the class 8F 2-8-2 proposal, and to flesh out the bones, as it were, the author once photographed a 9F with trailing wheelset removed for attention. To this has been pasted on a photograph of a 'Britannia' trailing truck, and the result, somewhat crude, appears on page 135.

9F 92006 outside Swindon works in 1954. When drawings for this superb design arrived at Swindon from Brighton, colleagues failed to understand the author's enthusiasm.

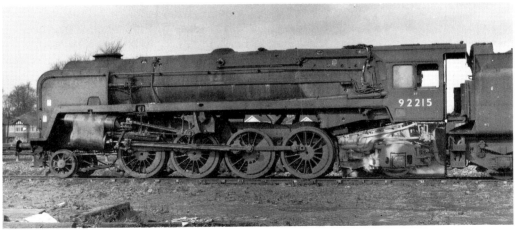

BR class 9F 92215 photographically "rebuilt" with a Britannia trailing truck to simulate the original design proposal.

Before Swindon completed any 9Fs, those first built at Crewe were allocated to the Western Region for trains hauling imported ore from Newport docks to Ebbw Vale steelworks. This had always been a motive power problem, and before the war the GWR carried out some interesting experiments using a couple of 'Kings' after which was schemed out a massive 2-10-2T using a 47XX boiler. This was all very well, but two such locos would still have been needed to move the traffic handled similarly by two 9Fs. The use of such engines on short distance traffic of this nature seemed incorrect, and the real solution seemed to me to be a massive tank engine. The 9F's only concession to curvature was in flangeless main drivers, with no designed sideplay in the coupled axles. On the continent I had seen 10-coupled designs with about $1\frac{1}{4}$ inches sideplay on the extreme axles, and which curved very freely. Reasoning that if the 9F's effectively rigid wheelbase could successfully traverse curvature up to Ebbw Vale, it was possible to flank five coupled axles with two more having about one inch sideplay which, with $\frac{3}{4}$-inch gauge widening would enable the resulting machine to traverse seven chain curves. The resulting 2-14-2T is shown in figure 7 and with a 22 ton axle load could have equalled the haulage capacity of two 9Fs! The original sketch, when shown to authority in Swindon drawing office produced reactions ranging from glassy eyed horror to accusations of consuming excessive draught Bass at the 'Bell'! Nobody was prepared to check the relevant calculations, and I suppose that even had they been proposed, the likelihood of Derby agreeing to such a machine was pretty remote, to say the least. I suppose a Garratt would have been a more acceptable solution but at that time the only such engines I had encountered were the miserable Midlandised monstrosities, which hardly encouraged thoughts along such lines.

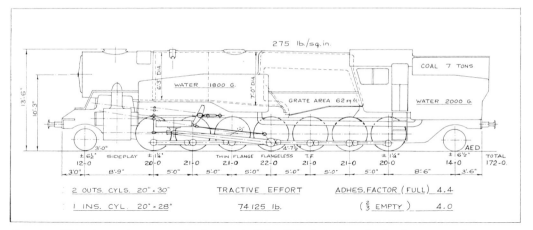

Two class 9F tender engines conveying iron up to Ebbw Vale, in tank engine territory, seemed wrong. Guided by a German wartime proposal, this 2-14-2T was schemed out to equal the capacity of two 9Fs up the valleys. An eight-coupled Garratt would have been more acceptable, but the author's current experience of these articulateds was limited to the unsatisfactory Midland contrivances. (Fig 7)

The idea of a 2-14-2T was not, perhaps, entirely original. Everybody knew that Russia had built a 4-14-4, and that it was unsuccessful. However, this was a large wheeled engine with enormously long wheelbase just over ten metres coupled, all but 33 feet in total. I had just purchased a book *25 Jahre Deutsche Einheitslokomotiven* (25 years German standard locomotives), and this contained a diagram of a fascinating wartime proposal for a 2-14-0 with smaller wheels and 9.3 metre (30' 6") coupled wheelbase, about the same as a Union Pacific 4-12-2, known to be successful. Whereas the Russian engine had three adjacent pairs of flangeless wheels, which almost certainly would have dropped off the track fairly frequently, the German had two and was designed to traverse curves of 140 metres radius, just about 7 chains in British measurements. Since Germany had experience with successful 12-coupled designs, it seemed logical that their 14-coupler might work and, given the same techniques, a 14-coupled tank for Monmouthshire!

As drawing office work became increasingly mundane with standardised designs plus lots of clerical work in adding to each drawing the batches of engines to which it applied, frustration escalated accordingly. Nearly a decade after war's end, British Railways was still 'recovering' from the conflict, a viewpoint embraced with comfort by those who found it an excuse for inaction. 'Ar, had a good trip up to Paddington, only twenty minutes late' was the sort of complacent remark which had me fuming, especially bearing in mind the slow schedules. Other, commercial, interests evidently thought the same way in basics, but instead of using such evidence as reasons for building steam loco-motives of higher capacity, it was insinuated that 'steam was finished – only diesels and electrics can produce the high powers needed in the future'. The latest generation of British steam, the BR standards, certainly tended to support such a viewpoint, as with the exception of the 9F, there was nothing whose performance in traffic could not be equalled or bettered by former company designs sometimes twenty years older. Even the 9F, superb though it was, was in basic capacity, as a freight hauler, only the equal of Gresley's P1 of thirty years earlier.

As this anti-steam syndrome began to gain ground, mainly on quite false premises, I began to investigate the possibilities of high powered steam within general British limitations. There were possibly others, at other design centres, with similar ideas, but I never met any, and being in a junior position was certainly not encouraged to pursue what amounted to radical ideas, against the prevailing fashions. I was even told off for writing to the 'Railway Gazette', because my Swindon address might give offence as indicating that people in Wiltshire were not toeing the party line!

There was really little to do in my later drawing office days, and whereas others in similar positions chatted about the local football team, I bent over my drawing board looking quite industrious, as in fact I was. However, I was investigating what could be done with steam traction, when authority had already decided that it was outmoded. Thankfully this was still Wiltshire, England. Had I been somewhere in Russia, similarly bucking the party line, the end result would have been the salt mines in Siberia! None of this work was official, nor of course carried any sort of drawing number (especially Swindon).

However, I had a large drawing board at my disposal, and it seemed a pity not to use it. There were also the office set of large radius wooden curves, upon which designs could be superimposed, and plenty of time!

Having always been rather freight engine minded, as the bread and butter earner of railways, the first really big engine tried out was a 3-cylinder 2-12-0, but the firebox, for high horsepower, was too long leading eventually to a rather ungainly 2-12-2 with firebox over the trailing coupled wheels. This caused all sort of restrictions including boiler diameter, firebox depth, and ashpan capacity. A corresponding 2-8-4 was proposed, for higher speeds, and this was again developed to a 2-8-6 with four outside cylinders, á la Pennsylvania T1, but with inside coupling rods between the two units, as on the PLM 2-10-2 compounds. As a design exercise, the 2-8-6 is shown in figure 8 but it suffered the restriction of being too specialised – there was no clearly defined extension of the design into a suitable freight version. Smallish wheels and short piston stroke would have enabled the attainment of high speeds, but it would have been a 'one-off' concept.

Apart from the obvious Pennsylvania inspiration behind the 2-8-4, the 2-8-6 version was sketched to include a boiler of the Brotan type, ie with water tube firebox. Locomotives having this type of boiler had been described in the press from time to time, and one had even been built for use in Britain, a small industrial engine for the Mannesman Steel Company in South Wales. The advantage of the Brotan type is in largely eliminating flat stayed surfaces, which

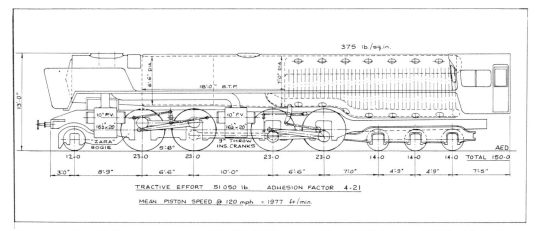

Assorted external influences are apparent in this 2-8-6 express scheme initiated about 1952 while in the army. Four outside cylinders like a Pennsylvania T1, but all wheels coupled as in the PLM 151A. Ultra short stroke for high speeds, and Brotan water tube firebox to allow high pressure. Piston speed at any rail velocity only 90 percent of a Gresley A4, from which it would probably have wrested the world speed record. Roller bearings throughout. Double Lemâitre exhaust. Possibly a steam competitor to today's HST! (Fig 8)

tend to give more or less trouble in conventional fireboxes, whilst at the same time restricting possible working pressures. Since none of the water tube types had been recorded as being successful and therefore multiplied, I had assumed them to be unsuccessful.

Only after visiting Jugoslavia was the true story revealed. Brotan-boilered locomotives were quite numerous in that country, all being ex-Hungarian State Railways, and some investigation showed that about a thousand Brotan boilers had been built by that country. The boiler design as sketched showed a lovely flowing series of lower mud tubes, of rather large diameter, for good water circulation. It took up quite a lot of room and was possibly heavy, hence the change to a six wheel trailing truck. After I had left railway service, some time was spent with the Superheater Company in London, dealing mainly with large, high pressure water tube boilers for power stations etc., thus providing some experience in such matters, from which was learned that the boiler on the 2-8-6 would have been excessively expensive to manufacture, amongst other defects. However, a more advanced and acceptable design was later evolved, but that falls outside the scope of this book.

The final pair of designs, for express passenger and heavy freight, although initiated at Swindon, were not fully developed until several years after departure. These are shown in figs 9 & 10, and are illustrated as straightforward two cylinder engines, although three-cylinder versions were always considered as alternatives. Important standardisation, in boiler and motion design, was included, and if conditions warranted, an intermediate 2-10-4 mixed traffic version would have been easily feasible. Locomotives of these dimensions

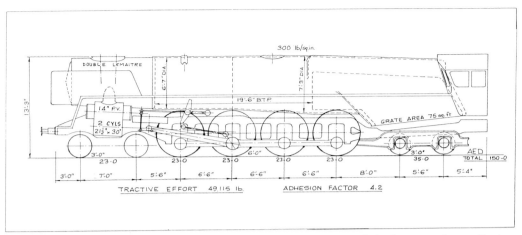

The two cylinder version (three cylinders also envisaged) of high powered simple express locomotive to equal electric traction output in Britain with far less civil engineering work and capital expenditure. Estimated drawbar horsepower about 4000. (Fig 9)

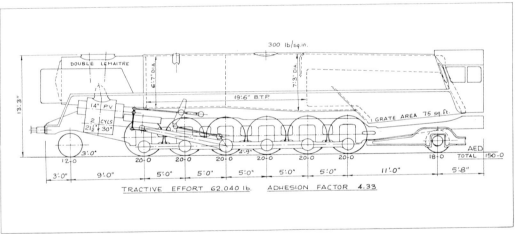

The heavy freight version of fig. 9, with identical boiler, cylinders, motion, etc. A possible third version, a mixed traffic 2-10-4 could also have been interpolated using these components. (Fig 10)

would be capable of 4000 drawbar horsepower, greatly exceeding the largest electric and diesel locomotives subsequently introduced by BR. Naturally, they would have been restricted to trunk routes only, and possibly some civil engineering may have been necessary to accommodate throwover on curves. However, compared with the civil engineering necessary to electrify main lines, raising of bridges, lowering track in tunnels, etc., this will have been minimal indeed. Equally, electric locomotives are restricted to routes which have concomitant fixed catenary, and large steam locomotives would be no more restricted in their routings than electrics. The largest diesels, such as the

Deltics, would have been completely outclassed, and indeed, in later days, it was found that Gresley Pacifics were able to fill in for the much vaunted Deltic diagrams at a moment's notice.

Some readers may query the validity for including non-official design schemes in such a book as this which otherwise records what actually happened at various times and places. In the first instance they show that finality in British steam development had not been reached, or even approached. Secondly it is an account of an apprenticeship, and whereas some, indeed most, apprentices are content to be taught the way things were always done, inevitably there would be some, like the author, of an inquisitive turn of mind, and who were not constrained by the 'party line'. That such people could turn up at Swindon was perhaps remarkable. Swindon had done little in the way of locomotive development since Churchward's days, and there was a very well developed attitude of resting forever on the master's laurels. Come nationalisation, Derby was in the ascendency over British Railways, and the BR standard designs, while including some refinement in detail, were in their way just as conservative with regard to the 1950s as were the 2P and 4F types thirty years earlier. There remained the inbuilt Derby resistance to size and power, culminating in the multiplicity of small engines, classes 2, 3, and 4. Thus there was no real feeling of belonging to a go-ahead organisation.

Thirdly, although in a junior position when these schemes were worked out, had not the accident of history condemned steam development to a premature demise, then it is possible that the author could have been in a senior, or even a commanding design position later on when realisation came that existing designs could not provide the power and speed necessary to compete with other forms of transport. Had this happened, then these early 'doodles', while primitive, could have formed the basis for discussions on finalised high-output designs. Those whose horizons had never expanded beyond a 'Castle' or a 'Britannia' would have been considerably inhibited in thinking big, as had happened so clearly fifty years before, at the start of the twentieth century. Amazingly enough, even the eventual BR diesel fleet was basically underpowered, and while using the term 'type' instead of 'class', clung to the traditional Derby power grades of 1, 2, 3, and 4!

Thus these early schemes, redrawn to a common style suitable for reproduction, show how a person's outlook, starting off purely 'Great Western' could, by cross-breeding firstly with other local ingredients, and later by foreign 'genes' proceed, as with animal husbandry, beyond previously constrained frontiers. The author claims no exclusivity for this, there were probably others in different centres who also doodled designs for what was to be a non-existent steam future, and perhaps in the goodness of time some of these alternative ideas may emerge in the printed word (and drawing).

FURTHER OVERSEAS

As mentioned earlier, staff status provided free travel, second class, on the continent, and no time was lost in taking advantage of this. For some time it had been evident that very interesting locomotives were to be found in Eastern Europe, and I was particularly attracted towards the Czechoslovakian designs described in that wonderful organ the *'Locomotive'* magazine. Equally, I was interested technically in the massive 2-12-4T used in Bulgaria, and in 1953 a visit was planned to see and experience these wonders. Free passes were applied for through official channels, and visits made to the consulates of Czechoslovakia, Hungary, Rumania and Bulgaria, applying for visas. In my naivety the 'reason for visiting' these communist countries was truthfully stated as studying and photographing their locomotives (!?) thinking that my job as a 'railway worker' would bring favourable status. I had no idea at that time how restrictive was a communist society, and despite several reminders, and repeated visits to these consulates, applications were never even acknowledged. Amazingly enough, the free passes, applied for via railway channels, were granted, and I found myself in the position of having free passes on railways in countries I could not enter! The only exception was Bulgaria who granted a transit visa for travel without break on the Orient Express on the way back from Istanbul, the ultimate destination.

Hence my outward journey was disjointed. I actually went up to the Czech frontier at Schnirding, on the through train to Warsaw, and was rewarded by seeing and photographing a pre-war 365.0 2-6-2 take the through carriages over the Iron Curtain. A freight came in headed by a 555.0 wartime ex-German 2-10-0, such that nothing was seen of the modern ČSD types which were the object of the exercise. I continued to Istanbul via Jugoslavia and Greece, having great fun in southern Serbia and Greece trying to make out where the train was, for station nameboards were entirely in Cyrillic and Greek characters respectively. Arrival in Thessalonika was about dawn, and I guessed where we were by the fact that it was a largish junction with terminal platforms. To my amazement, most of the locomotives were quite familiar – there were the US Army 0-6-0T and 2-8-0 wartime engines seen previously in Britain, Austrian Gölsdorf 0-10-0s and, surprise of suprises, British War Department 2-10-0s, one of which hauled my 'express', all stations across Thrace to Alexandroupolis. All such things became well known in later days, but in 1953 it represented original exploration. At Alexandroupolis the Hellenic State Railways petered out in a dusty bazaar area, full of people and noise, especially the latter, and one really felt the mysterious Orient was being penetrated, there being much Moslem influence. From here, where the train reversed, to the Turkish border, international traffic rolled over the Chemins de Fer Franco Hellenique, the still privately owned rump (with offices in Paris) of the former Compagnie Oriental, a once extensive system with tentacles running into what are today Turkey,

Greece, and Bulgaria, all but the Greek section having been absorbed into the respective national railways. Motive power, as noted, comprised two of the original CO 2-6-2 for passenger work, an ancient 4-4-0, evidently workable, as standby, and one or two Gölsdorf 0-10-0 from the batch supplied to the PLM in France, doubtless obtained cheaply via their 'French connection'. An ancient CO 0-6-0, derelict, completed the motive power visible during the lengthy station stop.

The train continued at incredibly slow speed, across the border into Turkey, eventually arriving at Istanbul well into daylight. En route were seen and photographed outside framed 0-6-0s dating back to the 1870s, as Alpullu and Uzunkopru, the latter name, when related to the tracers in Swindon drawing office, being frankly disbelieved. Considering that the next station down the line from Swindon was Wootton Bassett, one wonders at parochial self limitations. Probably there were Turks who could not believe that Wootton Bassett could be the name of a railway station! Today Turkey is a popular venue for British steam enthusiasts, every locomotive listed with its allocation and possible duties. Thirty-five years ago it was very much the 'mysterious Orient', and the author believes he was the first to report on the system, with details of nomenclature, locomotive classification etc, in an article published in the *Stephenson Locomotive Society* journal, in 1953.

Returning, through Bulgaria with limited transit visa, the train from Istanbul (devoid of the 'Orient Express' through coaches, which failed to arrive on the outward journey), was so late that the connection at the Bulgarian frontier was missed by several hours, leading to transit by daylight instead of the scheduled night. Bulgarian locomotives were magnificent, in the old Prussian livery of green with red wheels and frames, white tyres and running plates, set off with much polished brasswork. Even a Swindon-trained man, brought up on a diet of ex-works 'Kings' and 'Castles' could not fail to be impressed by the condition of BDZ locomotives, all of which were maintained in immaculate condition. Unfortunately, being a communist country, my camera and films were regarded with horror by the frontier authorities, evidently relating a locomotive enthusiast as a potential spy, and all were bundled, boxed up, and sealed with lead clips and wire. This sort of paranoia is still to be found in most communist countries (with the notable exception of China), and has even been exported to countries such as Zambia where authorities tend to become hysterical when cameras are produced near a railway train!

As a result, my daytime journey through Bulgaria was a highly frustrating experience, perfect weather, beautiful locomotives, and sealed camera equipment. Perhaps the most frustrating detail of the lot was coasting into Sofia station and running parallel to a gleaming 2-12-4T hauling coal empties, watching all those wheels revolving at just the distance for a perfect photograph, and being unable to act. Later on, after Stalin's death, things eased a little, I did make a couple of visits to Bulgaria and obtained some shots of those massive tank engines in action, these successes being balanced by continuing suspicion, the loss of several films apparently stolen from my bag by security police, and several other problems and adventures. What was important was that these massive 2-12-4T were clearly not experimental monstrosities, restricted to a single prototype, but successful designs engaged in everyday haulage over a difficult route. One was even seen to travel quite fast, accelerating through the suburbs of Sofia prior to rushing the bank up through Gorna Banja.

My 1954 and 1955 holidays were also spent down in Southeast Europe and Turkey, limited by time. We had annual holidays amounting to two weeks and three days, during which time it was possible to go into central Turkey and back. Railway free passes were available even in Iraq, such that it was theoretically possible to travel down to Baghdad or even Basra by train, but this would have made a four week holiday necessary.

A Robert Stephenson & Co 0-6-2T in Turkey in 1955 would have looked perfectly at home on the Brecon & Merthyr.

8

SECONDMENTS

With real design work rather thin, there was ample scope for being loaned or seconded to other sections, in or out of Swindon, to assist anybody short of staff. As a carefree bachelor with a yen for variety I was always happy to take on such duties, considered a nuisance for the ordinary married man with family commitments.

TRACK TESTING

Little appears in enthusiast literature concerning the track testing vehicle, an old clerestory coach fitted with a Hallade recorder to measure vertical and lateral oscillation, and roll. In charge of this was Bob Hancock who thus had a little niche for himself. The car itself was maintained in a standard condition as supervised by Bob, and a programme of runs was planned every year. Important main lines were track tested more frequently than secondary routes, and I think only those having express passenger traffic were tested, except perhaps for exceptional reasons. Certainly the several excursions I enjoyed in this vehicle were all behind express trains, whose drivers were instructed to run as briskly as possible, subject to official speed restrictions.

Most trains used were expresses from Paddington, which gave the main line to Reading plenty of workouts, but one interesting trip I made was from Newport to Hereford and back, which was probably only traversed annually. Normal procedure was for the test vehicle, known universally as the 'whitewash car' (for reasons which appear later) to be sent on a day or two ahead of the planned run, for forming into the intended train. Bob and his assistant would leave Swindon, usually on an early train the same day, for Paddington, where an 'OCS tea' would be consumed while awaiting arrival of the empty stock. Eventually the chaff-chaff-chaff-chaff of a pannier tank heralded the train's arrival, slowing down towards buffer stops with a pish-tish of vacuum pumps. The whitewash car was always at the rear of the train, to allow those on board to view the track as it receded at speed, and also to minimise the effect of traction forces and possibly poorly riding adjacent vehicles. For this second reason, couplings were invariably adjusted such that buffers were slightly apart, this being our first job to supervise.

Once aboard, the Hallade recorder, a classic piece of early instrumentation, made of brass and driven by clockwork, was set up. A roll of paper was fed in, motor wound up and the styli tested for operation and legibility. Various dignitaries from the civil engineer's department arrived, the district chiefs and the gangers over whose track we were about to speed, large bluff men with the ruddy features associated with their outdoor existence. The rear part of the car contained the Hallade machine mounted on a table, plus several large comfortable chairs of what might be termed 'GWR Executive' style, facing backwards to view through three large windows at the car's rear. Once under way, it was my job to keep the machine functioning smoothly, while another assistant from the CCE's department kept his eyes open and pressed a button with codes for mile and quarter mile posts, stations etc, causing blips to appear on the paper roll, from which the particular section of track could be identified.

When a poor section of track was encountered, an electric bell rang, while an exceptionally poor section operated a siren and deposited a dollop of whitewash on the sleepers for immediate identification and rapid rectification of the offending track. When this happened, very infrequently, the responsible ganger invariably looked most uncomfortable in the presence of his superiors, although they were certainly not there to create unpleasantness. Bob always had the Hallade rolls from the previous couple of trips on hand for comparison, and these bad spots tended to recur each trip, due mainly to extraneous conditions such as, for example, a section of swampy ground. Nobody could blame the ganger for this, but the whitewash dollop certainly kept him alert to provide extra care over such sections.

As we passed over different men's sections, they came and went from several normal passenger compartments to and from the rear saloon. From time to time tea was dispensed from a kettle located in a small galley, whose attendant also kept things spick and span. The chief civil engineer seemed to have more manpower than the CME, for on trips in the dynamometer car we had to do this sort of duty ourselves. Mealtimes also reflected differing styles between the two departments. Drinking on the job was always taboo on railway service, yet on the track testing car lunch, supplied by the CCE, was a real outdoor man's repast comprising good ham or beef sandwiches plus a bottle of blue triangle Bass for those who felt like one! Very pleasant outings, these track testing jaunts, travelling along in a smartly run steam express, and even getting paid for it!

WHEEL BALANCING

Another drawing office job which I inherited for a while was the almost daily walk down to the AW shop to check the wheel balancing. A pair of wheels ex overhaul would have mounted upon it weights at the crankpins to simulate the weights of connecting and coupling rods normally borne. The whole lot would then be spun at a predetermined speed according to locomotive class, and when out of balance was recorded, further weights were clamped on by fitters until the wheelset revolved smoothly. It was a bit hit-and-miss, with high spots recorded with a piece of chalk, but seemed to work. My job was to calculate the moments of the bolted on weights, and from these work out how much lead had to be added or removed from the pockets in the balance weights. If much adjustment was needed, the wheels were spun again to verify the calculations, but most wheelsets needed little adjustment.

Those were the days before electronic calculators, and all was done by slide rule and notebook, which apparently looked impressive to outsiders although simple enough in reality. Swindon entertained numerous locomotive engineering students from the Commonwealth, and one day some young Indians watched the procedures with evident fascination. After explaining what was happening one asked what formula I was using. I replied that there was no formula, it was just calculated from first principles. Pause for thought, then; 'What is the formula for first principles?' Evidently the university they attended simply filled students with masses of formulae without providing any real 'feel' of what engineering was all about, as was learned very effectively with a premium apprenticeship. They had with them some locomotive diagrams of existing and proposed Indian Railways steam locomotives, of which engines such as the WG and WP classes were familiar through the British railway press. However, I was intrigued to notice designs for two heavy shunting engines, both 2-10-6T of typical Indian style, one for broad and one for metre gauge, neither of which were built. Subsequent enquiries many years later revealed that although people *recalled* these designs, nobody seems able to find copies of those diagrams.

LOCOMOTIVE TESTING

During the time I was at Swindon, S.O. (Sam) Ell developed and refined the art and science of steam locomotive performance testing to levels never attained before or since. The Swindon locomotive test plant was uprated to absorb the power generated by modern locomotive types, the 'summation of increments' method of coal consumption measurement evolved, and a great deal of work done on front end proportions including fixing the steaming rate relative to blast pipe pressure. His principal assistant was one Titchener, and for juniors he had Wally Harland (junior), son of the assistant chief draughtsman, and

Mike Casey, who eventually succeeded in recent years to the top engineering job on British Railways. What is amazing today, is that all these men, engaged on mechanical engineering research of an enterprising and original nature, were classified simply as 'draughtsmen'! Today, people who barely know which is the sharp end of a pencil are designated 'draughtsmen', such has the term degenerated over about thirty years.

The test department occupied something of a rambling hutch over the B shed, reached through the print department who printed drawings produced in the main D.O., and which included one extraordinary character who will be excluded from these pages, but who might perhaps be commented upon after the third pint of beer! The eminence achieved by Sam Ell was jealously regarded by the rival Derby establishment who used the more modern test station at Rugby, had more modern dynamometer cars, and a 'mobile testing unit' which might be likened to dragging a couple of tramcars backwards in full fore gear, compared with Sam's method of hauling a real train of sufficient size to absorb the power output of the locomotive under test. Several books by London Midland men have made snide remarks about Swindon's work on testing, probably because in some cases it corrected Derby designs, and also because the train timing and motive power economy methods thus evolved were of such basic veracity as to be applicable to other forms of traction, as was actually done.

These Ivatt LMS light 2-6-0s, constructed at Swindon, needed redraughting by Sam Ell's team for their performance to equal the old locos they replaced.

2-6-2T version of the Ivatt 2-6-0 at Swindon in 1952. LMS blurb billed them as the first modern small engines, ignoring GWR 45XX, equally as modern when built, which could outperform the LMS tanks.

Naturally, Ell developed his work on a purely regional basis, with 'Kings' and 'Castles' having larger superheaters and double chimneys, but as word got around, he was called upon to test other locomotives. One early example, which caused much embarrassment to Derby, was when Swindon built a batch of Ivatt class 2 2-6-0 to replace old locomotives such as Swindon's 'Dean Goods' and the former Cambrian 0-6-0s. Now the Ivatt mogul was basically an excellent little engine with all mod cons, and very capable of producing economies of both fuel and maintenance while carrying out the duties formerly entrusted to Kirtley and Johnson 0-6-0s on that railway where little engines were treated like pets and worked gently. Along the near level lines bordering the valley of the turgid Trent, its power output was also considered satisfactory, but when pitted against the asperities of the Newport-Brecon line it was found totally inadequate. On the southbound run, the summit at Torpantau (pronounced *Tor*-pan-tah-ee, with Welsh double vowel) was approached by about ten miles of around 1 in 36, guaranteed to defeat any inadequate locomotive. When drivers complained that this 1946 design could not compete with an 1883 'Dean Goods', the usual runs with inspectors etc were made, and the verdict confirmed.

Probably even the most ardent 'Gurt Western' enthusiasts were insufficiently bigoted to really believe this, but tests were carried out on the Swindon plant, confirming enginemen's reports. All that were needed were better blast pipe and chimney proportions, and after these were provided the Ivatt 2-6-0 were found fully capable of replacing Dean's 0-6-0s. Derby apologists make remarks such as 'All they needed were copper capped chimneys', but the chimney proportions on those early Ivatt 2-6-0 (and 2-6-2T) looked remarkably like the malformed organs which sat atop those dreadful Fowler 2-6-2T of even feebler performance. It is not only Derby where reactionary conservatism prevailed. Under Collett, Swindon was similarly backward, and one may imagine that Churchward, given the requirement for a modern, light axle load, tender engine for such duties would have produced a tender version of a 45XX, a 2-6-0, to knock spots off any later contestant!

An LNER engine at Swindon works was a rare occurrence. In my early apprenticeship days, a K3 hauling the Sundays only Sheffield-Swansea ran a hot bearing, and was despatched to the works for rectification, providing the amazed denizens therein, their first sight of a Cyclopean single-cranked axle! Later, another Gresley engine in the shape of V2 60845 was to appear at Swindon for testing. Nobody doubted the V2's steaming in its original condition, but after fitting with self cleaning smokebox plates, they became unreliable, and Sam Ell was called upon to evaluate a remedy. Rather surprisingly he stayed with the single chimney original design, altered in proportions only. Possibly this was not fully conclusive, as later some were fitted with double plain blastpipes of rather 'Rebuilt Scot' proportions and sound effects, while a few had double Kylchap systems which Peter Townend (admittedly biassed, but probably rightly) claims was the best solution.

It was during the trials of 60845 that the author was called upon to supplement the normal testing staff in the dynamometer car. Running was from Reading to Stoke Gifford and back, in one day, with trains increasing up to 25 passenger coaches plus dynamometer car, about 800 tons, an unprecedented load later repeated with a high superheat, double chimney, 'King'. On the first week of testing the author stayed in the office and managed to get some sort of photograph of the V2 thundering by. The second week he spent in the dynamometer car, and was given the task of recording various temperatures with a Cambridge instrument mounted on a plain table.

Now Sam Ell's testing procedures were based upon constant steaming rate, as measured by two manometers, one in the dynamometer car for recording purposes and one in the loco's cab where Ernie Nutty was the footplate representative of the experimental section. The driver was instructed to maintain whichever steaming rate was being tested, and this could be maintained either at high speed with short cut-off, or low speeds with longer cut-offs. On one of these tests in the second week, we were belting along with 25 coaches plus the dynamometer car, en route from Reading to Stoke Gifford, when adverse signals were sighted approaching Swindon. The operating department were given strict instructions to keep a clear road for test specials, as a very expensive exercise could be ruined by stop and start running, and at the time an attempt was made by the engine crew to maintain full steaming by working with long cut-off and brakes hard on. All was to no avail, the signals did not clear in time, and we ground to a halt.

Now the dynamometer car has a very sensitive drawbar spring, with a long travel, and we stopped with the engine flat out against dragging brakes, drawbar fully stretched recording maximum tractive effort, which meant that the buffers of tender and dynamometer car were a good foot apart.

Having ground to a halt at full power brakes were well jammed and the V2 unable to restart the train. Guided by years of experience with normal trains, the driver did what all drivers would do under similar conditions – wound the gear into full backwards and opened the regulator. Propelled by the V2's power, *plus* the thirty thousand pounds force on the stretched drawbar of the dynamometer car, engine and tender shot across the intervening gap between buffers and slammed into the train. Force of impact shot the dynamometer car back some distance, while the delicate recording instrument in my charge, restrained by its own inertia, stayed put after supporting table disappeared, and crashed to the floor in a chaos of broken glass and waving springs, looking rather like a cartoonist's impression of a smashed watch, on a much larger scale. That was the end of temperature measurement for that day.

Gresley's V2 60845 thundering past the foundry, towing the Swindon dynamometer car and a score or so of empty stock, passes an old pannier tank shunting ex-works engines on to their tenders.

On the way back from Stoke Gifford, the day had become rather misty (not unusual in the Thames Valley), and by Didcot this massive train had been worked up to 71 mph. My task having perforce been eliminated, I had been given another intermittent job which left time to lean out of the window and enjoy the thunderous roar of the V2 going flat out. As we blasted through Didcot, an old porter, doubtless alerted by the very un-GWR sound effects of a V2, came out to watch us go by. His head could be seen oscillating from side to side as he presumably counted the vehicles trailing behind this thundering monstrosity, and my last sight of him was as he disappeared into the gathering gloom at about 22 or 23 coaches! At the time it must have been the longest train of passenger stock run through Didcot at speed, but later on similar trains on test were hauled by BR 8P 71000 and also high superheat, double chimney, 'King' class.

ASHFORD, SOUTHERN

A curious secondment took place while I was in the Swindon drawing office. The Southern had built a pair of 1600 horsepower diesel-electric locomotives, Nos 10201–2, and these had been joined by the former LMS pair, 10000–1, on the West of England main line. I had made a point of having runs behind these representatives of a new motive power form, and found them remarkably feeble. Twelve driving wheels *should* have produced superior acceleration, and they undoubtedly got off the mark better than a Bulleid Pacific but soon eased off into the low performance restricted by their power output. Even a 4-6-0 could out-perform them, apart from initial acceleration, and there was no doubt in my mind that a good 4-8-0 would knock spots off them at all stages. Much the same could be said of the two Gas turbines, 18000 and 18100, behind which I had several runs from Paddington to Swindon, on a Bristol train departing, I think, about 5.30 pm. There was nothing in their performance to indicate any advance over even Standard 4-6-0s, let alone steam of advanced design.

There came a call about 1954 for draughtsmen to converge upon Ashford works in Kent, to help with the design of Southern 10203, an uprated diesel of 1750 hp. At that time I was not really anti-diesel, but was willing to see what the alternative had to offer, and to evaluate any possible advantages one way or the other. Apparently 10203 had become an embarrassment. Ashford drawing office, headed by Percy Bollen, the CD, had announced that x percent of the drawings had been issued to shops, and as x was quite high, construction had started at Eastleigh. What Percy had not made clear was that the drawings issued were those identical to 10201–2, and that virtually nothing had been done about the new drawings required to cope with the increased power rating! A circular was distributed round the various BR drawing offices, asking for volunteers to temporarily expand the limited Ashford DO staff, and I was one of the respondents. Apparently something like six or ten additional men were needed but as I recall one chap from Doncaster and another from Horwich were my only companions on this exercise. Regrettably I fail to remember their names, but my section leader was George Baker, a large bluff, unflappable, character who had survived the design and development of Bulleid's 'Leader' class and who regaled me with many detailed anecdotes from this period.

'Design', on a diesel electric, proved quite disappointing. The major organs, engines, generators, and traction motors, were simply supplied by their respective manufacturers, and all that was necessary was to fit them into the locomotive's package. What this mainly amounted to was threading enlarged fans and ducting for cooling traction motors through existing framework. There was really nothing to it, and many years later while in Australia I landed a job designing air conditioning ducting for a large building in Perth, Western Australia, on the basis of having done the job on 10203! The 'Aussie' job was even easier, as everything was fixed – there were no bogies moving relative to the mainframe – and the American 'specialist engineer' in charge was seen to be particularly suitable for winter conditions inasmuch as he produced a vast volume of hot air!

However, being in a Southern drawing office, albeit on diesel work, had interesting steam sidelights. George Baker had several interesting anecdotes about Bulleid, some possibly apocryphal, especially concerning the 'Leader' class. The arrangement drawing of this machine's incredible valve gear was at Ashford, in print form, and I spent some time tracing the main features of this, although more recently they have been published. There was also a diagram for the original wartime lightweight 4-6-2, a sort of small 'Merchant Navy' with Q1 class cladding, again a discovery at the time. Axlebox suspension of the 'Leader' was based on Swiss electric practice with cylindrical guides surrounded by coiled springs, which worked perfectly. Unfortunately, on the 'Leader', the offset boiler caused them to jam up due to the unbalanced weight, and according to George, trial runs had to be made with the side corridor full of steel girders and sections to correct 'trim' and render axlebox guides workable. All this added to what was already an overweight locomotive unpopular with the civil engineer.

Another amusing feature concerned the ash chute built into the smokebox base. In order to try out this feature it was also built into another engine, I think a class U 2-6-0. A large open duct in the smokebox seems hardly conducive to creating a satisfactory draught for the fire, and objections were raised. Bulleid's reaction was of typical super-confidence – 'My multiple jet exhaust system will easily counter the loss of draught', or similar. When tried out, the locomotive steamed abominably, except when handled by a particular driver, who obtained magnificent results from it. This was a total mystery, and the successful driver refused to divulge his secret. Eventually, when the driver was away from his engine for a while, an examination was made, revealing a 'bloody great turnip' stuffed into the ash chute, effectively negating any draught loss!

The author saw N class in his early wartime days, but had no idea then how much the design owed to Swindon. Photographed near Gomshall in later days, 31868 has improved frames, cylinders and draughting arrangements.

Always eager to learn new techniques, I was most interested to discover how Bulleid's modified *Lemâitre* exhaust varied according to locomotive size, and extracted the relevant drawings for study. To my amazement, they were all virtually the same, five jets of $2\frac{5}{8}$ inches diameter on closely similar pitch circle. Only much later did the significance of this emerge. The original design was probably prepared for the 'Nelsons', and worked well. On the 'Schools', it was really too big, which is why no definitive results were obtained in its favour. When these same sized jets were applied to the far larger 'Merchant Navy' class, they created too much back pressure, as confirmed with the tested high fuel consumption, but also created so much draught that the boilers were unbeatable! At a fuel consumption price. By coincidence, the identical arrangement on the smaller Pacifics provided a less extravagent draught and back pressure, giving them their popular acceptance. It seems amazing that the jet and chimney dimensions were not varied according to locomotive size, this being one of those little mysteries which make locomotive history so rewarding.

BFB (Bulleid–Firth–Brown) wheels on an unrebuilt Bulleid pacific. Note: the more fussy design compared with the American Boxpok type; the crosshead and crankpin nuts, changed from the Bulleid originals.

While at Ashford, I spent several weekends back at Swindon, plus others with my parents in South East London. During the Monday morning returns, a number of interesting steam workings were sampled. The Southern electric system was fine for suburban passenger services, but early mornings (and I talk about 3 a.m.) several newspaper trains left City termini for country destinations, hauled by steam over otherwise all-electric routes. These were all sampled in turn, and it was vaguely satisfying to bowl through places like Dartford, on the only steam hauled passenger of the day, unknown to most of the inhabitants, still fast asleep. These trains tended to have rebuilt 4-4-0 of classes D1 and E1, excellent little engines which *looked* like a Midland 2P but would be halfway to Dartford before the Derby engine had managed its first painful wheel revolution!

One fine Saturday I walked cross country from Ashford to the Romney, Hythe, and Dymchurch Railway, a goodly hike, and rode a couple of their trains but was disappointed not to manage a run behind Britain's only 4-8-2 class neither of which were in service that day. Walking through Kent was a

A set of Boxpok wheels, with well laid out valve gear, on an American built 141R class. To the author, this design seemed simpler and more workmanlike than Bulleid's BFB wheel centres.

pleasant pastime, and on those long summer evenings I often escaped from my lodgings for a long stroll through the fields, perhaps stopping for a while to note the difference in shunting effectiveness between an old rebuilt Stirling '01' 0-6-0, struggling noisily, and the quiet competence of the 3-cylinder 'Z' class 0-8-0T nearby. Definitely, 'big' engines were better, although the total weight of the 0-6-0 with tender was nearly that of the 0-8-0T.

On some of these excursions I took my landlady's dog for a walk, invariably managing to return via a very pleasant pub just outside town which purveyed well kept bitter and provided biscuits for the dog. Oh, woe! One day the landlady, member of a temperance society, was walking with dog and local vicar when they chanced upon this by then well known pub which the dog refused to pass without its customary biscuit. Worse, somebody recognised the dog and emerged with the expected snack, to the landlady's acute embarrassment. Fortunately, the Ashford 'crisis' was by then nearly finished and I returned to Swindon, after spending two weeks in the Army Emergency Reserve, from Ashford base.

TO AFRICA!

One of my vaguely remembered relatives from early days was an uncle who worked as a missionary in Uganda, and probably unwittingly helped to pave the way for the later monstrosity known as Idi Amin. Africa always had an appeal, mainly from an interest in wild animals, and in schoolboy days seeing such films as 'Sanders of the River', in which even to my untutored mind several views of the canoe paddling along the river were identical and doubtless the same shot repeated again and again!

British Railways had announced their 'modernisation plan', detailed by one of those redundant army generals who always seem able to impress gullible politicians so divorced from realities, and steam was clearly 'out'. Enormous savings were to be made by eliminating this 'outmoded' form of traction, and when the dust had settled, and the whole lot scrapped in an incredible few years, the deficit had increased! The big thing was that 'Britain needed a home market as a shop window for diesel exports', so twenty thousand steam locomotives were scrapped, some in their prime of life, so that a few hundred diesels could be sold to a handful of obscure colonial, or recently ex-colonial, railways. Important developments, much needed, such as fitting continuous brakes to freight wagons, to make rail traffic competitive in speed and service with airbraked articulated lorries, were totally ignored.

Hence, while I was working on the motion arrangement of the BR class 3 2-6-0, a drawing in which I spent much effort and took equal pride, a circular came round the office advertising a need for draughtsmen on the East African Railways, in Nairobi. Why not, EAR had been well in the technical news with a succession of modern locomotive types, and as steam design was clearly finished on BR, I applied. Some three months went by with no result, and I was about to embark on a shedmaster's course in Wolverhampton when suddenly the Crown Agents for the Colonies etc wanted to see me for a technical interview with one of the EAR engineers home from leave. He was a running man, with little design experience, and when I asked what a draughtsman would actually do in Nairobi he thought I might be –'drawing loco. diagrams' which, for a smallish railway with few locomotive classes seemed unlikely. Anyway, we seemed to get on well, and that was that.

After another three month hiatus I was called upon to visit the Crown Agent's tame medico in Harley Street, the only time I have ever been able to patronise that august centre of medical elitism. I remember an embarrassing moment when an attractive young lady in spotless and gleaming white overall presented a flask and asked for a urine sample. Now I had been out with several nurses from the Swindon community, and found them pretty down to earth in such matters, so prepared to provide the 'nurse' with some instant urine on draught! Horror! It turned out that the lady in question was the doctor's *secretary*, and I was rapidly despatched down the corridor to deliver the required sample in more decorous privacy!

Another three months went by, making a total bureaucratic gestation period of nine months when suddenly I was accepted and they wanted me out of Swindon and on the 'plane with quite indecent haste. Belongings were packed for despatch by sea ahead of my departure by air, every possible excuse was made for recurrent farewell 'thrashes', and the more apprehensive colleagues predicted my imminent demise per good offices of the then very active Mau Mau. Somebody whose African geography was as vague as mine recalled that in Africa the natives referred to the white man as *Baas* and that this was possibly a good omen as indicating a plentiful supply of Bass! Apart from the fact that he was a couple of thousand miles, several countries, and numerous tribes adrift, it was a surprisingly erudite joke from a Wiltshireman to whom a journey to Devizes was a safari.

Came the great day, and I made my first journey by the alien mode of air travel. Set off from London airport early and flew over the Alps on a lovely October morn, a splendid sight. Called at Rome, landed at Cairo and 'engine trouble' was announced. B.O.A.C., as it then was, put us all up in a reasonable hotel, and the following day took passengers on a 'bus tour of the Sphinx and Pyramids, which otherwise I would not have seen. Also walked down to the nearest EGR station, inhabited mainly by Moguls and various tank engines but unfortunately my camera was empty, and expecting a 'non-stop' run to Nairobi I had no negotiable money in small denominations to buy a couple of films, so had to be content with having seen Egyptian steam without recording it on celluloid. I regret this today much more than at the time, when interests were more technical. Arrived in Nairobi exactly a day late and was met by a genial colleague-to-be, one Idwell Jones, probably born in Kenya as he exhibited no trace of Cymric accent! Idwell's religion was golf and we proceeded to the EAR offices via the local golf club, where a couple of welcome beers were consumed, although I disappointed him by admitting to being a non-golf 'Infidel'

NAIROBI

The East African Railways in Nairobi was quite a surprise to one who while brought up in England on a diet of British type railways, had explored the continent of Europe, and who had even penetrated the fringes of Asia, in Turkey. In my time there were still those who averred that abolition of Brunel's heroic seven foot gauge was a grave error, and that $4'8\frac{1}{2}''$ was 'narrow gauge'. Anything less than that was thought of as miniature, epitomised by the little Vale of Rheidol 2-6-2T which turned up at Swindon from time to time to be overhauled while supported on wooden packing over pits far too wide to accept their diminutive dimensions.

This mistaken idea that the distance between rails was directly proportional to high speed, performance, and economy, had already been examined, and it seems that George Stephenson, by some incredible intuition, had stumbled upon the optimum rail gauge. Certainly, one could look around the world, and the highest speeds, heaviest loads, etc, were all achieved on standard gauge. Broad gauge systems as found in India, Argentina, Australia, etc were inferior in all respects. On the other hand, slightly 'narrow' gauges, which today I like to refer to as 'medium' gauge, clearly had great possibilities, and one only had to peruse the pages of the *'Railway Gazette'* or the *'Locomotive'* to become aware of the fact that much larger locomotives had been built for South Africa's 3'6" gauge than for India's 5'6", and for that matter, also, Britain's 'standard'.

One's first impression of a variant gauge, as a railwayman, comes in the initial tour of the premises, when in the course of introduction to so many people that all their names are instantly forgotten upon presentation to the next, the rails seem too close together (or too far apart). Immediate office colleagues were Freddy Goundry, design engineer, ex-BR somewhere, Alan Williamson (chief draughtsman, ex Vulcan Foundry, arriving just after myself), Jeff Lovell from Crewe, Maurice Heery from Beyer Peacock, and on the carriage and wagon side, Albert Harris from Metro-Cammell in Saltley, representing a pretty good cross selection of relevant experience. The chief mechanical engineer, Willie Bulman, was a definite 'character', sounding of English origin, but having evidently arrived via Tanganyika Railways in Dar es Salaam with earlier experience in Canada. Swindon being the secretive, ingrowing, place that it was, I had never knowingly seen, let alone met the Wiltshire incumbent, and it was somewhat awe-inspiring to actually have to discuss technical matters with so elevated an authority.

Social life in Nairobi was totally different to that at Swindon. I was accomodated in the bachelor's mess run by the EAR, in a fairly remote situation adjacent to the local aboretum. This was run by one of the clerks in the personnel dept, Vernon Heever, who initially provided a lift to and from work until such time, as was absolutely necessary, I purchased my first motor car, a 1949 Ford Anglia. Without a car one was totally dependent on others, quite unacceptable to one so independently minded as this author. Accommodation was full board, and we returned daily for lunch. Modern social practice, such as the five day week had yet to penetrate this colonial outpost and we still worked Saturday mornings. There was no pub close by, and to start with I enjoyed other's hospitality until mobile myself and able to reciprocate. Kenya did not have draught beer and one had to rough it in darkest Africa by bottled beverages of which the least potable to my palate was Allsop's. A good local brew was 'Tusker', with label depicting a charging elephant, while my favourite was 'White Cap', showing the snow capped peak of Kilimanjaro.

Wild life was a frequent topic of conversation, and Nairobi had its own small, but well stocked, game reserve, bounded on the north side by the main line from Athi River into Nairobi. Many were the Sunday mornings when, to clear the vapours from Saturday night's activities, I would watch the African dawn from the middle of a herd of Grant's or Thompson's gazelles while listening to a

59 class bellowing inland from the Athi River water stop. Not too far from the mess by car (but a rather long walk) was an establishment called the 'Swiss Grill' where I frequently watered after work. It was also not far from the line inland to Nakuru and I delighted to sit there relaxing with a cold 'White Cap' in the tropical dusk, birds twittering in the foliage all around, while an evening train, usually hauled by a 58 class, wound its way in almost a semi circle around, the two units wandering in and out of synchronisation in that fascinating Garratt rhythm – Bam, bam, bam, bam, dada, dada, dada, dada, bam, bam, bam, bam, dada, dada, dada, dada –!

In Nairobi, the railway separated the 'posh' part of town from the hoi polloi. At the 'town' side of the station was the general manager's office, a modern, multi storey block known to us as the 'Kremlin'. The CME occupied a suite of wooden, single storey, colonial type buildings south of the tracks, handy for both the works and the running shed, and the drawing office looked out directly onto the back of Nairobi station, separated from it by the shunting yard where continuous activity took place. In 1955 all locomotives were being outshopped in the magnificent maroon livery inherited from Tanganyika, but many older engines were in graphited black, the old Uganda Railway colours. Passenger stock was in familiar GWR chocolate and cream. All stock was airbraked, as befitted a railway which climbed to over 9000 feet altitude, where there would be very limited 'suck' in a vacuum system, but couplings were the very crude 'chopper' type, inherited from India with the metre gauge, and really quite inadequate for the type of traffic then handled by EAR. All modern locomotives and rolling stock were built for easy conversion to 3'6" gauge and the more modern knuckle couplers (at greater height) as used elsewhere in southern Africa, but in the event this change has yet to materialise over thirty years later.

As a locomotive man, motive power was first consideration in a bewildering kaleidoscope of new experiences, and the initial surprise was Garratts. In Britain, apart from the LNER U1 which I never saw on home ground at work, Garratts were represented by plodding Midland monsters roughly equalling two Midland 0-6-0s in both output and sluggishness, and boasting the highest axle load of any purely freight locomotive in the country. In Nairobi it was quite different, as they knew how to exploit this unique concept. Some 150 Garratts of eleven different classes graced the stock list and they handled most of the main line work. In fact they were very much 'standard' power, and by no means regarded as special purpose machines. Pride of place were the 59 class, massive 4-8-2 + 2-8-4 with the same 21 ton axle load as the Midland Garratts. There the similarity ended, for the 59's had bar frames, roller bearings on all axles plus the driving crankpins, a boiler 7'6" diameter, and 83,350 pounds tractive effort. Beside such a monster, a Swindon 'King' was quite puny, with less than half the tractive effort and half the grate area, although the 59's, built as oil burners, did not have a grate as such. More than double the largest GWR

East Africa's last new Garratt, 5934, emerges resplendent in maroon livery from Nairobi works in 1955. It has been commissioned after haulage upcountry from Mombasa.

locomotive, on less than half Brunel's broad gauge, a sure lesson that rail gauge is not an important criterion. Even the total width was about a foot more than on GWR locomotives, regarded in Britain as enjoying a 'generous' loading gauge!

Next in size were the wartime 54 class, rather too big for their plate frames, with over 58,000 pounds tractive effort, yet treading lightly on a 14 ton axle load, suitable for all but the lightest of British branchlines. The real eye openers were the 57 and 58 classes, which at 4-8-4 + 4-8-4 wheel arrangement had the largest number of wheels I had ever seen under a locomotive. The 58's were slightly larger with 49,000 pounds tractive effort on an axle load which, in GWR terms, was in line with a '1901' class baby pannier! Grate area about the same as BR 71000, and driving wheel diameter 4'6", or relative to gauge, 6'5½" on 'standard'! These were the express engines, and hauled most principal passenger trains at the time, down to Mombasa and upcountry from Nairobi. By coincidence, the 57 plus 58 classes totalled thirty locomotives, the same as GWR's 'King' class.

The remaining Garratts were for lightly laid lines, with eleven ton axle loads, and were all 4-8-2 + 2-8-4, ranging from the 1928 vintage 50 class to modern 60 class. Despite their tiptoe axle loadings, less than the Beattie well tanks kept for the Wenford Bridge branch in Britain, all boasted tractive efforts, boiler diam-

Second largest EAR Garratts were the 54 class, heavy wartime 4-8-2 + 2-8-4 whose design suffered somewhat by the inclusion of plate frames.

Brand new and just up from Mombasa, lightweight 2-8-4 3145 is in grey undercoat but will later reappear in glossy maroon.

eters, and grate areas in line with the BR standard class 9F 2-10-0! A totally new set of values had been learned.

Non-articulated locomotives were mainly for secondary work and comprised old narrow firebox 4-8-0s of classes 22, 23, and 24, ranging in technical features from saturated slide valves to superheated and piston valves in modern cylinders. The older Garratts, classes 50 to 53, were in detail virtually a pair of 24 class. There were three post war classes of tender locos, the 29 class 2-8-2 with 13 ton axle load, but nearly 30,000 pounds tractive effort and 38 sq ft grate area, based on the Nigerian 'River' class. Similar in size was the 30 class 2-8-4 for Tanganyika, quite potent secondary engines but rather slippery when starting. Smallest of the modern types were the 31 class, another 2-8-4 on 11 ton axle load, yet with nearly 'Hall' class tractive effort and 'Castle' sized grate area!

There was only one class of 'large' unarticulated tender engines, the six examples of class 28, 2-8-2. These dated back to 1928 and were an outstanding design when built. Bearing in mind that they were for a metre gauge colonial railway which had been open only thirty years, built through an area including man-eating lion and some of the most primitive African tribes, they were immense! Overall dimensions were remarkably similar to Gresley's class P1 of the same wheel arrangement, while they were little inferior to the BR class 9F of the following generation. It is, in fact, worth tabulating a few major dimensions of these three classes, just to demonstrate this relativity.

East Africa's largest non-articulated locos were the class 28 mikados, of similar size and capacity to a Gresley P1 or BR 9F. 2801 at Nairobi's alfresco works section.

Railway	EAR(KUR)	LNER	BR
Gauge	metre	standard	standard
Loco class	28(EA)	P1	9F
Type	2-8-2	2-8-2	2-10-0
date introduced	1928	1925	1953
Tractive effort lb	37,938	38,500	39,667
Max boiler dia	6'2"	6'5"	6'1"
Grate area sq ft	40.5	41.25	40.2
Loco only weight tons	90.7	100.0	86.7

Tank engines were used for much shunting, the old 10 class 2-6-4T and 11 class 2-6-2T being based on Indian practice. The 12 class 2-6-2T was a modern derivative in Tanganyika, and Nairobi had most of the dreadful 13 class, a 4-8-2T produced in large numbers by North British for industrial users in South Africa. These were based on a turn-of-century 4-10-2T built for Natal for heavy gradients, most of which had the trailing pair of coupled wheels filleted when reduced to shunting work on sharper curves. EAR's locomotives must have been the largest order placed for this type. Many of the SA industrials had frames cut in such a manner that easy conversion to 4-10-2T was possible, but for some reason the EAR locos would have entailed extra alteration.

What they really needed was that extra pair of coupled wheels! Never before, or since, have I encountered such slippery shunting engines. 29,134 pounds tractive effort on 52 tons adhesion gave an adhesion factor of 4.0 with tanks full, grossly inadequate especially on a railway using oil fuel with its perpetual spillage onto tracks. This was recognised as a problem, but for the wrong reasons, as operating simply complained that they failed to complete a shunting shift without running out of water. That a great deal of steam (and hence water) was being wasted with each slip, occurring every time the regulator was opened seemed self evident to me, hearing them continuously from the adjacent drawing office. What they needed was more adhesion, and since their 13 ton axle loads trod rails upon which mighty 59 class Garratts arrived and departed, this could have been achieved by increased axle loading. However, when I arrived, the solution had already started to go the wrong way. To counter 'shortage of water', one engine, no 1308 was superheated. This apparently helped a little, but it (and others) still went to work trailing an old Garratt front tank on a four wheeled goods truck frame. Willie Bulman then decided to superheat the whole class and convert them to 4-8-4T using trailing bogies off old 4-8-0s and Garratts, plus superheater elements from withdrawn 24 class 4-8-0s. All this was really an expensive exercise in futility, for the 24 class, unaltered, were more effective! Converting to 4-10-2T, with enlarged supplies could have given more effective adhesion, but the whole thing was already under way. The final result was a 4-8-4T, just as slippery, but with a larger water supply to waste!

Actually, EAR had prepared designs for shunting engines of the 0-8-0 tender type, with 10, 13, and 17/18 ton axle loads, but these, far more effective, were never built.

Work in the EAR DO provided plenty of variety, and one of my first efforts was to rearrange the tubeplates of the 57 class in order to eliminate thermic syphons, considered a maintenance nuisance. Without any heavy presses I wondered how Nairobi was going to make the new tubeplates needed and was shown just such an operation in action. In Swindon, a massive press performed such flanging operations with a single stroke of its hydraulic rams. In Nairobi, the plate was heated locally by gas jets while brawny Africans armed with heavy hammers belted the plate over a former. It looked crude by 'Gurt Western' standards, but worked.

Another job which came my way was designing a new refrigerator wagon, totally outside both practical and theoretical experience, although the basics of refrigeration had been taught in heat engines classes. Willie knew what he wanted, and Idwell Jones was my mentor in detail design, being experienced in such matters. It was the type of wagon where ice was introduced to roof tanks and allowed to dribble down the sides, thereby cooling whatever was inside. Questions of possible corrosion entered my inexperienced mind during the course of design, countered by Idwell with his standard remedy consisting of a 'good coating of bituminous paint', heard several times thereafter, and apparently his universal cure for possible carriage and wagon ailments.

At the time I served in Kenya, all locomotives were oil fired in both Kenya, Uganda, and most of Tanganyika, although a few woodburners survived in the 'deep south' of Tanganyika. East Africa had always been an excellent example of the way steam locomotives could burn almost any available fuel, and in the earliest days had burned mainly wood. As locomotives increased in size and available forests were depleted, coal was used, obtained mainly from India and South Africa. At my time, 'bunker C' residual oil was the approved economic fuel, a tar like substance which even in EAR's equatorial climate needed steam heat coils to render it inviscid. Nevertheless, even the 59 class had been designed such that mechanical stokers could be applied should coal once again become the most economical fuel, and at the back of Nairobi shed the old coaling plant remained in existence just in case.

Oil fuel itself presented several problems, as had been discovered earlier by British Railways when a massive panic programme of oil burning had been initiated while I was in my apprenticeship. Large numbers of oil tanks for tenders were made, and scattered around the works, and about a couple of dozen locos, mainly 'Halls' and 28XX fitted out, plus one or two other locos. One was a 2-6-0, 6320 which was transformed by oil burning, probably because the grate area on the standard 4 boiler was really too small. Burning oil, no such limitation existed, and for a week·6320 hauled the 9 a.m. Bristol to Paddington express (normally 'King' or 'Castle' hauled) and was noted belting past Swindon works while we had our morning tea break. I must confess to taking little interest in oil burning at the time, as it seemed so totally wrong for Britain.

In Nairobi, it was a different matter, and one had to be interested. The system used was called the 'Mexican trough', comprising a rather phallic casting protruding into the firebox, with a lower passage containing steam, exhausting through a narrow slit to form a fine spray. Above this was a passage for oil, heated by the steam beneath, which dribbled onto the steam spray and was theoretically atomised while being sprayed across the firebox. In practice this happened imperfectly, with rumbles and thumps of erratically ignited oil being the aural hall mark of an oil burning locomotive. From time to time, too much oil dribbled into the flame pan, causing almost an explosion upon eventual ignition. Quite a lot of drawing office time was spent devising new arrangements of flame pans, fire bricks, and burner positions and angles to try and optimise arrangements, but basically we were guessing all the time, everybody with his own pet theory. After leaving EAR I later worked for the Superheater Company in London, where we carried out tests on an oil fired power station near Dartford, where the same pattern of irregular combustion seemed to take place, despite the far vaster facilities and qualifications available to the CEGB.

Willie Bulman was a man with a particularly lively mind, and quite the opposite to the stodginess encountered at Swindon. While in Wiltshire, on a continental trip, I had seen the strange-looking oblong chimneys on a couple of Austrian engines, and later read of the Giesl ejector in British technical magazines. Mention of such matters at Swindon produced little other than ridicule, but I wrote to Dr Giesl and received much data by return post shortly before leaving for Nairobi. Bulman was far more positive, and when I showed him this correspondence he became immediately interested, such that in good time, after initial experiments, most of the more modern EAR classes were fitted with Giesl ejectors. Only after returning to Britain did I actually meet Dr Giesl, commencing a long friendship continuing over thirty years.

The major project Bulman was concerned with was his 61 class gigantic Garratt with 27 ton axle load and 110,000 pounds tractive effort – all on metre gauge! He regaled us on several occasions with stories of how he had to battle with Beyer Peacock when the 59 class was on order, as they wanted to use the 7'3" diameter flanging blocks as already existing for several SAR loco classes. 'I am not going to have a big engine with a small (!) boiler', quoth Willie, and eventually the 7'6" boiler was agreed upon. The 61 class design made even the 59s look small, although the overall appearance was quite similar. Maurice Heery, as an ex-Beyer Peacock man, did most of these schemes, which eventually expanded to double 4-8-4 arrangement, plus also a condensing Garratt. The very high axle load was proposed for their existing track, using an empirical formula concerning tapered axle loadings, and, possibly fortunately, was never put to test.

Having seen in Europe, and even on the BR class 9F locos, how successful was a ten-coupled arrangement, and having even seen twelve-coupled loco-motives in evidently successful operation, I spent some of EAR's time and drawing paper on a couple of schemes, one for a double 4-10-2 Garratt to equal the proposed 61 class without exceeding the 59 class axle loading, plus another for a 4-12-2 Garratt of even greater power than the 61 class, still on a 59 class axle load. Regrettably, these drawings were regarded as impertinences, as new ideas are supposed to come from the top, and not from the most junior design draughtsman! One thing never taught in a purely engineering education, always concerned with stresses, strains, efforts and pressures, is the theory of management, which level every successful engineer will eventually attain; the psychology of getting the boss to accept one's ideas (usually with the painful realisation that he will claim credit for *your* thinking); and the essential dis-cipline of costing, usually left for accountants to provide as a horrified historical fact after the deed has been done. Possibly things are better arranged today, but conversations with younger people seem to indicate that things are much as before except that one now blames it on the computer!

A few non-railway experiences to round off my eventual departure from Nairobi, and departure from direct railway employment, although I have mainly since then worked for commercial firms engaged in supplying rolling stock or components for railway work. Over the years photography has become an increasingly fascinating hobby, aimed mainly at locomotives and trains as principal subjects. Whilst actually working on railways themselves, this was very much a secondary interest, and in particular I regret that both expertise and depth of coverage is lacking in the EAR photos included in this book. Expertise is always an ongoing thing, but I really made little effort to go out and 'shoot' all those locos in action. In part, there was the restriction that many of the more remote areas, where the most spectacular shots might be obtained, were dangerous due to the presence of the Mau Mau, but where railway interests are mainly technical, I found more inspiration in photo-graphing wildlife. Included in this were sequences of lion mating, and later on of some lovely cuddly cubs which may or may not have been the outcome.

Social life for a young draughtsman in Nairobi, at that time, was mainly alcoholic! The 'fair sex' were comparatively few in number, and tended quite realistically to attach themselves either to wealthy farmers and planters, or to dashing young officers out to combat the Mau Mau. We more lowly civilians were left with either tremendous 'thrashes' (nonetheless enjoyable), a handful of pale and uninteresting females, or the indigenous versions which, as the old story went, became whiter every day!

Living in the EAR mess, there were a couple of interesting occurrences when my car was out of action for servicing. In each case I had walked to the 'Swiss

Grill' for the evening, and on the first occasion was almost home when a small animal was perceived in the road. Thinking it was a dog or cat I crouched and made 'tsk tsk' noises whereupon it approached cautiously until about six feet from me, suddenly turned sideways and fled. It was a lovely silver backed mongoose, incredibly approaching so close to a human before deciding I might be dangerous. On another similar occasion, in the same area, I was again plodding home from my failed internal combustion conveyance, but had in mind the fact that several domestic dogs had fallen prey to leopard who had established themselves in the heavily wooded valley. In the still of the night, a large animal could be heard crashing through the undergrowth, heading in a beeline for me. I thought the best ploy was to stand stock still, hoping not to be noticed, so stopped with heart beating rapidly. Eventually the animal broke out of the bush – jumped at me, and licked me all over – it was an enormous labrador! Was I delighted?! Later, of course, I learned that leopards hunt by stealth, and never by crashing through undergrowth.

While in Nairobi, new steam locomotives were still being delivered to EAR, and one of the accompanying photographs shows a 31 class lightweight 2-8-4 just arrived outside the works after haulage from Mombasa. New locomotives arrived in an undercoat, in this case grey, and were finally assembled and painted in the superb maroon livery, within EAR workshops. I also photographed the last 59 class Garratt as it emerged brand new from shops, and for some time tried to obtain photographs of the 30 class, larger 2-8-4, all of which went to Tanganyika, and were something of a mystery engine in Nairobi. What disappointed me greatly was the decision, whilst there, that future traction would be diesel. Willie Bulman would certainly have preferred his 61 class, but it seems that even in railway managerial circles, fashions are as stupidly inconsistent as hemlines for women's skirts. *Haute couture* in motive power was dictated by various Generals in the USA and slavishly emulated by the unthinking sheep elsewhere in the world. Thus I learned that there would be no 61 class, let alone any 10 or 12 coupled version thereof, and in fact after moving to Africa to escape the end of steam in Britain, found eventually that the last new steam locomotive for BR was delivered about five years after the last EAR locomotive!

What seemed then obvious was that my chosen career as a *steam* locomotive engineer had been shot out from beneath my feet. As a result, it seemed that the next best alternative would be in strengthening the 'enthusiast' side of my interests, and see as much steam as possible, worldwide, before it all went. In retrospect, my subsequent movements were precipitate – I should have stayed on EAR longer, seen more of the system, done much more photography, and explored the adjacent railways of the Belgian Congo, which in 1956 could have been done safely and in the event were never covered properly by dedicated enthusiasts. However, an advertisement in the *'Railway Gazette'* outlined a position for assistant works manager on the Antofogasta Chile and Bolivia

Railway, so I applied by post. They were very interested, but would not appoint from such far places without an interview, so I resigned and saw their people at their City of London offices. The engineer who interviewed me said I was the best candidate he had seen, and recommended me for the job. However, the directors decided they wanted the 'status' of a universary graduate, and appointed one of the alternatives who, I understand, lasted only a month or so at their workshops at Uyuni before being repatriated as of little use, possibly to his intense relief, speaking as one who has subsequently seen something of that barren republic!

As it was, I returned to Britain, somewhat disillusioned, by a delightful airline called Hunting Clan, taking three days from Nairobi to London, flying by day in a smallish twin-engined craft and with overnight stops at hotels in Khartoum and Malta. At the time I had not realised that Africa is not only a continent but an addiction. Flying over those beautiful hills and valleys of Kenya and Uganda, and later over the deserts of Sudan and Egypt, there was a recurrent thought that I had done the wrong thing – somehow, sometime, I would return to Africa. This later occurred, is another story, but ends this narrative.

9

THE CHURCHWARD LEGEND

Much has been written about George Jackson Churchward, the man and his locomotives, undoubtedly the most able and gifted British locomotive engineer from about 1898, when he started to understudy for the weakening William Dean, until his retirement at the end of 1921. It is a rather curious coincidence that during the 'steam years' of the twentieth century, each of the eventual 'big four' railway groups took turns in having the most outstanding locomotive engineer in charge. After Churchward's retirement, his successor, Collett, seemed to show a continuation of Churchward's success, with the 'Castle' class running on both the LMS and LNE Railways, beating the indigenous classes in the process. However, this can be seen in retrospect as the basically Churchward flywheel continuing its momentum, and in the course of time Nigel Gresley became 'top CME' with sufficient fame to gain eventually a knighthood. William Stanier, from Swindon, and a Churchward protégé became third top man, for the LMS, and after his retirement, Oliver Bulleid, on the Southern, became the man with all the bright ideas. Stanier also gained a knighthood, but for wartime rather than railway work. After nationalisation, the inevitable committee situation took over, preventing any outstanding characters from showing their paces. On the design side, E. S. Cox produced several competent, but not outstanding designs, mainly to replace existing types. Midland-style thinking restrained the BR standards into a group of generally small engines, with no less than seven classes to cover power ranges 2, 3, and 4. Like Maunsell of the Southern, whose single outstanding design was the combination of several existing components into the brilliant 'Schools' class, Cox's *magnum opus* was a similarly concocted 9F 2-10-0, from standard parts, to comprise the most outstanding locomotive to run in Britain. It was fitting that this class, which included so many ideas inherited from Churchward's practice, should have its last example built at Swindon.

Having said all this, is there anything new to be said about a well aired subject? It was been acknowledged several times that one of Churchward's

Churchward Star class 4061 *Glastonbury Abbey*, stationed at Wolverhampton, on a north to west express at Exeter St. David's. (*J. B. Cornish*)

strengths was his ability to pick and select excellent subordinate staff to whom he could delegate work with complete confidence. Swindon became a byword for good locomotive design, with such men as Holcroft and Stanier moving to other groups in senior positions, whilst many went into private industry or overseas railway work, such as H. M. le Fleming, assistant CME to the Federated Malayan State Railways, an example known personally to the author and paralleled by numerous others.

What has never been expanded on, despite adequate evidence, was Churchward's equally uncanny ability to spot a good design feature, and to copy or adapt it to his own requirements. There is nothing derogatory in saying this, rather the opposite, but in general many sycophantic accounts of his work have tended to treat all his design success as almost divine inspiration. Design is not a chief mechanical engineer's main responsibility, and in later days, for example, Swindon's annual capacity was roughly 150 new locomotives, mainly to existing designs, plus say two thousand overhauls, to which should be added overhauls at other main works at Wolverhampton and Caerphilly, plus further work at smaller depot workshops. On top of this is carriage and wagon work, the maintenance of all sorts of outdoor machinery, pumps, turntables, etc, and in the case of the Great Western, even shipping used on the Irish and cross-Channel services, some of which marine machinery was dealt with at Swindon. Locomotive design can then, perhaps, be seen as about two or three percent of a CME's responsibilities. Humans being what they are, they tend to do the jobs in which they are most interested, and whereas people like Fowler delegated locomotive design to subordinates, Churchward took personal interest in this aspect, doubtless by delegating other duties less interesting to himself. Even so, he perhaps was able to divert only twenty percent of his time to locomotive design, even in his early development years.

Perhaps Churchward's greatest design strength lay in his totally unparochial outlook, a very rare virtue at a time when most British locomotive engineers worked on the principle of 'same as last time, but half an inch more here and three inches extra there'. Looking around other British railways he would have seen that little real change was evident over the previous forty or fifty years, but fortunately there were two excellent journals, 'The Engineer' and 'Engineering' which during that critical turn-of-century period devoted a great deal of space to locomotives both at home and abroad. At that time, overseas practice was developing far faster than British, there being four major schools of thought, each with their own specialities. In America, power and speed at all costs seemed to be the objective, with locomotive design rapidly exploring the then thresholds of maximum size. This was combined with simplicity of construction, suited to the perhaps crude conditions of a pioneering country.

The opposite prevailed in France, where fuel economy was paramount, and any sort of complexity considered worth the effort if a kilogramme or so of coal were thus saved. Compounding and complex valve gears were rife, and designers appeared to find some sort of challenge in testing the ingenuity of the most skilful fitters. German practice tended to follow French, except that complexity for its own sake was less revered, and the lopsided two-cylinder compound was commonly employed. Schmidt of Prussia is credited with perfecting the smoke tube superheater, which revolutionised steam practice throughout the world. The principle of drying, or superheating steam goes back to early days, to a smokebox drier by R. & W. Hawthorn, patented in 1839. Moncheuil, in 1850, invented the smoke tube superheater as we know it today; but difficulties in manufacture and lubrication probably rendered it a useless invention in those early days. The fourth design school was that of central Europe, where Karl Gölsdorf held sway in Austria, producing locomotives of high capacity within extremely limited axle and total weights.

All these diverse schools of thought provided points of interest, often apparently conflicting in principle. Churchward, in seeking to bring Great Western practice to a point well ahead of contemporary British conservatism, used a most skilful blend of what he saw to be good and appropriate. Such a statement in no way accuses him of plagiarism, but rather compares him to the master blender of, say, Scotch whisky, or a French restaurant *Chef*, who with a *soupçon* of known ingredients produces a gastronomic masterpiece totally unattainable by lesser cooks of inferior imagination.

Practically, for a man in a hurry, such as Churchward, this method produces better and faster results than doing everything from scratch, and wastefully researching things to which somebody else has already found the answer. Thus, few Churchward features were truly original, but his blend of other's bests, gleaned worldwide, put him in the forefront of British practice for at least a quarter-century. Past accounts of his work have referred vaguely to American practice regarding cylinder design and the partially bar type frames used on his two-cylinder locomotives. French practice has been confined, in comment, to the Nord and Paris-Orleans 4-4-2 purchased by Churchward, and German practice referred to only in respect of the Schmidt superheater. Let us now look more deeply into where Churchward obtained his ideas.

AMERICAN PRACTICE

Whilst uniform in the use of bar frames, two outside cylinders, and inside Stephenson valve gear, there were important variations in American practice at the time when Churchward became interested in transatlantic practice. The largest, and best-known firm was Baldwin, who clave very much to the traditional American way of things, and had a very active export section which ensured that wherever an overseas country decided to try out US practice against British or European, the Baldwin salesman was instantly to be found panting at the front door, order book in hand. Unfortunately, the Baldwin products of that time were on the crude side, and their export efforts probably did the American locomotive industry a disservice where competition was against more sophisticated products. Churchward was particularly friendly with officials of the Pennsylvania Railroad, good Baldwin customers, but their favourite contractor had nothing really to show the Great Western.

The company with the really brilliant design team was Brooks Locomotive Works, of Dunkirk, NJ, later amalgamated with other firms into the American Locomotive Company. Brooks were head and shoulders above the rest of the World in both cylinder and boiler design, and Churchward was happy to incorporate Brooks style cylinders immediately into his own practice, and after some hesitation, probably due to cost factors, eventually adopted the Brooks style boiler. There seems some circumstantial evidence that Brooks had at least two design teams, one of whom excelled on cylinders and the other on boilers, since there are many interesting cases of domestic locomotives having one or the other feature in its optimum style.

CYLINDERS

Brooks were perhaps the first in the world to appreciate that the use of piston valves permitted straight, direct, passages, from steam chest to cylinders. The concept of piston valves dates well back to the early days of steam, but as so often is the case, thinking was ahead of practical technology. The first apparently successful and large scale application of piston valves was in France, in the 1880s, by Ricours, and while he apparently succeeded in overcoming the problems inherent in the use of piston valves *per se*, he failed to grasp the opportunities they gave for straight, direct, ports.

At about the same time, Mr A. J. Stevens of the Central Pacific Railroad had worked out the advantages of direct ports, but not of piston valves, and in place of the usual slide valves with their tortuous 'Z' shaped ports, built some 4-8-0 and an incredible 4-10-0 with straight ports and a separate slide valve at each end of the cylinder. It seems to have been some brilliant but unknown draughtsman at Brooks who first combined the use of piston valves with straight direct ports, which features were certainly in use by 1900, possibly slightly earlier.

One may claim that the prototype Churchward locomotive, upon which he based his outstanding 4-6-0 No 100 (later 'William Dean') was a remarkably similar machine in both size and main features, to No 613 of the Lake Shore and Michigan Southern RR, built by Brooks in 1900. This superb locomotive had all the 'Churchward' features except the Belpaire boiler, and photographs of the two locomotives reveal these remarkable similarities. The American locomotive was somewhat larger, but as an astute student of the best in foreign practice, Churchward will have been well aware of its features, and may even have experienced the locomotive itself. It may be of interest here to tabulate several of the main comparative dimensions.

Railway	LS & MS	GWR
Locomotive	613	100
Type	4-6-0	4-6-0
Cylinders (in)	20 × 28	18 × 30
Wheels	6′ 8″	6′ 8″
Boiler Pressure	200	200psi
Grate area	36.6	27.6sq ft
Max boiler dia	6′ 3″	5′ 0″
Loco weight	77.0	67.8 tons
Adhesive	60.3	52.5 tons
Tractive effort	23800	20530 lb @ 85%

Almost certainly the inspiration behind Churchward's epoch making 4-6-0 number 100, Lake Shore and Michigan Southern no. 613 by Brooks with piston valves actuated by Stephenson valve gear. Built 1900.
(Alco Historic Photos, courtesy R. Koch)

The Lake Shore locomotive had a round top firebox, the major feature in which it differed from 'William Dean', but we may go back to 1898 to another Brooks 4-6-0 built for the Wisconsin Central Railway which contained further advanced features, notably 12″ piston valves for 19″ × 26″ cylinders, an extremely generous size, although the cylinders were not straight ported. Inside Stephenson valve gear was used, indirectly actuating the valves via rocking levers, as in 100, but the outstanding feature was the boiler and firebox.

Churchward's earlier boilers had Belpaire fireboxes with flat, parallel surfaces, and these apparently gave problems with water circulation. The usual account given out is that the eventual shape, with tapered barrel and tapered firebox, the latter with curved instead of flat surfaces, was 'developed' at Swindon under Churchward's supervision. In fact, such boilers were already in production by Brooks as early as 1898, and what seems more probable was that GJC, the man in a hurry, instructed his subordinates to build a Brooks type

The Brooks boiler, with tapered barrel and tapered Belpaire firebox as later adopted by Churchward and transplanted by Holcroft to Ashford and the LMS by Stanier, finally appearing on the BR Standard locos. Wisconsin Central 227 was built by Brooks in 1898.   (*Alco Historic Photos, courtesy R. Koch*)

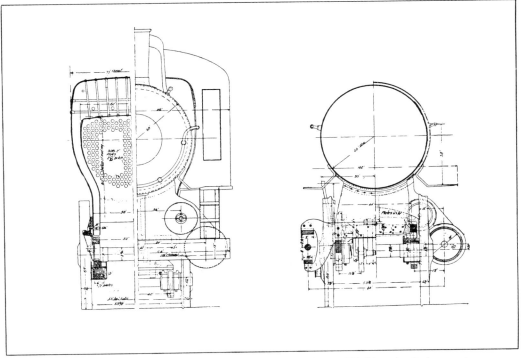

Cross section through the Wisconsin Central 4-6-0 built by Brooks in 1898. Note the firebox contours as later adopted by Churchward, and the generous sized piston valves, actuated by inside Stephenson valve motion. From *The Railway Engineer*, September 1898. (Fig 11)

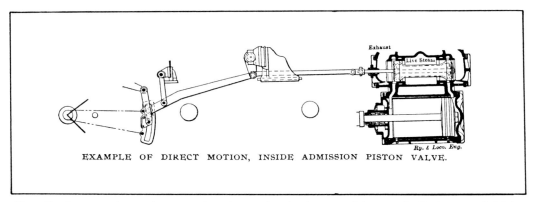

EXAMPLE OF DIRECT MOTION, INSIDE ADMISSION PISTON VALVE.

Direct Stephenson valve motion, actuating piston valves in almost straight ported cylinders, on a 2-8-0 for the Michigan Central Railroad. This type of cylinder and motion design was adopted by Churchward, and formed the basis of the highly successful Great Western "marque" until the end of GWR steam. (Fig 12)

boiler and, finding it solved the problem, adopted it as standard. That the Brooks design was fully satisfactory is shown that in addition to its adoption by Swindon, it was transplanted by Holcroft to the SE&CR and Southern, by Stanier to the LMS, and from there incorporated into the British Railways standard designs! Very few people appreciate the history behind this boiler design.

VALVE GEAR

Apart from No 100, which used rocking levers to give indirect motion, Churchward used, from No 98 onwards, built March 1903, a direct action Stephenson motion in which the rocking levers moved the action laterally from between the frames to the piston valves over the cylinders. This also seems to have originated in the USA, by the Schenectady works, particularly for the Michigan Central RR, under the requirements of Messrs J. F. Deems and E. D. Bronner, of whom the latter was superintendent of motive power. The earliest illustration of this gear which the author has been able to discover is in 'Railway and Locomotive Engineering' for May 1904, dealing specifically with some Atlantic type express locomotives, but indicating that this type of motion was in general use and proving very satisfactory. Indeed, the drawing reproduced appears to apply to a 2-8-0 type. Publication of this application thus seems to be a year after Churchward used it, but indications are that it was already well established in the USA by then. It seems probable that Churchward knew about the design, was attracted by its advantages, and adopted the arrangement for his own locomotives.

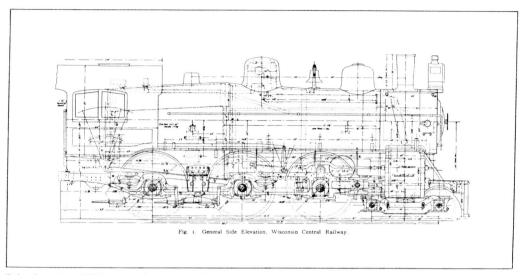

Fig. 1. General Side Elevation, Wisconsin Central Railway.

Side elevation of Wisconsin Central 4-6-0 by Brooks, showing tapered firebox mounted over bar frames. The British loading gauge virtually precluded such an arrangement without restricting firebox depth. (Fig 13)

THE TEUTONIC CONNECTION

As one of the major locomotive 'schools' then developing, Churchward would have been aware of German design practices. In adopting the American practice of two cylinder castings bolted back-to-back, he was faced with a problem in how to arrange frames for the narrow fireboxes envisaged. Bar frames themselves were, at that period, about 4" thick compared with about 1" for plate frames, such that a firebox *between* the frames would need to be 6" narrower were it to sit between bar frames. This imposed undue restrictions on grate area which, in the USA was met by sitting the firebox *above* the frames, gaining thereby a couple of inches in width. With the generous American loading gauge this was very practical, but in Britain, especially on the GWR with its reliance on Welsh coal, a deep firebox was necessary and impossible to fit above a bar frame assembly.

Fortunately again, an established solution was at hand from the Prussian State Railways who in their von Borries, four-cylinder compound, locomotives had evolved a mixed plate and bar framing. The class S5[1] designed in 1898 and first produced by Hanomag in 1900 had just such frames, plate round the narrow firebox and bar at the front end, to which were bolted four compound cylinders, all driving the leading axle. In the German engine this was possibly done to improve accessibility, as they had inside Walschaerts gear, actuating the outside valves by means of rocker arms. About fifty of these 4-4-0 were built, and the framing evidently gave satisfaction as they were developed into an 'Atlantic' type, class S9 with the same hybrid framing. Later on there were

Prussian State Railways class S5[1] compound 4-4-0 built 1900, with combined plate and bar frames as later adopted by Churchward for his standard two-cylinder locos.   (*A. E. Durrant collection*)

several hundred 4-6-0 of series S10 (4-cylinder simple), S10[1] (4-cyl. compound) and S10[2] (3-cyl. simple). The final Germanic manifestation was in fifteen three-cylinder 4-6-2 for the Saxon State Railways, built 1917–18.

Both the Prussian 4-6-0 and the Saxon 'Pacifics', with three cylinders, used conjugated valve gear for the inside valve, of two different types as represented by the development of this device by H. Holcroft, one of Churchward's proté-gés. There thus seemed a channel of communication, double acting, between Swindon and the Prussian State Railways, but not with the locomotive industry of southern Germany. Possibly this was due to language difficulties – one suspects that Churchward, like most Englishmen, was no linguist, and he had to conduct his continental investigations where somebody could speak adequate technical English!

The major German importation, on the Great Western as on every other railway worldwide, was the Schmidt smoke tube superheater. E. S. Cox, in his various writings has tried to make out a case for the 4-4-0 of the Lancashire & Yorkshire Railway as being the first truly modern British locomotives, with high degree superheat, together with long lap, long travel valves. The first L&Y locomotive superheated was no. 1112 in April 1908, and the first to combine superheat with improved valves was 1104, a month later. Meanwhile, Churchward, in May 1906, ie *two years earlier* had built 2901 with Schmidt high degree superheat, and whereas L&Y engines needed cylinder and valve gear alterations to bring them into line with modern practice, Churchward's engine already possessed these features as standard! Highly superheated steam, in those days, gave lubrication problems with piston valves and whilst the L&Y took the easy way out by reverting to slide valves, Churchward simply reduced the degree of superheat and continued with his otherwise modern front end, thereby ensuring that GWR locomotives were the most effective in the country for another twenty to thirty years.

Reverting to the Prussian type of hybrid frame, the author, while in Swindon drawing office, was asked to produce a three-dimensional sketch showing just how the two cylinders on a 7800 class were bolted together and mounted on the hybrid frame. This drawing (Swindon 133 725, dated 30.4.54), see fig 21, is believed to have been used in a last ditch stand to build yet another batch of 78's for the Cambrian section, as opposed to BR's proposal for their class 4, 4-6-0. In the event, BR standard policy of course won, and this final batch of 'Manors' never saw the light of day.

THE FRENCH CONNECTION

The 'standard' account, as included even in the authoritative RCTS history, indicates that the three French 'Atlantics' purchased by the Great Western in 1903 and 1905 were a sort of second opinion decided upon after completion of his outstanding 4-6-0 No 100. However, evidence shows that Churchward was deeply interested in French compound practice at least as far back as August 1899. A letter in the author's possession, dated 17 Aug 1899, is reproduced in

GWR's three de Glehn atlantics were scrapped before the author was born, so it was pleasing, in late 1952, to find ex-Nord Railway 221A30 at Creil, near Paris.

Compound County? Swindon drawing 56767 was a diagram of these Western Railway of France de Glehn
4-4-0, sent with a letter to G. J. Churchward in August 1899.   (*Locomotive Pub. Co.*)

C 91 - Les Locomotives FRANÇAISES (État)

Machine Nº 230-134, compound à 4 cylindres, tiroirs plans, vapeur saturée, pour
trains express. Série 230-126 à 230-140, ancien 2526-2540 Ouest.
Construite en 1899.

Swindon drawing 56768 was a small compound 4-6-0 of the French Western Railway, roughly comparable
with the later Manor class.   (*F. Fleury*)

full, as a most valuable piece of historical evidence. It indicates that for some time before that, Churchward had not only been in contact with the Western Railway of France (his most logical equivalent), but the French official had apparently visited Swindon. In the absence of further available departmental correspondence, the author is unaware of preceding negotiations but Churchward's French confrere sent him drawings of the latest express and general passenger engines (both de Glehn compounds) plus a suburban tank engine, all listed in the letter. Furthermore, there was a diagram of Nord's then latest express engine. These four diagrams were only given Swindon drawing numbers in 1918, presumably having remained attached to the correspondence which, in turn, may have been retained in Churchward's personal papers. They were, in fact, the original French diagrams with Swindon numbers stencilled on. Details of these diagrams are:

Swindon Drawing no.	Type	Class
56767	4-4-0 compound	Ouest 503-22
56768	4-6-0 compound	Ouest 2501-25
56769	4-6-0T simple	Ouest 3701-10
56770	4-4-0 compound	Nord 2161-80

Only the tank engine was really irrelevant in respect of not being a compound, although it was rather modern for 1893, as a six-coupled machine with outside cylinders and Walschaerts valve gear built for suburban work.

In 1901, Churchward produced his well known diagram sheet showing six types of locomotive for express, mixed traffic, and heavy freight work, using common cylinders and two boiler designs. By the following year his 4-6-0 No 100 had been turned out in February, he had taken over from Dean, and further thoughts on compounding came to the fore. If compounding were to prove substantially superior to simple expansion, as was claimed by its protagonists, then it may have been necessary to revise his standard types to include double expansion, and from 1902 to 1904 several French compound classes were examined for suitability (see table on p. 182).

As is well known, Churchward's simple locomotives, with modern front ends, proved at least the equal to the French compounds at that time, although several French details, notably the bogie side bearer, were adopted for all future builds, while the four-cylinder arrangement, with divided drive, was adopted for GWR express locomotives retaining simple expansion. A selection of these diagrams is reproduced here, for the first time, together with photographs of the locomotives as used in France.

Before embarking on the *Great Bear*, Churchward studied the initial pacific design on the French Western Railway, their nos. 2901 & 2902, shown on Swindon drawing 56829.   (*A. E. Durrant collection*)

Swindon Drg no.	Date	Type	Railway & class	Notes
20560	26.6.02	4-4-0	Est 2401-08	Compound County equivalent
20798	19.8.02	4-4-2	Nord 2641-2	GWR 102 'La France'
20799	6.10.02	4-4-2	Nord 2641-2	End view, superimposed on GWR loading gauge
21355	4.11.02	4-4-2	PO 3001-8	GWR 103-04
22732	29.6.03	2-8-0	Midi 4001-18	Compound 28XX equivalent
25903	19.9.04	4-4-2	PO 3001-18	Later diagram
25904	19.9.04	4-6-0	PO 4001-12	Mixed traffic type, 5'11" wheels, equivalent to a compound 'Hall'.

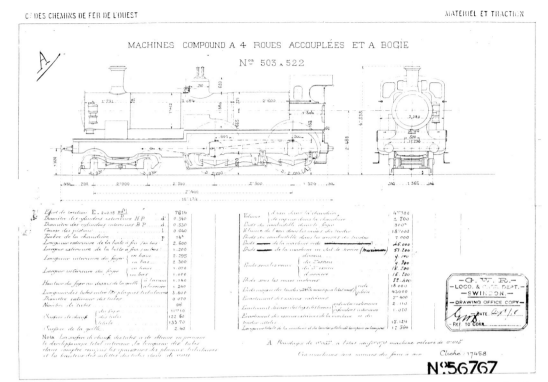

Swindon drawing 56767 showing Western Railway of France compound 4-4-0 as sent to Churchward with letter dated 17th August 1899. (Fig 14)

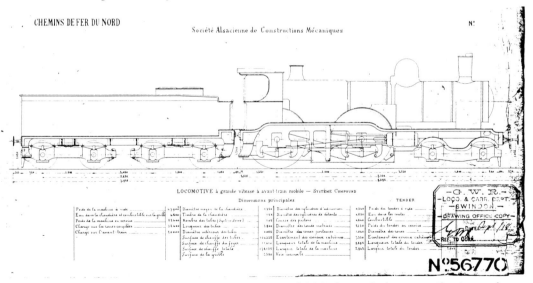

Swindon drawing 56770, showing an oldish Nord compound 4-4-0 of no real relevance to the sizes and powers of locomotives as envisaged by Churchward at that time. One of these locomotives was noted by the author, out of use, at Paris La Chapelle depot as late as 1949. (Fig 15)

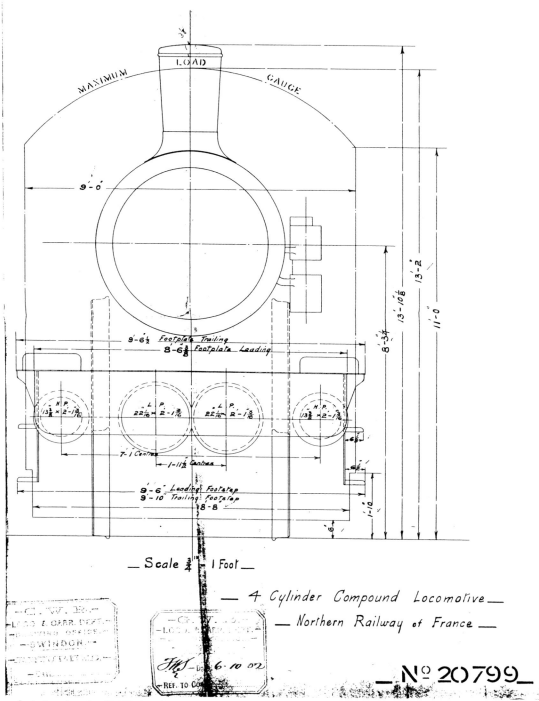

Swindon drawing 20799 showing cross section of French Northern Railway 4-4-2 compound superimposed on GWR loading gauge. Dated 6 Oct 1902. (Fig 16)

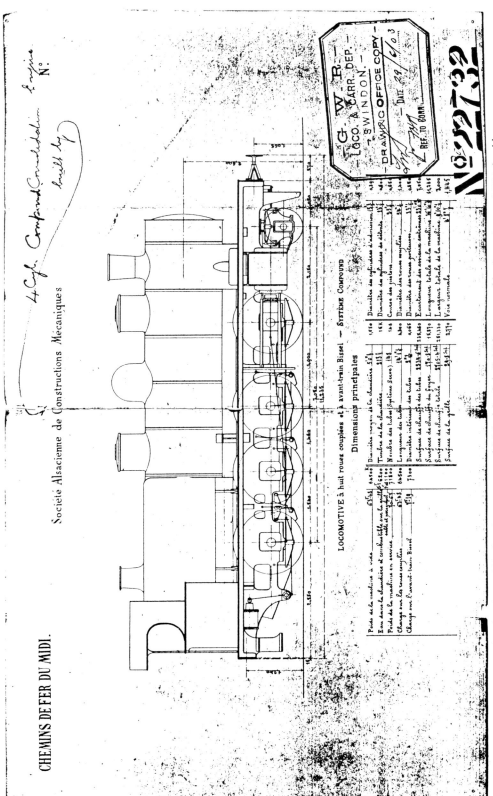

Swindon drawing 22732 dated 29 June 1903, showing a compound 2-8-0 of the C de F. Midi, as a possible alternative to a 28XX should compound expansion have proved beneficial. (Fig 17)

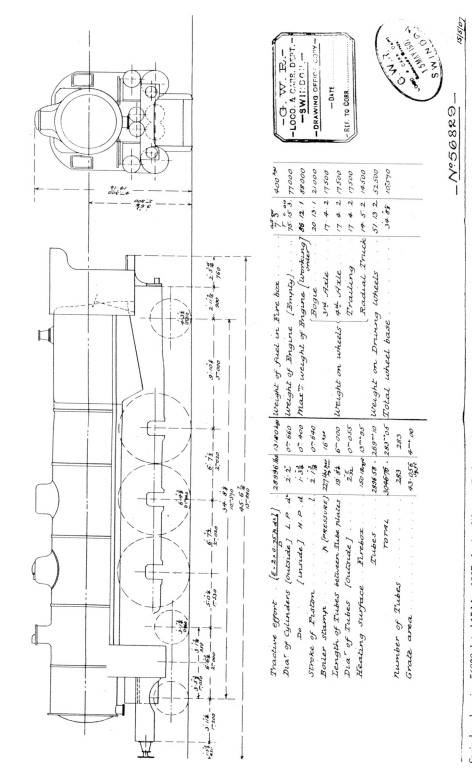

N°56829

15/5/07

Swindon drawing 56829 dated 15 May 1907, depicts Western Railway of France's initial and clumsy compound 4-6-2 which, like the *Great Bear* were only built the following year. Knowing Churchward's close connections with that railway, this was probably a careful cross-check to see how weight estimates agreed or differed, prior to embarking on actual construction. (Fig 18)

Compagnie des Chemins de fer de l'Ouest

Matériel et Traction
Rue de Rome 44
N° 171

Paris, le **17**th August 1899.

Dear Sir,

Your letter of the 8th instant in hands, I am glad to state
that the included informations suit thoroughly the purpose & I am
very grateful to you for *your* kindness in sending them. Should I however,
without abusing, ask you to be kind enough to address me a copy
of the Regulations of the G.W.R.,we have spoken of when last month
at Swindon ?

Since I am back from England, I have prepared all informations you requested respecting our Ry system (Western of France)
& as soon as your letter has reached me, I have sent a messenger
to the Northern Ry for the particulars you want .

I send you by the same post :

I - Three brief drawings of our new engines :

A - 503-522: Compound for fast & heavy passengers trains (twenty
now in order, 523-542)

B - 2501-2525: Compound, for heavy, but rather slow, passengers
trains (speed not exceeding 55 miles per hour) & for goods trains

G.J. Churchward Esq. - first assistant
to the Loco & carriage Superintendent G.W.R.

Swindon - England.

C - 3701-3710: tank engines, for goods & passengers trains on the short & hilly lines (fifteen now in order, 3711-3725).

D - A special notice enclosed giving the conditions under which the weight has been indicated.

2 - Three photos of the same locomotives.

3 - five photos :

    1 : first classe passenger carriage with lavatory (26 places),

    2 : the same with four beds in the end compartments,

    3 : waggon to carry :

        20^T in goods slow trains,

        10^T in passengers trains & international transit,

    4 : waggon for international transit.

    5 : waggon for passengers trains & international transit, fitted with Westinghouse automatic air brake.

4 - Ten diagrams of several engines Compound or not (taken by means of the "Auto indicateur Ouest"[1].

5 - Four drawings of the piston used on the Compound loco of the Northern Ry of France.

6 - The drawing of the piston used on our Rw O^y (Western of France) for the similar engines.

7 - Analyses of several kinds of coal on our Ry system & on the Northern Ry of France.

8 - The indication of consumption of coal on the Western of France Ry.

I will send you the same information about the Northern Ry of France, when I will have it which I have asked for.

I annex a small pamphlet I have written on the conditions of power

(1) See "Revue Générale des Chemins de fer" N. of September 1896, March, May & June 1898)

used by various tools when working or not.

Hoping such informations will be of some interest for you, I remain of course at your entire disposal for any further statement you would happen to desire.

With many grateful thanks,

Yours sincerely

J. Huilly

THE GREAT BEAR

The reasons behind this locomotive have been discussed at length in previous books, and its history recorded in detail, such that there is no need to repeat this detail here. It is well known, of course, that 'The Great Bear' was the first 4-6-2 to run in Britain, and the author has seen in print a comment that the type was well established in America and on the continent. Certainly this is true as regards the USA, but only two continental railways placed 'Pacifics' in service before GWR 111, and then by less than a year. In France, the Paris Orleans put their first two locomotives, nos 4501 and 4502, in service in July and September 1907, and Lucien Vilain in his history of that company's locomotives claims them as the first Pacifics in Europe. These were unsuperheated de Glehn compounds, and a further sixty-eight followed on in 1908–9, plus thirty super-heated versions in 1910, making them a substantially numerous series.

The first German 'Pacifics' also appeared in 1907, and were built by Maffei for the Baden State Railways, class IVf, numbers 751-53. These were an absolutely magnificent design, superheated, bar frames, and four compound cylinders in line with piston valves about 12 inches diameter on both high and low pressure cylinders. They were the forerunners of the famous Bavarian Pacifics, of similar features, which appeared the following year.

Several European railways introduced Pacifics in 1908, but as 'The Great Bear' was outshopped in February it seems probable that it was the third of its type in Europe. The only contact Churchward seems to have had in this respect was again with the Western Railway of France, who built two enormous and very clumsy engines, Nos 2901-02, in 1908, the same year as No 111. Swindon drawing 56829, dated 15.5.07 is a diagram of these locomotives, drawn at Swindon, and with dual metric/imperial dimensions. Similarities with 'The Great Bear' (or vice versa) were a Belpaire firebox without combustion chamber, a fairly long boiler, and inside bearings on trailing truck. It is believed that like 111, these two engines were not too successful, although further, better pro-portioned 4-6-2 were built for the Ouest.

THE PO SIMPLE 4-6-2

An intriguing drawing in the Swindon files was No 63144, dated July 1922, shortly after Churchward's retirement. After the 1919 Armistice, the Paris Orleans bought two hundred locomotives from the American Locomotive Company, of which 150 were mixed traffic 2-8-2 and fifty were express pas-senger 4-6-2. Like most American locomotives, they were simple expansion, two-cylinder, locomotives, with bar frames. Only the 4-6-2 diagram and data seems to have been acquired by Swindon, and several major dimensions have been converted from metric to imperial dimensions. The cylinders, at 24.4" diameter were far too large to run in Britain, but as pressure was only 171 psi the whole locomotive, with higher pressure, could have been fitted in and would have then been somewhat akin to the British Railways 'Britannia' of thirty years later. Piston valves, no less than $13\frac{3}{4}$ inches diameter, with valve travel $6\frac{1}{2}$ inches, would have made them fairly free running, and 250 of a French version of the 'Mikados' were later built for the Etat, or State railway, formerly the Ouest. It is interesting to speculate on what Swindon drawing office had in mind when this design was studied, but probably all other reference to it has been destroyed.

EARLIER BRITISH PACIFICS

While *'The Great Bear'* was the first 4-6-2 to run on a British railway, the type was no novelty to commercial locomotive builders. Between 1903 and 1907 some 29 such locomotives were built, to six designs, for three railways in South Africa. Of these, one locomotive for the Cape Government Railway, in 1907, was a three-cylinder compound, while five by Vulcan Foundry for the Central South African Railways were bar framed jobs with narrow fireboxes. Forty-five of another narrow firebox 4-6-2 were built in 1902–3, by Nasmyth Wilson and Vulcan Foundry, for Western Australia, all the above being on 3' 6" gauge.

THE CHURCHWARD INFLUENCE

The design practices standardised by Churchward permeated through the whole of Britain's domestic locomotive industry. Holcroft took the Brooks type boilers and straight-ported cylinders with long lap valves to the SE&CR after which they remained standard on the Southern. Even Bulleid, despite his Doncaster training, retained the finely shaped Belpaire firebox on his Pacifics and Q1 0-6-0. Gresley, at Doncaster, used Swindon's cylinder and valve gear principles, but stuck with round topped fireboxes and, often, parallel boilers. LMS motive power remained largely a disaster until Stanier was wooed from Swindon to set matters right, and his detailing developed naturally into the British Railways' standard designs. Thus the last steam locomotive built for British Railways, appropriately at Swindon, in 1960, included features which can be traced to Churchward's interest in overseas practice at the end of the nineteenth century – a fascinating saga.

CHURCHWARD AND WIDE FIREBOXES

The first GWR 4-6-0, No 36, built by William Dean, was also the first British locomotive with a wide firebox, of which Churchward had possibly some say. Certainly the ten 'Krugers' of 1899–1903 were clearly very much Churchward influenced, and the initial two locomotives were built before Ivatt's prototype wide firebox 'Atlantic'. In the event, the only other GWR locomotive built with

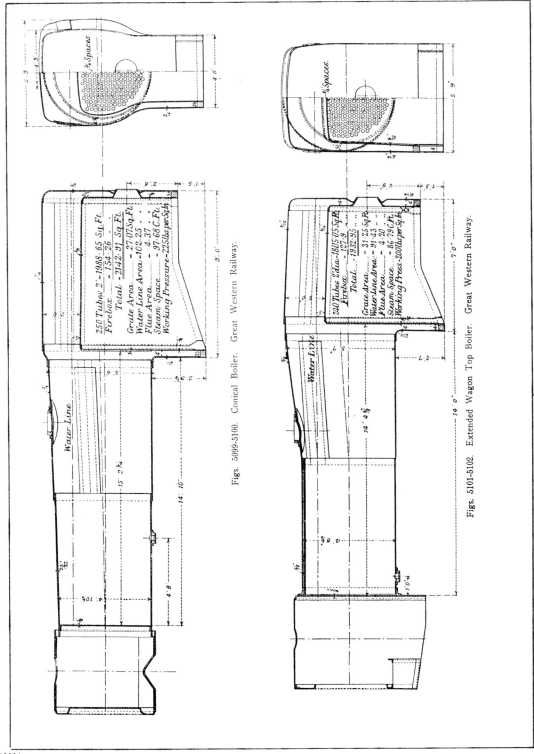

250 Tubes 2″-1988·65 Sq.Ft.
Firebox - 154·26 "
Total - 2142·91 Sq.Ft.
Grate Area - 27·07 Sq.Ft.
Water Line Area - 102·25 "
Flue Area - 4·37 "
Steam Space - 97·68 C.Ft.
Working Pressure - 225 lbs.per Sq.In.

Figs. 5099-5100. Conical Boiler. Great Western Railway.

240 Tubes 2″dia - 1805·05 Sq.Ft.
Firebox - 127·9 "
Total - 1932·95 "
Grate Area - 31·25 Sq.Ft.
Water Line Area - 91·43 "
Flue Area - 4·20 "
Steam Space - 86·79 C.Ft.
Working Press - 200 lbs.per Sq.In.

Figs. 5101-5102. Extended Wagon Top Boiler. Great Western Railway.

Two Churchward boilers as published in America in 1906. Upper is the standard number 1 full cone boiler while below is an apparent wide firebox version as discussed in the text. (Fig 19) a wide firebox was 111, *'The Great Bear'*, and apart from the hazy Hawksworth 'Pacific' proposal, wide fireboxes fade out from GWR literature.

Fascinating information can sometimes be obtained from the most unlikely sources, and while preparing this book the author purchased a copy of the 1906 edition of the American *Locomotive Dictionary*, an unlikely source of GWR history! There is a section on British locomotives and page 515 is reproduced (fig 19). The upper drawing is the standard 1 full coned boiler, in unsuperheated state, but underneath, shown without comment, as though it existed, is a wide firebox version thereof. The question is, for what locomotive or locomotives was this intended? The curious smokebox suggests fitting to a 'Kruger', and indeed the barrel length of 14' 0" just equals the 10' 6" barrel plus 3' 6" combustion chamber on these engines. As is known, no such boilers were built, and the 'Krugers' were scrapped mainly in 1906, the date this drawing was published.

Possibly Churchward considered using these engines as guinea pigs to gain experience with wide fireboxes in case traffic demands rendered them necessary. The boiler as shown could have been fitted to 4-4-2 and 2-8-0 types, but not to large wheeled 4-6-0 which would have needed complete redesign as 2-6-2 to accomodate them. Thus is a curious detail of GWR history found in an American publication of over eighty years ago!

AN AUSTRIAN ENIGMA

At the turn of the century, when Churchward was consolidating his position, he kept very much in touch with locomotive practice worldwide. At the same time, Karl Gölsdorf in Austria was producing locomotives of unprecedented power/weight ratio with most of his designs appearing in the British technical press, with whom he even corresponded. It seems thus very possible that he and Churchward were in contact at some time. An intriguing proposal for an early four-cylinder compound 2-6-2 was published in *'The Locomotive'* for June 1902, with several Churchward features including domeless boiler with central safety valve in GWR-type casing, an apparently Belpaire firebox containing steam collector, and rather GWR style smokebox door. The eventual locomotives as built in 1906 were quite different in detail, and it seems rather that the diagram illustrated shows an early proposal containing quite a lot of Churchward influence, which certainly will be very interesting to learn more of.

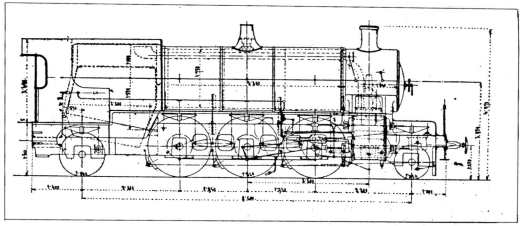

A proposed express passenger compound 2-6-2 by Gölsdorf in Austria, including several features evidently inspired by Churchward but in the event excluded from the locomotives as produced. The GWR outline is quite pronounced. (Fig 20)

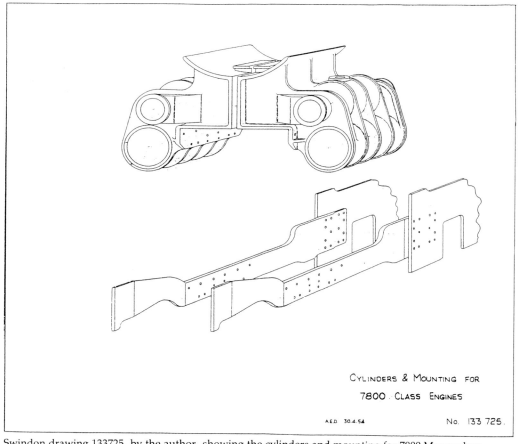

CYLINDERS & MOUNTING FOR

7800 CLASS ENGINES

A.E.D. 30.4.54   No. 133 725.

Swindon drawing 133725, by the author, showing the cylinders and mounting for 7800 Manor class. (Fig 21)

RELICS

Swindon was one of the most venerable railway owned workshops in Britain, with several buildings dating back to earliest days. In addition, several other oddities of historical interest accumulated over the years, and were photographed by the author in later days. Some of these are illustrated in this section.

An old Taff Vale tender, converted to water wagon, stands outside A shop Swindon.

The replica *North Star*, the first satisfactory broad gauge loco, in Swindon's A shop. In front are the driving wheels from 4-2-2 *Lord of the Isles*.

Wheels from an ex-Bristol & Exeter 4-2-4T, outside Swindon's G shop. The caption is incorrect, the original Rothwell engines having been replaced by similar locos in 1873. The large balance weight on one wheel only suggests that these may have been used for stationary work, thus accounting for their survival.

Mixed gauge turntable outside Swindon G shop. Broad gauge was used for 54 years, but this turntable with its stub of broad gauge track, survived over 70 **further** years.

With wide fireboxes, combustion chambers and Belpaire configuration, the boilers built for the Kruger class were very modern in concept for 1899. Indeed, the GWR introduced the wide firebox into British practice, a development usually claimed for Ivatt's atlantic on the GNR. In service the Kruger boilers proved unsatisfactory, for unstated reasons, yet continued at work, at lower pressure, in Swindon wagon works for 60 years after their locos had been scrapped! Here are two, being finally scrapped, in the 1960s.

Rear view of Kruger firebox showing outward flanged backplate.

The central boiler house at Swindon had eight enormous chimneys, each made from six old 2301 class boiler barrels. This shot was taken in the 1960s after they had been truncated, but patches over the former dome openings can be seen.

SWINDON REVISITED

After departure to East Africa, I had no idea if, how, or when Swindon would be revisited. As it was, by 1959 I had joined the staff of Beclawat, a London firm making components for the transport industry, and not unnaturally Swindon was very much on the itinerary for somebody involved in technical sales to railway manufacturing establishments. It was a great pleasure to meet up again with my old colleagues, although initially somewhat embarrassing to approach them for business, a feeling not encountered at 'foreign' establishments such as Derby or Doncaster. Even more pleasant was the fact that this new process in the employment chain meant that I could entertain my old 'mates' for lunch, at company expense, and at Swindon there was none of the problem of 'getting to know' the relevant staff. One only disappointment was experienced – the night I went to the Bell Hotel in Old Town. In October 1955, just before departure for Nairobi, it was my local hostelry, and upon entry to the bar, virtually every face was familiar. Four years later I entered the well remembered premises to find not a single familiar face! Even the staff were strange, an interesting commentary on how change takes place continuously but is really only noticed by the spasmodic visitor.

Many of the photographs illustrating this book were taken in these later years, from 1959 to 1965, when I started to 'shoot' many interesting relics formerly taken as everyday and commonplace. Others had disappeared, but it is surprising how many of the really important ones survived. Swindon was full of amazing artifacts dating from the earliest years of the Great Western, and such that I photographed are illustrated here.

This period, armed with a better camera than owned during the actual Swindon employment period, enabled the author to record Swindon built steam in action in a better manner than formerly possible, while the use of a company motor car made better locations accessible.

Stanier's first design for the LMS were his most Swindon orientated, with domeless boilers and horizontal cylinders, and was possibly a pointer to Swindon practice had he been appointed CME instead of Collett. Perhaps appropriately, some of these engines had their final overhauls at Swindon in the 1960s.

7002 *Devizes Castle* rolls under the combined road and rail bridge at the east end of Old Oak Common yard with an express from Bristol. Built new with larger superheater, it later acquired a double chimney, as shown.

6014 retained its streamlined V-fronted cab until scrapped. Here it swings off the main line with a Birmingham train in the mid 1960s.

THE LAST NEW STEAM

During this period, in March 1960, Swindon built the last new steam loco-motive for British Railways, No 92220, *'Evening Star'*, which perpetuated in name the first successful broad gauge type of 1837, and concluded 114 years of steam locomotive construction. The author was not on the official guest list, but gained entry the following morning where 92220 was available, uncluttered, for some historic photographs to be taken. In works at that time were 4-4-0 *'City of Truro'*, very relevant, and an extraordinary visitor in the shape of Caledonian 4-2-2 No 123. Several photographs reproduced here record that historic occasion.

BR's last new steam locomotive, 92220 *Evening Star*, the morning after the official naming ceremony.

Close up of nameplate and dedication plate on 92220 *Evening Star*.

While *Evening Star* was being named at Swindon, *City of Truro* was on display for guests at the ceremony. It is an interesting comment on steam locomotive development that a ten-coupled freight design of the 1950s should be capable of attaining a maximum speed **ninety per cent** of the record breaking express engine half a century before.

Caledonian 4-2-2 no. 123 in A shop at the time of 92220s dedication.

Not quite two prototypes. Outside Swindon foundry are BR class 8, 71000, awaiting dynamometer car tests, and 9F 92001 up from South Wales for attention to regulator problems. The tall building is the pattern store.

Close up of poppet valve motion, 71000 at Swindon, 1954.

On the original 9Fs, regulator linkage was faulty in design, resulting in uncontrollable slipping when hauling heavy ore traffic from Newport to Ebbw Vale. 92004, in for attention at Swindon in 1954, seems to have damaged itself, and with fall plate removed exudes a particularly continental identity.

The GWR standard 0-6-0 pannier tank was really quite archaic, with basic layout dating from the late 19th century. Nevertheless they were quite powerful shunters and were surprisingly sprightly on local passenger duties

The first 1500 class 0-6-0PT on empty stock work at Old Oak Common, hardly the type of duty to extract maximum benefit from its short wheelbase.

The neat layout of outside Walschaerts valve gear on a 1500 class. Note welded crosshead and single slide bar. Future Swindon designs may well have moved in this direction.

ABBREVIATIONS

ATC	Automatic Train Control
BDZ	Blgarski Drzavni Zeleznitsa (Bulgarian State Railways)
B&MR	Brecon & Merthyr Railway
BOAC	British Overseas Airways Corporation
BPGV	Burry Port & Gwendraeth Valley Railway
BR	British Railways
C de F	Chemins de Fer
CCE	Chief Civil Engineer
CD	Chief Draughtsman
CEGB	Central Electricity Generating Board
CO	Compagnie Oriental (of Turkey)
CSD	Československe Statni Drahy (Czechoslovakian State Railways)
DO	Drawing Office
EAR	East African Railways
EGR	Egyptian Government Railways
GER	Great Eastern Railway
GCR	Great Central Railway
GNR	Great Northern Railway
GWR	Great Western Railway
JDŽ	Jugoslovenske Državni Železnice (Jugoslavian State Railways)
KUR	Kenya Uganda Railway
LDEC	Lancashire Derbyshire & East Coast Railway
LMS	London Midland & Scottish Railway
LNER	London & North Eastern Railway
LNWR	London & North Western Railway
LTSR	London Tilbury & Southend Railway
L&Y	Lancashire & Yorkshire Railway
M&SWJR	Midland & South Western Junction Railway
NE	North Eastern Railway
NCO	Non Commissioned Officer
NJ	New Jersey
OCS	On Company Service
PLM	Paris Lyon & Mediterranean Railway
PTR	Port Talbot Railway
REME	Royal Electrical & Mechanical Engineers
ROD	Railway Operating Department (of Royal Engineers)
RR	Rhymney Railway
SAR	South African Railways
SNCF	Societe Nationale des Chemins de Fer Francais (French Railways)
TV	Taff Vale Railway
US	United States
VE	Victory in Europe
WD	War Department
YMCA	Young Men's Christian Association

BIBLIOGRAPHY

The Locomotives of the Great Western Railway, in 12 parts, published by the Railway Correspondence & Travel Society.
A Pictorial Record of Great Western Engines, by J. H. Russell
The Great Western at Swindon Works, by Alan S. Peck
La Machine Locomotive by E. Sauvage et A. Chapelon
25 Jahre Deutsche Einheitslokomotiven by Hanns Stockklausner
Un Siècle de Matériel et Traction sur le Réseau d'Orléans, L. M. Vilain.

Magazines

The Locomotive
The Railway Gazette
The Engineer
Engineering

Dates as shown in text.

ACKNOWLEDGEMENTS

Thanks are extended to Bob Koch for obtaining the Brooks photographs from the USA, and to my wife, Christine, for her usual patience and fortitude whilst I am incarcerated in study or darkroom, emerging only at meal times or to commandeer her dining room table for use as a drawing board! Thanks also to all the Swindon characters, named and unnamed, without whose diverse personalities this would have been a very dull book indeed. Further thanks are due to my publisher, Stephen Mourton, for the care taken in producing this book and for making it bigger and better than originally envisaged.

INDEX